Give Me Liberty

THE UNCOMPROMISING STATESMANSHIP OF PATRICK HENRY

DAVID J. VAUGHAN

GENERAL EDITOR, GEORGE GRANT

LEADERS IN ACTION SERIES

CUMBERLAND HOUSE

PUBLISHING INC.

All Scripture quotations, unless otherwise noted, are taken from the Holy
Bible: King James Version.

Published by Cumberland House Publishing, Inc., 431 Harding Industrial
Drive, Nashville, Tennessee 37211, by license from Highland Books, 229
South Bridge Street, P.O. Box 254, Elkton, Maryland 21922-0254.

Library of Congress Cataloging-in-Publication Data

Vaughan, David, 1955–
    Give me liberty : the uncompromising statesmanship of Patrick
Henry / David Vaughan.
        p.   cm. — (Leaders in action series)
    Includes bibliographical references
    ISBN 1-888952-22-9 (hb. alk. paper)
    ISBN 1-58182-323-1 (pb. alk. paper)
    1. Henry, Patrick, 1736–1799. 2. Legislators—United States—
Biography. 3. Virginia—Politics and government—1775–1783.
4. United States—Politics and government—1775–1783. 5. United
States. Continental Congress—Biography. I. Title. II. Series.
E302.6H5V38 1997
973.3'092—dc21
[B]   97-5773
                                                         CIP

Printed in the United States of America

    4 5 6 7 8 9—08 07

To My Son, Ethan:
Destined to be a Leader

TABLE OF CONTENTS

Foreword by George Grant
Acknowledgments
Introduction
Chronology

Part II: The Character of Patrick Henry

FOREWORD

BY GEORGE GRANT

*A*ccording to G.K. Chesterton, "The real hero is not he who is bold enough to fulfill the predictions, but he who is bold enough to falsify them." By all counts, Patrick Henry was a real hero–he upended every expectation, confounded every prophecy, and falsified every prediction. And thus he laid enduring foundations of greatness in his own life and in his beloved nation.

To begin with, he was a most unlikely revolutionary. As was the case with so many of his fellow patriots–from Samuel Adams and John Hancock to Richard Henry Lee and George Washington, from James Iredell and Henry Laurens to Samuel Chase and John Dickinson–he was profoundly conservative. He was loathe to indulge in any kind of radicalism that might erupt into violence–rhetorical, political, or martial. Indeed, he was the faithful heir of the settled colonial gentry. He was devoted to conventional Whig principles: the rule of law, *noblesse oblige*, unswerving honor, squirey superintendence, and the maintenance of corporate order. He believed in a tranquil and serene society free of the raucous upsets and tumults of agitation, activism, and unrest–hardly the stuff of revolution.

His initial reticence to squabble with the crown was obvious to even the most casual observer. He desired to exhaust every recourse to law before even entertaining a resort to armed resistance. For more than a decade, he supported the innumerable appeals, suits, and petitions which colonial leaders sent to both parliament and king. Even after American blood had been spilled, he refrained from embracing impulsive insurrection.

He was, at best, a reluctant revolutionary.

Why then did he finally throw in his lot with the rebellion–indeed, why did he become the revolutions most articulate champion? What could possibly have so overcome his native conservatism?

Actually, it was his traditionalism–his commitment to those lasting things that transcend the ever-shifting tides of situation and circumstance–which finally drove him to arms. He urged his fellow patriots to fight against king and motherland in order to preserve all that which king and motherland were supposed to represent.

He asserted that it was only a grave responsibility which the leaders held to God and countrymen that could possibly compel the peace-loving people of America to fight. He believed that the combined tyranny of economic mercantilism–the politicalization of matters of commerce–and legislative despotism–the politicalization of matters of conscience–had insured that "an appeal to arms and the God of Hosts" was "all that was left" to them. It was appallingly evident to him that their colonial charters had been "subverted or even abrogated," their "citizenship rights" according to English common law had been "violated," and their "freedom of religious practice" and "moral witness" had been "curtailed." Thus, rule of the colonies had become "arbitrary and capricious;" it had become "supra-legal;" it had become "intolerable." Under such circumstances "a holy duty" demanded "a holy response."

Henry's reluctant conclusion–that ideological and political encroachments upon the whole of society could not be any longer ignored–was shared by many of those who faithfully occupied American pulpits across the land. The very conservative colonial pastors certainly did not set out to "stir up strife or political tumult at the cost of the proclamation of the Gospel" as Charles Lane of Savannah put it. On the other hand, "The Gospel naturally mitigates against lawless tyranny, in whatever form it may take," said Ebenezer Smith of Lowell. Indeed, as Charles Turner of Duxbury asserted, "The Scriptures cannot be rightfully expounded without explaining them in a manner friendly to the cause of freedom." Thus, "Where the spirit of the Lord is, there is liberty" was a favorite pastoral text–as were "Ye shall know the truth and the truth shall make you free" and "Take away your exactions from my people, saith the Lord God." The leading churchmen of America were generally agreed with Henry that "Where political tyranny begins true government ends"; as Samuel West of Dartmouth declared, "and the good Christian must needs be certain to oppose such lawless encroachments, however bland or bold."

It was not a love of firebrand Enlightenment rhetoric, or a passion for political upheaval, or even a restless vision for social reform that drove Patrick Henry from hearth and home to the forefront of the American Revolution. It was the certainty that God had called him to an inescapable accountability. It was the conviction that he was covenantally honor-bound to uphold the standard of impartial justice and broadcast the blessings of liberty afar. It was the firm conviction that it was his Christian duty to vindicate the cause of freedom.

In the end, he was forced to arms by a recognition of the fact that "resistance to tyrants is obedience to God." And thus, was birthed an unflinching stalwartness: "Is life so dear or peace so sweet, as to be purchased at the price of chains and slavery? Forbid it, Almighty God! I know not what course others may take, but as for me, give me liberty or give me death!"

In this examination of Patrick Henry's unlikely heroism, David Vaughan has afforded us with a remarkably vivid glimpse into the workings of the great man's life, career, and character. In so doing, he has done us all real service.

At a time when heroism is an all but extinct attribute, we need to be reminded of its unlikely boldness more than ever. Indeed, it is hoped that the example of this reluctant revolutionary will stir us all toward the falsification of predominant predictions of our day.

Acknowledgments

*T*he essayist Hilaire Belloc once sarcastically commented on the custom of beginning a book with acknowledgments. "Now there is another thing book writers do in their prefaces," he said, [which is] "to introduce a mass of nincompoops of whom no one ever heard, to say 'my thanks are due to such-and-such,' all in a litany, as though anyone cared a farthing for the rats!"

Belloc notwithstanding, the lesson to be learned by this custom is that no significant accomplishment is ever the product of one man's efforts alone. As the saying goes, "No man is an island." And whatever successes we attain in life should be causes for humility and gratitude rather than trophies to pride and self-satisfaction.

While I am indebted to many people for the completion of this project, first place is due to my wife, Diane, whose faith, prayers, and encouragement were the hidden origin of this book. Moreover, she suffered the solitude of my study without a word of complaint, freeing me from many domestic duties and distractions so I could work undisturbed. Her patient and faithful labor in the home, though hidden and unacknowledged by the world, will one day earn her the reward of hearing her children, Hannah, Lydia, and Ethan, rise up and call her "blessed." She is a "wise woman" who knows how to build her house.

Next to my wife, special thanks is due to the inimitable George Grant, whose confidence in me has been a fountain of encouragement. George is one of those Christian leaders who not only believes what he says, but more importantly, practices what he preaches. Living as we do in an era of Christian celebrities and ministry scandals (the two often go hand in hand), George's leadership and ministry are a breath of fresh air and a reason for hope. While not all that glitters is gold, some that glitters is; and George not only shines in public, he also sparkles in private. He is an unalloyed coin whose worth can only be appreciated by those fortunate enough to know him.

A number of friends have gone beyond the sphere of duty in supporting both this project and my ministry in general. Tim ("Braveheart") Ward and his lovely wife Kim are sterling models of self-sacrifice and have taught me much about loyalty, while Jim ("Scottish Chief") Cummings and his godly wife Cathy live out the true meaning of fidelity. Both of these families stood with me during my hour of trial and demonstrated a courage rarely seen in our age of "tolerant" Evangelicalism.

Also, Dave Wilson, president of PC Innovators, and his kind wife Cindy, are living examples of generosity. Dave's vision for my writing ministry and his gracious gift of computer equipment has made my work more effective and enjoyable. His generosity, industry, and honesty make him a shining light in the often shady world of business.

Jim Day, the publisher of the St. Louis MetroVoice, also deserves special thanks for allowing me to work with him and hone my writing skills at his newspaper's expense. Jim is a rare journalist dedicated to knowing and publishing the whole truth, even if unpopular.

Others to whom I am indebted are the "Volz Clan" for boosting me to 100 megs; Dave Volz for his administrative leadership that frees my time to write; Marty Kinsey for his musical inspiration; John and Mona Maynard, Rick and Gina

Fister, Todd and Jackie Jaeger, and Bryan and Deborah Short for their many years of support and friendship.

Speaking of friendship, my wife and I are deeply indebted to Rob and Karen Graham for continually encouraging us and believing in us when we felt like retreating from the battle. Their hospitality and acceptance have been "the balm of Gilead" to my war-torn family; and for that I will be forever grateful.

Last but not least, I could not have finished this project without the patient efficiency of Debbie Durso, who typed the original manuscript. She laboriously interpreted my illegible scrawl, transforming it into the readable text you now have before your eyes.

To all these, as well as many other friends and family members, I render sincere appreciation and affection; while acknowledging that apart from the good providence of God this book would never have been completed. He alone deserves all the honor for all the truth it unfolds and all the good it may accomplish. May He use it to raise up a new generation of leaders who, like Patrick Henry, are valiant warriors for His truth.

INTRODUCTION

*I*n the center of Richmond's Capital Square stands a monument to three of Virginia's greatest sons, and three of America's greatest heroes: George Washington, Thomas Jefferson, and Patrick Henry. George Washington is seated upon his steed and flanked by the standing figures of Thomas Jefferson and Patrick Henry. Each member of this talented trio of valiant Virginians was, within his own sphere and according to his own ability, a great man, a noble patriot, and a legendary leader. Thus, history has coined them, respectively, as the Sword, the Pen, and the Trumpet of the American Revolution.

What is surprising to learn about this triumphant trio is that, among them, Patrick Henry was the recognized leader. It is one thing to capture the imagination of the masses or arouse the passions of the populace; it is quite another thing to earn the reverence of the respected and marshall the loyalty of leaders. Yet this is precisely what Patrick Henry accomplished.

Some of the greatest men in American history (Washington, Jefferson, and others) looked to Patrick Henry as a man worthy to follow. As one historian has written, "The historian-detective is greatly impressed by the man's tremendous power, his persuasive talents, his unequaled popularity. Again and again he finds Jefferson, Madison, Washington, and others asking just how Henry stood on such and such an issue–and just how he stood often, if not always, meant its success or failure."[1] Later in his life Thomas Jefferson confided in Daniel Webster that not only was Patrick Henry's eloquence "sublime," but as "our leader he was far above all…in the Revolution." Indeed, confessed Jefferson, "It is not now easy to say what we should have done without Patrick Henry."[2]

How do we account for Patrick Henry's stature as the leader of some of our nations most gifted men? That question is not so easily answered, for several reasons. First of all, contrary to the custom of many of his contemporaries, Patrick Henry did not keep a personal journal. Nor was he particularly fond of writing letters. Compared to the voluminous writings of both Washington (39 volumes) and Jefferson (over 50 volumes), Henry paled in comparison. He has left us only one meager volume of letters and recorded speeches. Thus it is often difficult to pry into the mind and motivations of this master-leader. Henry's paucity of pen has undoubtedly also led to a certain neglect by historians.

In addition, although Henry was the undisputed leader in Virginia during the revolutionary period, and was nationally recognized as a patriot, he never assumed a national office even though several were offered to him. Thus his stature as a "national" figure has been obscured.

But perhaps there is another and more profound reason that historian Bernard Mayo, quoting Churchill, said that Henry was "a riddle wrapped in a mystery inside an enigma."[3]

That reason being, that the essence of leadership is itself a mystery.

Contrary to many popular books on the subject, leadership is not simply the ability to employ techniques or to imitate traits. True leadership is more than the possession of a special quality like courage or vision–both of which are common to great leaders–and it is more than simply the combination of several such qualities. As in philosophy, so with leadership: the whole is greater than the sum of the parts. Real leadership of the kind evinced in the life of Patrick Henry–the kind that inspired educated, gifted, and brave men to follow him–is more like a force or an energy than a trait. It is a power that animates action, demands daring deeds, and excites exertion for noble causes.

If we were to reduce the essence of leadership to a single word, we might call it "integrity," although that word is too pristine. The Greeks would probably have termed it "semnous," and the Romans, "gravitas." The fundamental idea lurking behind these inadequate epithets is this: the sense of character that a person holds which inspires in others reverence or respect. A good modern equivalent would be "moral authority." And it is this quality that Patrick Henry possessed in full. When he spoke, men listened. When he acted, men followed. Why? Because he was a man of deep religious faith and virtue; and when he spoke he awed men with not only his rhetorical gifts, but also with "the trumpet resonance of his moral authority."[4] As we look at Patrick Henry's life, we will see that his character is inseparable from his accomplishments, and his virtue from his valor.

As with any renowned leader, there is always an additional element that lends to the mystery of his greatness: namely, God's providence. The ways of God are ultimately inscrutable to man, and why He should choose to raise up one man rather than another is a question we can never fully answer. We will see in Patrick Henry's life, however, that God's good providence was continually at work to fulfill a divine plan.

CHRONOLOGY OF PATRICK HENRY'S LIFE

1733,   Marriage of John Henry and Sarah Winston (Syme).

1736,   May 29–Birth of Patrick Henry at Studley Plantation in Hanover County.

1747,   Reverend Samuel Davies comes to Hanover and establishes the Presbyterian Church there.

1749,   Henry family moves to Mount Brilliant, known as "The Retreat."

1751,   Patrick, at age 15, apprenticed as a merchant.

1752,   Patrick and brother, William, open their own country store.

1754,   The Henry brothers' business fails.

1754,   Patrick marries Sarah Shelton in the fall, and establishes a home at Pine Slash.

1757,   A fire destroys Henry's home and a large part of his possessions.

1758,   Spring–Patrick opens a country store while still maintaining a small farm.

1760,   Failure of second business. Henry decides to try the legal profession.

1760,   August 15–Henry sworn in as a lawyer and begins law practice.

1763,   December 1–Henry pleads the "Parson Cause" and becomes a local celebrity.

1765,   Stamp Act passes House of Commons and Lords and is given Royal assent.

1765,   May 20–Henry is admitted to the Virginia House of Burgesses and takes his seat.

1765,   May 23–Henry makes his Bank Loan speech.

1765,	May 29–Henry's twenty-ninth birthday. He makes his famous Stamp Act speech and the Stamp Act Resolutions are passed.
1766,	March 18–Repeal of the Stamp Act.
1769,	Henry and family move to Scotchtown. Henry admitted to bar of the General Court in Williamsburg.
1771,	Henry defends the Baptist dissenter John Waller.
1773,	March 12–Henry helps to establish colonial "Committees of Correspondence."
1774,	May–Henry, Jefferson, and others develop plan for Continental Congress.
1774,	August 1–First Virginia Convention convenes.
1774,	September 5–Henry sent as a delegate to the First Continental Congress in Philadelphia.
1775,	February–Death of Henry's first wife, Sallie.
1775,	March 20–Second Virginia Convention convenes.
1775,	March 23–Henry delivers his famous "Give Me Liberty" speech. Passage of measures to arm Virginia.
1775,	April 19–Battle at Lexington, Massachusetts–the "shot heard 'round the world."
1775,	April 20–Governor Dunmore steals gunpowder from Williamsburg magazine.
1775,	May 2-4–Henry leads armed militia against Dunmore to retrieve gunpowder.
1775,	May 10–Second Continental Congress in Philadelphia. Henry takes his seat on May 18.
1775,	July–Third Virginia Convention convenes.
1775,	August 5–Third Convention appoints Henry as colonel of the First Regiment and commander-in-chief of the Virginia regular forces.
1775,	December 1–Fourth Virginia Convention convenes.
1776,	February 28–Henry resigns his military commission.
1776,	May 6–Fourth and final Virginia Convention meets.
1776,	May 15–Convention instructs Congressional delegates to adopt American Declaration of Independence.

1776, June 12–Convention adopts the Virginia Bill of Rights.

1776, June 29–Virginia's Declaration of Independence and Constitution formally adopted. Henry elected as first governor of the new state of Virginia.

1776, July 4–Congress adopts the American Declaration of Independence.

1776, July 5–Henry sworn in as first governor of Virginia.

1777, May 27–Henry elected for second annual term as governor.

1777, October 9–Henry marries Dorothea Dandridge.

1777, Winter–Henry supports Washington's army at Valley Forge.

1778, May 29–Henry elected governor for a third consecutive term.

1779, June 1–Henry retires as governor; Thomas Jefferson elected to succeed him. Henry moves to Leatherwood.

1780, May–Henry returns to Virginia legislature as its leading member.

1781, October–American victory at Yorktown.

1781, December 12–Report to the Virginia House by committee appointed to investigate Jefferson's conduct as governor.

1783, September 3–America passes treaty with Great Britain.

1784, November–Henry proposes "assessment" for plural establishment of Christianity.

1784, November 17–Henry elected governor for fourth term.

1785, November 25–Henry elected governor for fifth term.

1786, April–Colonel Christian, Henry's brother-in-law, killed by Indians.

1786, November–Henry declines appointment to sixth term as governor.

1787, February 13–Henry declines to become a delegate to the Constitutional Convention in Philadelphia.

1787, October–Henry returns to the Virginia Assembly as its leading member.

1788, June 2–Virginia Constitution Convention. Henry leads fight against adoption of federal Constitution without prior amendments.

1788, June 25–Virginia Convention ratifies the federal Constitution against Henry's objections.

1788-1791, Henry is the leading advocate in the Virginia Assembly for Constitutional amendments.

1791,   November–Henry retires from the Virginia legislature.

1791,   November–Henry appears in the British Debt Case.

1791,   December–States ratify the federal Bill of Rights.

1791-1794,   Henry appears in many criminal and civil cases, including the Randolph murder case.

1795-1799,   Henry retires from legal practice to Red Hill. He declines the offers of several high governmental positions including secretary of state and chief justice of the United States Supreme Court.

1799,   March–Henry makes his last speech at Charlotte Courthouse, and warns of civil war. Elected to Virginia legislature.

1799,   June 6–The Trumpet of the Revolution hears the trumpet of God.

PART I:
THE LIFE OF PATRICK HENRY

જ્∘   જ્∘   જ્∘

The American Revolution was the grand operation,
which seemed to be assigned by the Deity to the men
of this age in our country, over and above the common
duties of life. I ever prized the superior privilege of
being one in that chosen age, to which providence
entrusted its favorite work.[5]

Is life so dear, or peace so sweet, as to be purchased at the
price of chains and slavery? Forbid it, Almighty God![6]

Early Life

*T*he early life of Patrick Henry augured nothing of the future greatness for which he was destined. This fact should not surprise us, however: both nature and Scripture reveal a providential pattern of greatness springing out of obscurity. The small acorn grows into the strong and stately oak, and the minute mustard seed blossoms into a haven for the fowls of the air. Thus it was with Patrick Henry.

Born in Hanover County, Virginia, on May 29, 1736, Patrick was the second of nine children–two boys and seven girls. His father, John Henry, was a well-respected member of the Hanover community, and throughout his life held such positions as county surveyor and presiding magistrate of Hanover County. He was also a colonel of Hanover's regiment of the state militia. John Henry's political sympathies lay with the monarchy, and his religious affiliation was with the established church–the Anglican church. Those who personally knew him described him as a man of "plain but solid understanding," whose life was an example of "integrity and piety."[7]

In 1731, John Henry was employed as a surveyor by a Colonel John Syme, who died that same year. John Henry stayed on at Studley Plantation, helping widow Syme manage her affairs. Two years thereafter, in 1733, John Henry and the widow were wed.

Sarah Winston (her maiden name) was an attractive woman with a cheerful disposition. William Byrd, a well-known aristocrat of the day, who happened to visit Sarah shortly after her first husband's death, described her as a "portly, handsome dame," of a "lively and cheerful conversation."[8] Indeed, the art of conversation was a trait that marked the Winston clan, and it was probably from his mother that Patrick acquired those oratorical gifts that later made him so famous.[9] But more importantly, Sarah was a devoted Christian who set before her children an example of "fervent piety."[10]

The Studley Plantation was a fairly prosperous farm with woodlands, open fields, and a small meandering stream–Totopotomoy Creek. And it was here that young Patrick, together with his cousins and neighbors, spent his early years fishing, hunting, and exploring the beautiful Virginia woods and countryside.

As a young boy, Patrick was "remarkably fond of fun" and "indulged much in innocent amusements."[11] Henry's love for his rod and gun, undoubtedly a common trait for Virginia lads raised in the country, has been misconstrued by some biographers to suggest that Patrick was lazy and indolent, with a positive "enmity" to books and learning. William Wirt, whose biography has influenced many that have followed, claimed that Patrick "was passionately addicted to the sports of the field, and could not support the confinement and toil which education required."[12] And A. G. Bradley, who was strongly influenced by Wirt, has said that Patrick "was a wastrel and an idler, a reputed hater of books and work, a loud-tongued joker at the village tavern."[13] Fortunately, later and more thorough research has demonstrated that these characterizations are false.[14]

Nevertheless, it is true that Henry had a great love for the outdoors–a love that remained throughout his life. In addition to his boyish love for the outdoors and hunting, Henry also had a more pensive and thoughtful side. His solitary roaming in the woods, instead of being wasted hours, were times of deep reflection and meditation–an almost forgotten art in our age of incessant noise and unceasing activity.[15] Contrary to Wirt, Henry developed a fondness for reading that gave his fertile mind ample matter for his quiet meditations.[16]

Henry's early education was fairly typical for his times. Until the age of ten he studied at an English common school where he learned the rudiments of reading, writing, and arithmetic. Afterwards, for about the next five years, he was educated by his father, who tutored several other students for pay. His father, who had himself received a classical education in England, taught Patrick Latin, Greek, math, and ancient and modern history.[17] His uncle, the Rev. Patrick Henry, also had a hand in the young boy's education, instructing him "not only in the catechism, but in the Greek and Latin classics."[18] By the time Henry was fifteen, he could read Virgil and Livy in the original. We also know from his writings that Patrick acquired some French and had an astounding command of the English language.[19]

Young Patrick's interest in the song of the birds and the melody of the meadows was undoubtedly a token of his natural ear for music. He was an excellent violinist. At the age of twelve he broke his collarbone and while recuperating, he mastered the flute. He also found time, during these early years, to learn a little lute and harpsichord.[20] Although Henry's educational achievements might strike us as extraordinary, they were fairly common for his day. In fact, there was nothing really exceptional about him as a young boy, except perhaps his tendency to be a careful observer of others, a trait noticed by those who knew him well.[21]

In a word, Henry's childhood was ordinary. "He was a normal boy, who liked work as little as a colt likes the cart. Unaware of his own latent powers, he did as other boys in Hanover were doing–went barefoot in summer, fished, swam, sang, fought, did 'chores,' and in fall and winter roamed the forests with his flintlock."[22] There is much testimony of Henry's "fondness for the woods and streams and of his fun-loving spirit, normal for a youth in his times."[23] But instead of being an impediment to his later greatness, Henry's "normal" childhood was the rich soil that nourished his love for both land and liberty and fueled his fiery rhetoric in their defense. "The frontier…helped to make Patrick Henry a fiery apostle of American democracy."[24]

Lessons in Rhetoric and Religion

*A*s with all great leaders, the providential hand of God was at work in Henry's youth. At the age of 12, Patrick first began to sit under the masterful preaching of the Rev. Samuel Davies, "the prince of American preachers." Davies' sermons were so telling that he was unequaled in the pulpit except by the eloquent evangelist George Whitefield himself. "Indeed, his manner of delivery as to pronunciation, gesture and modulation of voice was a perfect model of the most moving and striking oratory, while the sublimity and perspicuity of his discourses rendered his sermons...models for all who heard them..."[25]

The solemn and dignified sermons of Davies surely made a profound and lasting impact on the young and impressionable Patrick. Under Davies' eloquent and spell-binding preaching, he observed an exalted model of oratory worthy of imitation in his later political discourses. Henry is even reported to have confessed that Davies was "the greatest orator" he had ever heard.[26] If one compares some of Davies' sermons to Henry's later speeches, the influence is almost undeniable.[27]

Davies was more than a model of rhetoric, however. He was also a teacher of theology. And it was from Davies, and perhaps Patrick's mother, that he learned the outline and rudiments of Calvinist theology, which played a leading role in the colonial struggle for religious and political freedom. Henry later became a champion of both freedoms, and his views on liberty were probably derived from the Calvinistic doctrine "that the sovereign and supreme God alone is Lord of the conscience." Throughout his later political career, Henry advocated not only religious freedom, but also the justness of revolution, a view he may have inherited from the Calvinist John Knox.[28]

Although Henry's father was an Episcopalian, his mother became a Presbyterian and joined the "Fork Church" where Davies regularly preached. It was here that she brought young Patrick to church in 1748–riding in a double rig–and quizzed him after the service on the main points of the sermon. Because his parents and other relatives were members of different denominations, it is understandable why Henry, while remaining in the established church, was a recognized friend of all Christian denominations and a champion of religious toleration.[29]

Henry's early religious training was augmented by his clergyman uncle who drilled Patrick in the basic maxims of conduct. According to Henry, his uncle taught him the following practical precepts: "To be true and just in all my dealings. To bear no malice nor hatred in my heart. To keep my hands from picking and stealing. Not to covet other men's goods; but to learn and labor truly to get my own living, and to do my duty in that state of life unto which it shall please God to call me".[30]

FIRST FAILURES AND FIRST LOVE

*I*n 1749, the Henrys moved from the home of Patrick's birth in Studley to Mount Brilliant about 22 miles from Richmond. Also located in Hanover County, Mount Brilliant was later named, "The Retreat." Two years later, armed with the example of his parents' piety and the lessons from his uncle's catechism, Henry graduated his domestic school at the tender age of 15, and was apprenticed as a clerk in a country store. A year later, his father bought a stock of goods and set up Patrick and his brother, William, in business for themselves. Young Patrick was on his way "to learn and labor truly to get his own living."

The country store, of which he was now a joint proprietor, was an important economic agency and a hub of social activity in colonial Virginia. If we could for a moment step back in time and loiter in Henry's store, we would experience a microcosm of colonial life, "for in front of the counters a thousand scenes were enacted, stories told, characters revealed–all reflecting the familiar life of high families and mean–white and black–through the Old Dominion."[31] While Henry was weighing sugar and drawing molasses, his maturing mind was developing that faculty of keen observation which was to become a key ingredient in his success as both an orator and lawyer. For Henry, the country store was another school for the study of human nature. When his customers were engaged in unreserved conversation, Henry "would take no part in their discussions, but listen with a silence as deep and attentive as if under the influence of some potent charm." On the other hand, when there was little conversation, "nothing suited him better than to start a debate and then watch the debaters."[32]

There is an old and dogged anecdote about young Patrick's mercantile mismanagement. One day Henry was supposedly stretched out at full length on a sack filled with salt, engaged in a theoretical discussion, when a customer entered the store.

"Have you any salt, sir?" he inquired.

"Just sold the last peck," said Patrick.

Although it is probably spurious, this anecdote–and others like it–was a product of Henry's short-lived experience as an entrepreneur. Within a year, the Henry brothers had to close shop, having granted their delinquent customers too much credit. To Patrick fell the task of closing out the business and settling the accounts. Patrick's good nature was not good business. His generosity was his undoing.[33]

While finalizing the closure of the store, in the fall of 1754, Patrick married his first wife, Sarah Shelton. The Sheltons were a "respectable family who lived at Rural Plains, a few miles from Studley. John Shelton, her father, was a successful farmer and owned a profitable tavern near the Hanover Court House."[34] Sarah, or "Sallie" as her family called her, "had a pretty, round face, dark brown hair, and deep brown eyes." Apparently, Patrick and Sarah had known each other from childhood.[35] Since both bride and groom were legal minors, (Sarah was sixteen, and Patrick eighteen) parental consent was required–and reluctantly given.

In October 1754, the two families attended the wedding ceremony held in a small parlor at the Sheltons' Rural Plains home.[36] As part of the dowry, Sarah brought with her 300 acres of worn and sandy land, called "Pine Slash," and six young slaves. Pine Slash was a tract of land partially worn by previous use and partially in need of clearing for new crops– stumps had to be removed, grass burned away, and land plowed and hoed. The main crops were wheat, corn, oats, and tobacco; but only the tobacco was salable, the rest being used on the farm.[37]

Patrick's parents gave him a little property also, and with these meager resources the young newlyweds began to build a family and life together.

In the early summer of 1755, as Patrick labored in the field, his wife Sarah labored to bring forth Martha, their first-born child–afterward nicknamed "Patsy." But as his family grew, so did his misfortune. In that first year, Henry's crops were plagued with both a summer drought and then an early frost. Moreover, most small farmers in the colonies were beginning to feel the economic consequences of Britain's battle with France for colonial dominion. As Francis Jerdone, a merchant, stated in 1756, "the poor people are now very much pinched."[38]

While some of his contemporaries, such as George Washington, were going off to fight the French on the frontier, Henry stayed home to battle the soil and care for his young family. In the spring of 1757, his first son, John, was born, which must have given Patrick great joy. Shortly thereafter, however, the Henrys were struck by a fire that destroyed their house and nearly all their possessions. With his house in ashes and his family in tow, Henry took up residence in his father-in-law's tavern, and once again made a try at success-fully operating a country store. This second effort, however, proved no more lucrative than the first. Times were hard in 1758, the year he opened, and the next year the tobacco crop again failed. His customers were, again, unable to make good on their accounts, and Henry was forced to close his store, los-ing his capital and going into debt. Thus, by 1759, Patrick Henry had failed–not once, but three times–and was virtually a pauper.

In spite of his difficulties, Henry maintained a "cheerful and self-reliant spirit which no misfortune could benumb."[39] It was this buoyant spirit that Thomas Jefferson noticed when he first met Henry in 1759. It was Christmas, and Patrick took his family to visit his parents at Mount Brilliant. A nearby neighbor, the well-to-do Colonel Nathaniel West Dandridge, was entertaining holiday guests, one of whom was young Tom Jefferson, and another, Patrick Henry. Years later, Jefferson recalled that Patrick had "a passion for music and dancing and pleasantry." And although he was beset with troubles, there was no trace of them "either in his countenance or con-duct."[40] Little did these two young men–one an aspiring student and the other a struggling father–realize that one day soon they would labor together for the cause of American independence.

To the Law and Testimony

*I*t was at this troubled time in Henry's life that he determined to try the law profession. Having failed at his other ventures, and being struck with adversity, God was using necessity to redirect Henry's path according to His plan. Necessity actually proved to be a blessing because it forced Henry into the field where he had to double his efforts to succeed and tap into his heretofore unused powers of mind and soul. Henry later realized the blessing of adversity and wrote to a young friend who was experiencing business problems:

> *Looking forward into life and to those
> prospects which seem to be commensurate with
> your talents…you may justly esteem those inci-
> dents fortunate which compel an exertion of
> mental power, maturity of which is rarely seen
> growing out of an uninterrupted tranquillity.
> Adversity toughens manhood, and the charac-
> teristic of the good or the great man, is not that
> he has been exempted from the evils of life, but
> that he has surmounted them.*[41]

Henry knew what he was talking about. Having decided to enter law, he was compelled to "an exertion of mental power" in preparation for licensure. Although the custom for aspiring law students was to either work as an apprentice under an experienced lawyer, or, if money was not an issue, to study law in London at the Inns of Court, Henry chose the more diffucult route of self-education. Accordingly, he borrowed a copy of *Coke upon Littleton* (Blackstone's famous commentaries not yet being published), a *Digest of Virginia Acts*, and Bacon's *Abridgement of the Laws* and began his preparation for the bar. Spurred by necessity, Henry devoured these volumes in the short span of six weeks. This was no small feat when we realize that Coke's tome was a huge folio volume of "closely printed columns, one for Littleton's original text in a mixture of legal French and Latin, a second for Coke's translation into English, and a third for the comments"–some of which ran longer than the texts themselves, and covered legal philosophy, philology and precedent.[42]

Virginia law required that a candidate for the legal profession apply to a panel of examiners in Williamsburg appointed by the General Court. Thus, after finishing his abbreviated preparation, Henry then rode off to Williamsburg, making the 50-mile trip in two days, to appear before the board of examiners. The board consisted of George Wythe, who later held the first law professorship in America; John and Peyton Randolph, each of whom at different times served as Virginia's attorney general; and Robert Carter Nicholas. All of these men sat in the Virginia House of Burgesses and were of considerable wealth and influence.

There are conflicting reports concerning the examination by the board, but all accounts agree that there was an initial reluctance by the board to examine the coarse-looking and unprepared candidate. John Randolph, a man of great polish and refinement, was put off by Henry's plain country clothes, and at first refused to examine him. After learning that two of the other examiners had already signed Henry's application, Randolph agreed to quiz him. Much to his surprise, Randolph found that although Henry was inadequate with regard to many of the finer points of the law, he had a strong grasp of natural law, feudal law and general history. After a lengthy discussion, Randolph said to Henry, "You defend your opinions well, sir, but now to the law and to the testimony." He then led Henry to his office, and opening a variety of legal authorities he said to him: "Behold the force of natural reason; you have never seen these books, nor this principle of the law; yet you are right and I am wrong; and from this lesson which you have given me (you must excuse me for saying it), I will never trust to appearances again. Mr. Henry, if your industry be only half equal to your genius I augur that you will do well, and become an ornament and an honor to your profession."[43]

With his license in hand, and the ordeal behind him, Henry rode back to Hanover. A week later, on August 15, 1760, he rode 30 miles west to Goochland Court House on the Upper James and was sworn in as a practicing lawyer. Later in the same court session he filed the first of many legal papers. In fact, the records show that by early September, Henry had handled 176 cases for 75 clients, and had collected about half of the £123 in fees.[44] Over the next three years, Henry performed a number of standard services as he traveled the circuit of county courthouses of Cumberland, Louisa, Albemarle, Chesterfield, and Augusta. By 1763, his practice had more than doubled.

Randolph's prophecy was coming true: by his industry Henry was becoming an "ornament and an honor" to his profession. As his practice grew so did his reputation as a hard-working and conscientious attorney. But more importantly, Henry was now in the line of work that paved the way for his later exploits as an American patriot. For without his entrance into law, Henry would have never pled the Parson's Cause, the legal case that earned him a widespread popularity and launched his entrance into politics.

THE PARSON'S CAUSE

*H*enry's entrance into the legal profession was the critical move of his early career. He not only developed a successful practice by industrious habits, but he also paid off his lingering debts, and acquired an expanding knowledge of law and human nature. After three years in practice in Hanover and the surrounding counties, he had gained an excellent reputation as an advocate. But his true claim to fame occurred when he was engaged in the so-called Parson's Cause.

This celebrated case derived its name from the plaintiff's involved–clergymen. Almost from the inception of the Virginia colony, the Anglican church was the established church, which meant that the Anglican clergy were servants of state who were paid through taxation. Throughout the colony it was the duty of the vestrymen, or town's officials, to hire a local minister and set his salary. Since the vestrymen were usually owners of tobacco plantations, the custom was to pay the parsons in tobacco.

In 1748, the Virginia House of Burgesses had set a minister's salary at 16,000 pounds of tobacco annually. If the vestrymen failed to meet this quota, they could be sued for damages. In 1755, and then again in 1758, the vestrymen altered the quota due to bad crops and forced the parsons to accept depreciated paper money at a rate of "two pence" for every pound of tobacco–that law appropriately being called the "Two Penny Act." The net result was that ministers were receiving only about one-third of their lawful wages.[45] But instead of accepting their lowered standard of living in the spirit of the beatitude, "Blessed are the poor," many of the clergy sued. One such litigant was the Reverend Maury, former instructor of Thomas Jefferson, who filed suit in the courthouse of Hanover.

In November 1763, the case came to trial, and the court ruled that since the King had never agreed to the Two Penny Act, the law was void, and the vestrymen had thus acted illegally. The defendant, Thomas Johnson, was liable for damages, and a hearing to assess them was set for December 1, 1763. In the meantime, Johnson retained Henry to represent him at the hearing.[46]

On the first of December, the Hanover courthouse, a quaint, roomy building made from English brick, was filled with spectators–lawyers and clergy, commoners and aristocrats. When Patrick Henry's uncle, the Reverend Henry, arrived at the courthouse, Patrick ran to his carriage and begged him not to come to court that day.

"Why?" asked Reverend Henry.

"Because I am engaged in opposition to the clergy," said Patrick, "and your appearance there might strike me with such awe as to prevent me from doing justice to my clients. Besides, sir, I shall be obliged to say some hard things of the clergy, and I am very unwilling to give pain to your feelings."[47]

The elder Henry complied and rode off to his parsonage.

The case began with Henry's father sitting as the presiding judge, and after the jury was chosen, the only question to be determined was the amount of damages to be awarded to Reverend Maury. His counsel, Peter Lyons, argued that his client deserved at least triple the £144 actually paid. In addition, Lyons made what would prove to be a serious tactical error by incidentally praising the Anglican church and its clergy. Henry's reply is best described by one biographer:

> *He rose to reply to Mr. Lyons with apparent embarrassment and some awkwardness, and began a faltering exordium .The people hung their heads at the unpromising commencement, and the clergy were observed to exchange sly looks with each other, while his father sank back in his chair in evident confusion. All this was of short duration however. As he proceeded and warmed up with his subject, a wondrous change came over him. His attitude became erect and lofty, his face lighted up with genius, and his eyes seemed to flash fire; his gesture became graceful and impressive, his voice and his emphasis peculiarly charming. His appeals to the passions were overpowering. In the language of those who heard him, 'he made their blood to run cold, and their hair to rise on end.' In a word, to the astonishment of all, he suddenly burst upon them as an orator of the highest order. The surprise of the people was only equaled by their delight, and so overcome was his father that tears flowed profusely down his cheeks.*[48]

Citing a basic constitutional principle in English law, that only a representative assembly has the power to levy taxes on the people it represents, Henry claimed that the King had no authority to annul the law in question, and implied that by doing so he was a tyrant. Mr. Lyons objected, "The gentleman has spoken treason…" And murmurs of "Treason! Treason!" were heard throughout the courtroom. But the court over-ruled and Henry continued.

He now directed his shafts toward the clergy. Since the established clergy were servants of the state, their obligation was to encourage obedience to civil law, he argued. But look at them, he said with disdain, they are challenging the law, and have thus forfeited their positions as useful members of the community. The court had already determined that Reverend Maury should be paid damages, yet Henry argued that what he *really* deserved was punishment. He then unleashed the fatal blow.

> *We have heard a great deal about the benevo-*
> *lence and holy zeal of our reverend clergy, but*
> *how is this manifested? Do they manifest their*
> *zeal in the cause of religion and humanity by*
> *practicing the mild and benevolent precepts of*
> *the Gospel of Jesus? Do they feed the hungry*
> *and clothe the naked? Oh, no, gentlemen!*
> *Instead of feeding the hungry and clothing the*
> *naked, these rapacious harpies would, were*
> *their powers equal to their will, snatch from the*
> *hearth of their honest parishioner his last hoe-*
> *cake, from the widow and her orphan children*
> *their last milch cow! The last bed, nay, the last*
> *blanket from the lying-in woman!*[49]

Henry then concluded by reminding the jury that even though they must find for the plaintiff, "they need not give him more than a farthing."[50] As he turned from the jury, the courtroom erupted into a wild clamor, and before the bailiff could restore order, the jury returned with their verdict: the Reverend Maury was to receive damages in the amount of one penny! At the jury's announcement, the spectators burst into an uproar and drowned out Lyon's objections. The people then "pressed around Henry, seized him, lifted him to willing shoulders, and with shouts of jubilation, bore him into the court-yard, where he was lionized…"[51] The man and the hour had met.

As a result of the Parson's Cause, Henry leapt from obscurity. His name was now a household word in Hanover and the surrounding counties. His law practice began to flourish and he was recruited for political office as a champion of the people's rights. But Henry was not yet ready for a larger stage. His heart was at home and his head was in the woods. He was still so fond of hunting that he would often appear in court to plead a case "fresh from the chase," wearing his leathers with gun in hand.

A broader result of the Parson's Cause was the established clergy's loss of respect in the eyes of the public and a growing spirit of dissent against the monarchy. "Henry's speech in the Parson's Cause and the verdict of the jury may be said, in a certain sense, to have been the commencement of the Revolution in Virginia; and Hanover, where dissent had appeared, was the starting point."[52] Thus, the celebrated case that led to Henry's professional independence led also to America's political independence. And the independence of both Henry and America were from now on inextricably linked.

British Blunders

While Henry was enjoying fame throughout Virginia as "the orator of nature," and pursuing success as a lawyer, the relations between England and America were becoming increasingly strained as a result of British blunders in colonial policy.

The British crown had, from the inception of colonial America, recognized that all colonists and their descendants should enjoy all the "liberties, franchises, and immunities" of free-born Englishmen. Thus said the original charter that King James granted to the London Company in 1606, and all subsequent charters made similar provisions.

Once established, the colonies naturally organized local self-government to protect their ancient rights and liberties. As early as 1619, the Virginia Assembly was convened; and five years later, in 1624, the Assembly declared that "the Governor shall not lay any taxes or imposition upon the colony"…except by "the authority of the General Assembly."[53] This claim, formalized in the infancy of colonial history, established the right of the American people to have a voice in matters of internal taxation.

Nevertheless, Britain passed a series of maritime laws that encroached on this right. Between 1651 and 1663 Parliament passed legislation designed to eliminate Dutch competition and to grant British vessels a monopoly on colonial shipping. A consequence, however, was the suppression of colonial free trade, and a duty laid on inter-colonial commerce. This "external taxation," as it was called, was considered an oppressive, though legal, burden. Moreover, laws were passed in England that granted customs officers the authority to conduct searches, without cause or warrant, whenever they pleased. The colonists considered this practice a gross violation of their rights, further alienating their loyalty and exacerbating their resentment.

Relations between the Crown and the colonies further deteriorated because of the King's authority over colonial assemblies. In order for a measure passed by an assembly to become law, it first needed the King's assent. His distance from the colonies, as well as his ignorance of their condition, made for continual confusion in the colonies and poor judgment on the part of the King. Needed laws were often annulled or delayed, much to the detriment of the colonies. To make matters worse, the Lords of Trade, who stood between the King and the colonies, were guilty of "criminal mismanagement."[54]

With this subterranean river of resentment flowing through the colonial legislatures, Parliament passed the Sugar Act in 1763, which renewed a tax on imported sugar and molasses. By this act, all officials of the Crown were designated as custom house officials and given wide powers to make seizures of suspected illicit traffic. Moreover, all cases of this nature were now referred to courts of admiralty which were presided over by Crown appointees, and where trial by jury was not allowed. This practice was viewed by the colonists as a grievous infringement of their right to trial by jury.[55]

Colonial suspicions of the Crown were further inflamed by rumors traveling from England. The word coming from Crown representatives was that the young King George III was planning radical and oppressive measures against the colonies: to alter original colonial charters, to quarter a standing army in the colonies, and to impose a direct tax to support that army. Although the plan to alter the charters was never acted on, the Crown did decide to levy a direct tax on the colonies in the form of a stamp tax. The Stamp Act required that, after November 1, 1765, stamps be affixed to all legal papers, commercial papers, liquor licenses, land documents, indentures, cards, dice, pamphlets, newspapers, advertisements, almanacs, academic degrees, and appointments to office. The money collected from the sale of these revenue (not postage) stamps was designated for the British treasury to be used for expenses incurred in America. This act was the most flagrant departure from tradition yet made by the Crown, for it placed a direct tax on the Americans, something that had never been done before. More importantly, it fell upon some of the most outspoken and influential people in America: lawyers and publishers.[56]

The original resolution for the Stamp Act, proposed by the infamous George Grenville, was agreed upon by the House of Commons in March of 1764. The execution of the measures was deferred, however, until the colonial legislatures could be heard from. As a gesture of goodwill, Parliament stipulated that if the stamp tax was not acceptable to the colonies, they might recommend a different form of taxation; however, the legality of the right to tax the colonies was not open to question.

These Declamatory Resolves, as they were called, united the colonies in protest to Great Britain. Beginning with a town meeting in Boston on May 24, 1764, the colonists instructed their representatives to oppose the tax as a direct violation of their rights. Nearly every colonial assembly sent papers of remonstrance to both the King and Parliament. Yet, in spite of the protest, the Stamp Act was passed by Parliament in March, 1765, and was to go into effect on the first of November. Once passed, the leading figures in the colonies generally agreed that the proper course of action was submission. The American people were despondent–and even resentful–but they were not inclined toward rebellion. James Otis, of the Boston Assembly, summed up their submissive sentiments: "It is the duty of all humbly, and silently, to acquiesce in all the decisions of the supreme legislature."[57]

It seemed, then, that the Stamp Act would be executed by Parliament and accepted by the colonists. Even though "the great mass of the people were thoroughly convinced that the act was in violation of their rights, and an unjustifiable wrong inflicted on them," there was no leader "around whom they could rally in opposing its execution."[58] That is, until Patrick Henry, the Son of Thunder, arrived at the capitol, resolved to resist the encroaching tyranny.

THE STAMP ACT RESOLUTIONS

*W*hen the Virginia House of Burgesses convened in 1765, one of their first orders of business was to fill several vacancies that had occurred during the recess. Patrick Henry was chosen to fill the vacancy left by William Johnson of Louisa County, who had accepted the office of coroner. On May 20, Henry arrived in Williamsburg, entered the H-shaped capitol building, and proceeded to the east-wing chamber where the Assembly convened. After taking the prescribed oaths, he was duly "admitted to his place in the House."[59]

Although the formal House rules permitted every member equal privileges in debate, custom accorded power to the "aristocratic gentlemen" of long-standing–men like John Robinson, for thirty years Speaker of the House; Peyton Randolph, the attorney general since 1744, whose opinions in constitutional matters were highly respected; Edmund Pendleton, whom Jefferson claimed was "the ablest man in debate"; George Wythe, considered the most learned jurist in the colonies; Richard Bland, skilled parliamentarian and political philosopher; and George Washington, the wealthy Mount

Vernon planter and admired military leader in the French and Indian War. Other men of great character and learning, such as Thomas Jefferson, Robert Nicholas Carter, and Richard Henry Lee, were also members of this Assembly. "History does not tell us of a state of the same size as Virginia which could, at any one period, furnish such a galaxy of great names as is found on the roll of this House."[60] Yet it was this august body of men who had, for all intents and purposes, acquiesced to the inevitability of the Stamp Act which was to go into effect on November 1.

Henry, however, was of a different mind. In league with George Johnson, the delegate for Fairfax, and John Fleming, the member for Cumberland, Henry quickly drew up his now famous Stamp Act Resolves. Only nine days after accepting his seat in the House, the neophyte assemblyman offered the following resolutions in opposition to the Stamp Act:

> RESOLVED, *That the first adventurers and settlers of this his Majesty's colony and dominion brought with them, and transmitted to their posterity, and all other his Majesty's subjects since inhabiting in this his Majesty's said colony, all the privileges, franchises, and immunities that have at any time been held, enjoyed, and possessed by the people of Great Britain.*

> RESOLVED, *That by two royal charters, granted by King James the First, the colonists aforesaid are declared entitled to all the privileges, liberties, and immunities of citizens and natural-born subjects, to all intents and purposes as if they had been abiding and born within the realm of England.*

RESOLVED, *That the taxation of the people by themselves, or by persons chosen by themselves to represent them, who can only know what taxes the people are able to bear, and the easiest mode of raising them, and are equally affected by such taxes themselves, is the distinguishing characteristic of British freedom, and without which the ancient Constitution cannot subsist.*

RESOLVED, *That his Majesty's liege people of this most ancient colony have uninterruptedly enjoyed the right of being thus governed by their own Assembly in the article of their taxes and internal police, and that the same hath never been forfeited or any other way given up, but hath been constantly recognized by the kings and people of Great Britain.*

RESOLVED, *therefore, That the General Assembly of this colony has the only and sole exclusive right and power to lay taxes and impositions upon the inhabitants of this colony, and that every attempt to vest such power in any person or persons whatsoever, other than the General Assembly aforesaid, has a manifest tendency to destroy British as well as American freedom.*[61]

A "most bloody debate" ensued: Henry, backed by Johnson and Fleming, against the entrenched aristocracy of Randolph, Bland, Pendleton, and others. The dispute lasted for two days, at the height of which Henry displayed his great and overpowering gifts of oratory. "They were great indeed,"

Thomas Jefferson later said, "such as I have never heard from any other man. He appeared to me to speak as Homer wrote."[62] Judge John Tyler, who was standing next to Jefferson in the lobby of the House, recalled Henry's "treason" speech.

> *Caesar had his Brutus; Charles the First, his Cromwell; and George the Third ("Treason," shouted the speaker. "Treason, treason," rose from all sides of the room. The orator paused in stately defiance till these rude exclamations were ended and then, rearing himself with a look and bearing of still prouder and fiercer determination, he so closed the sentence as to baffle his accusers, without the least flinching from his own position,)–"and if this be treason, make the most of it."[63]*

Judge Paul Carrington, delegate from Charlotte, declared that Henry's eloquence in this debate was "beyond his powers of description."[64] In the end, Henry's fiery and thunderous rhetoric carried the day and the resolutions were passed. It was a decisive victory; for "by these resolutions," said Jefferson, "Mr. Henry took the lead out of the hands of those who heretofore guided the proceedings of the House."[65] Thus, on his twenty-ninth birthday, Patrick Henry had established himself as the acknowledged leader of the colony of Virginia.

A day later, he left Williamsburg on horseback, assuming his work was done. The House, however, reassembled the next day and attempted to expunge the resolves from the record. After another debate, only four of the resolutions stayed in the House Journal. Nevertheless, Henry's resolves were leaked to the press and soon spread like wildfire throughout the colonies, burning away American apathy

toward British tyranny. The *Newport Mercury* printed six resolutions on June 24; the *Boston Gazette* printed a preamble
and seven resolves on July 1; and the *Maryland Gazette*, on
July 4, printed seven resolves without a preamble. In all the
newspaper versions, the final two resolutions read:

> RESOLVED, *that his Majesty's liege people, the*
> *inhabitants of this colony, are not bound to*
> *yield obedience to any law or ordinance what-*
> *soever, designed to impose any taxation*
> *whatsoever upon them, other than the laws or*
> *ordinances of the General Assembly aforesaid.*

> RESOLVED, *That any person, who shall, by*
> *speaking or writing, assert or maintain, that*
> *any person or persons, other than the General*
> *Assembly of this colony, have any right or*
> *authority to impose or lay any taxation on the*
> *people here, shall be deemed an enemy of this*
> *his Majesty's colony.*[66]

These resolves were seen, not as a protest, but as a virtual
declaration of resistance by the legislature of the great colony
of Virginia.[67] Some, such as Mr. Otis, declared them treason-
able, but a majority of colonists rallied around them as their
standard of resistance.

"The Virginia action, like an alarm, roused the patriots to
pass similar resolves."[68] During the fall of 1765, all of the colonial assemblies that met adopted resolutions closely parallel
to those enumerated by Henry in Virginia. The Sons of
Liberty, then organizing in the various colonies, also published their own resolves that closely reflected Henry's
words.[69] As a result, several public disturbances broke out,

stamp distributors were burned in effigy, and many of them resigned or agreed not to sell the loathed stamps. By the time the act was supposed to become effective–November 1, 1765–every stamp distributor had resigned and all stamps had been destroyed.

Thus, it was Patrick Henry and his opposition to the Stamp Act that proved to be the "alarm bell" of resistance and the beginning of the revolution. As Jefferson said, "Mr. Henry certainly gave the first impulse to the ball of the revolution." [70] According to historian William Cabell Rives, Henry played a "distinguished and splendid role" in propelling the revolution.

> *By his ever memorable resolutions in opposition to the Stamp Act, and the lofty eloquence with which he sustained them, he struck a timely blow which resounded throughout America and the world, and roused a spirit that never slumbered till its great work was accomplished. The moment was opportune and critical; and he seized it with a bold and felicitous energy that belonged to his ardent and impassioned nature. His was the temperament and the genius of the great popular orator, that fitted him to lead at such a moment, and, like Aaron, to proclaim the divine message of freedom to his countrymen, and of wrath and denunciation to their oppressors.* [71]

Henry's resolutions changed the American mind. "No man ever thought just the same after he had read them." [72]

PERSONAL AND PROFESSIONAL PROGRESS

*P*atrick Henry's custom was to retreat into private life after a session in the House. And as he rode back to Hanover after this conclusive victory, he was undoubtedly longing for family and farm, friends and fields. Henry's family was growing as rapidly as his fame. In the summer of 1767, his wife Sallie gave birth to another daughter, named Anne. Their eldest daughter, Patsy, had by now passed her twelfth birthday. Two young sons, Johnny and Billy, replicated their father's own boyhood ways by running "as wild as young colts."[73] Plantation life for the Henrys was simple and enjoyable. When visitors dropped in (as they frequently did), they were always met with cordiality and a taste of "Virginia hospitality," not to mention recreational dancing accompanied by Henry on the fiddle.

Henry's home at Roundabout is described by a later visitor as a "story-and-a-half structure, about 20 by 18 feet, with a shed on the north side. This shed was well finished off as a bedroom, which, added to one and often two bedrooms upstairs in the main building, furnished the sleeping apartments for the household." Around the mansion there were "several small buildings which served the purpose of kitchens, lumber-rooms, pantries, and smoke-houses; and there was almost always one which was fitted up as a bedroom for the boys of the establishment." The manse was on a hill which commanded a beautiful view of the Roundabout Valley, and was about three hundred yards from the little creek of that name. "It was just between two great thoroughfares that led from the mountains to the seaboard; and tradition says that the location was then considered one of the best in this region."[74]

In addition to his wife and children, it fell upon Henry to financially help both his father and father-in-law. His own father had contracted a number of small debts which Patrick helped relieve. Sallie's father, John Shelton, also experienced some financial reverses, and Henry "acquired some money for him" in exchange for an interest in some land holdings. Henry also raised some funds for Shelton by selling "Pine Slash," Sallie's dowry.[75] Like other successful lawyers, Henry tutored aspiring law students at this time. Two cousins, Isaac Coles and Edmund Winston, studied with Henry during the 1760's, and William Christian, another student, became so close to the Henry family that he married Patrick's sister Anne in 1768. Moreover, Henry began to take on greater responsibilities in the community after 1765 as a member of the vestry of Trinity Parish.[76]

Like many aspiring Virginians, Henry realized that property was a means to personal independence and wealth. George Washington, reflecting the sentiments of many of his contemporaries, noted that anyone who "rejects the present opportunity of hunting out good lands and in some measure working and distinguishing them for their own will never regain it."[77] Henry wisely seized the opportunity and invested both time and money in land speculation, acquiring 3,335 acres on Moccasin Creek and Houlston. Of his several purchases, one of his most cherished was a plantation known as Scotchtown. According to the newspaper notices advertising its sale, it was a "valuable tract of land, lying on New Found River in Hanover County, about sixteen miles above the courthouse." The advertisement further claimed that Scotchtown produced the "finest sweet-scented tobacco" much sought after by cash purchasers, and that the soil was "exceeding good for wheat." Of the three thousand available acres, Henry purchased only one thousand, including "the manor house and working farms." [78]

In the spring of 1769, Henry moved his family to this hilly northwestern corner of Hanover. Shortly thereafter, his family was enlarged to six; Betsy was born in April 1769, and baby Edward in early 1771. The main house, or manor, was a long rectangular building with a one-story facade that actually had three floors of living space. There were rooms for spinning, food storage, and living quarters. There was also a large unpartitioned attic that provided ample space for either children's play or entertaining guests. The manor was surrounded by several smaller buildings, one of which served as Henry's law office. [79]

Henry's law practice had for several years provided a steady source of work when he was out of session. For example, in 1765 Henry handled 547 cases and in 1766, 144 cases. In the two following years, he charged fees in a total of 908 cases. In 1769, Henry won admission to the bar of the General Court in Williamsburg, which meant that he generally took only major cases before that court, attending less to smaller cases in the local courts. Accordingly, his fee books show a significant decline in the number of cases he handled in 1769. Jefferson's later criticism of Henry–that he was "woefully deficient as a lawyer" and "little acquainted with the fundamental principles of his profession"–is easily refuted by

the above-mentioned facts. Moreover, in 1771 Robert Carter
Nicholas, who stood at the head of the Virginia bar, retired
and entrusted his clientele to Henry–an unlikely choice had
Henry been lacking in legal knowledge or experience.[80]

Henry's manner as an advocate, as well as his personal
appearance at this period of his life, is best described by Judge
Tucker, one of his younger contemporaries.

> *The General Court met in April [1773]. Mr.*
> *Henry practiced as a lawyer in it. I attended*
> *very frequently; generally sat near the clerk's*
> *table, directly opposite to the bar. I had now for*
> *the first time a near view of Mr. Henry's face.*
> *He wore a black suit of clothes and (as was the*
> *custom of the bar then) a tie-wig. His visage*
> *was long, thin, but not sharp, dark, without any*
> *appearance of blood in his cheeks, somewhat*
> *inclining to sallowness; his profile was of the*
> *Roman cast; …his eyebrows dark, long, and*
> *full; his eyes a dark gray…; his cheekbones*
> *rather high, but not like a Scots-man's; they*
> *were neither as large, as near the eyes, nor as*
> *far apart as [are those of] the natives of*
> *Scotland; his cheeks hollow; his chin long but*
> *well-formed, and rounded at the end, so as to*
> *form a proper counterpart to the upper part of*
> *the face. I find it difficult to describe his mouth,*
> *which there was nothing remarkable, except*
> *when about to express a modest dissent from*
> *some opinion upon which he was commenting;*
> *he then had a half sort of smile, in which the*
> *want of conviction was, perhaps, more strongly*
> *expressed than that cynical or satirical emotion*

*which probably prompted it. His manner and
address to the court and jury might be deemed
the excess of humility, diffidence, and modesty.*

*In his reply to counsel, his remarks on the evi-
dence and on the conduct of the parties, he
preserved the same distinguished deference and
politeness, still accompanied by the never-
failing index of this skeptical smile when the
occasion prompted. His manner was solemn
and impressive; his voice neither remarkable for
its pleasing tones or the variety of its cadence,
nor for harshness. If it was never melodious (as
I think), it was never, however, raised harsh. It
was clear, distinct, and capable of that emphasis which I incline to believe constituted one of
the greatest charms in Mr. Henry's manner. His
countenance was grave (even when clothed
with the half smile I have mentioned), penetrating, and marked with the strong lineaments of
deep reflection. When speaking in public, he
never (even on occasions when he excited it in
others) had anything like pleasantry in his
countenance, his manner, or the tone of his
voice. You would swear he had never uttered or
laughed at a joke. In short, in debate either at
the bar or elsewhere, his manner was so earnest
and impressive, united with a contraction or
knitting of his brows which appeared habitual,
as to give his countenance a severity sometimes
bordering upon the appearance of anger or
contempt suppressed, while his language
and gesture exhibited nothing but what was*

perfectly decorous. He was emphatic, without
vehemence or declamation; animated, but
never boisterous; nervous, without recourse to
intemperate language; and clear, though not
always methodical.[81]

As a lawyer, Henry had a wonderful sway over the minds and emotions of a jury, due to both his gifts as an orator and his insight into human nature. Regarding his power over juries, his first biographer stated: "In short, he understood the human character so perfectly, knew so well all its strength and all its weakness, together with every path and by-way which winds around to the citadel of the best fortified heart and mind, that he never failed to take them, either by strata-gem or storm. Hence he was, beyond doubt, the ablest defender of criminals in Virginia, and will probably never be equaled again."[82]

One class of "criminals" that Henry freely defended were the dissenting Baptists and Quakers. Since the Baptists were the most aggressive in their public evangelism, they were also the most fiercely persecuted. Indeed, Baptist historians chroni-cled the persecution of their itinerants. They were "pulled down while preaching," "dragged out amidst clenched fists," "pelted with apples and stone," "commanded to take a dram or be whipped," "brutally assaulted by a mob," "arrested, abused, and released," and–over and over again–"jailed for preaching."[83] In response to their repeated cries for help, Henry successfully intervened on their behalf in a number of legal cases.

Persistence, passion, and perception–each combined to make Henry a successful man in his private and professional capacities. The 1760's were for him a time of progress and growth. An enlarged family, expanding properties, and grow-ing legal employment made Henry a man whose accomplish-ments as a citizen matched his achievements as a statesman.

THE ROAD TO REVOLUTION

*F*rom the time of his decisive victory in the Stamp
Act crisis, in the spring of 1765, to his first term in
the Continental Congress in the fall of 1774, Patrick Henry not
only prospered in his private life but also advanced in his
political career. For these nine years he served in the Virginia
Assembly when in session, and practiced the "dull virtues of
patience, competence, and dependability."[84] Throughout this
period Henry gained experience by serving on numerous
standing and special committess in the House. For instance,
he was a member of the committee to resolve the financial
problems of the treasurer's office; a committee for resolving
currency problems; and the standing Committee of Privileges
and Elections, just to name a few. Through unremitting and
tedious labor, Henry became an experienced and prudent
politician. But more importantly, as a maturing master-
statesman, he helped guide the ship of state through the rough
waters of political turmoil to the safe haven of independence.

The repeal of the Stamp Act was signed by the King on
March 18, 1766, due to Henry's resolve, the colonists resistance, and the Parliament's reluctance to push the colonies

toward separation. Parliament itself was divided on the issue of British foreign policy toward the colonies, some denying that they had the right to lay a direct tax on the colonies. Thus, Lord Camden, Edmund Burke, and others championed the liberties of America, and prevailed. News of the Stamp Act's repeal brought great joy and celebration on both sides of the Atlantic. In London, the King was cheered by multitudes and merchant ships on the Thames displayed their colors. In America, loyal addresses were made to both Crown and Parliament, expressing dependence and devotion. The crisis had been averted–at least for now.[85]

But American joy over the repeal of the Stamp Act was unfortunately short-lived. In spite of colonial remonstrance and resistance, the King and Parliament were determined to claim the right to tax the colonies. In 1767, the leadership of the House of Commons passed from Pitt to Charles Townshend, chancellor of the exchequer, who foolishly promoted taxing the colonies. The "Townshend Acts," named after him, placed import duties (taxes, in other words) on glass, lead, painter's colors, paper, and tea. Since these duties were considered "external" taxes, Townshend reasoned, the colonies would comply with them. The Acts also granted royal commissioners broad powers of search and seizure.

Parliament further aggravated the delicate relationship with the colonies by passing legislation designed to strengthen its grip on the colonies. According to Clarence Carson:

> *Another act, passed at the same time, was the American Board of Customs Act. This established a board of customs for America, to be composed of five commissioners, and to be located at Boston. A little later in the year, an*

act was passed suspending the New York legis-
lature for not providing troop supplies. In a
similar vein, an act in September 1767 cur-
tailed the power of colonial legislatures
generally. The tenor of these acts was not only
to facilitate the raising of revenue but also to
reduce colonial control over their own affairs.
Along these same lines, an act passed in July of
1768 extended and spelled out the jurisdictions
of vice-admiralty courts in the colonies and
increased the number of courts in America from
one to four. These were, in effect, military
(naval) courts being given jurisdiction over
civilians.[86]

The colonial reaction to this renewed oppression was slow but unanimous resistance. The basic principles previously enunciated by Henry and others–that taxation without representation was both unjust and unconstitutional–were now firmly rooted in American soil, and several American writers, most notably John Dickinson, the "Maryland Farmer," espoused this and other arguments through the colonial tabloids.[87]

Colonial legislatures began to act in short order. The Massachusetts Assembly, under the guidance of Samuel Adams, petitioned the King for a repeal of the recent Acts of Parliament, and again asserted American rights. He then sent a Circular Letter to the other colonial assemblies informing them of his petition and encouraging them to issue similar appeals. When the Virginia Assembly convened in the spring of 1768, it drew up a similar but bolder petition, and replied to the Massachusetts Assembly, applauding the members for their faithful stand for American liberty. The assemblies of

New Hampshire, Maryland, Connecticut, Rhode Island, Georgia, and South Carolina followed suit. When the Circular Letter reached London via the Massachusetts' Governor, a Cabinet meeting was held on August 15. Not only was the Circular condemned as "rebellious," but royal orders were issued commanding the Massachusetts Assembly to "rescind" their Circular Letter; and also ordering the other colonial legislatures to not receive the Circular but "treat it with contempt." The royal governors were also told to dissolve or dismiss any Assembly disposed "to receive or give any countenance to this seditious paper."[88]

The colonies, however, were defiant. When the Massachusetts Assembly gathered in June, 1768, they found British ships in Boston harbor and troops stationed in the town. Nevertheless, they resolutely refused to rescind their letter and were immediately dissolved. In November, Parliament proposed that the leaders in Massachusetts be tried for treason, and that the colony be isolated from its American allies.

When the Virginia Assembly convened in May of 1769 under Baron de Botetourt, the new governor, he reassured them that he would act on their behalf before the Crown, thereby hoping to subdue their resistance to Britain. But he could not have been more mistaken. Virginia declared by resolution its intention to stand with Massachusetts against any and all attempts by Parliament to deny them their rights as "free-born Englishmen." Henry was appointed to the committee that drafted a petition to the King, and a copy of both the Resolutions and petition were ordered to be sent to the other colonial legislatures, requesting their agreement.

When the Governor learned of the resolutions, he dissolved the Assembly. The principal members, under Henry's leadership, reassembled nearby in the long-room of the Raleigh Tavern, known as the "Apollo." It was here that they agreed to boycott any of the taxed goods. By their "industry and frugality," they vowed, British trade would suffer from British tyranny.[89] The colonial boycott, aided by the restoration in early 1770 of the conciliatory Pitt, led to the repeal of the Townshend duties in April of that year. The contest was far from over, however, for the Crown still maintained its "right" to tax the colonies.

The repeal of the Duty Act could have gone a long way toward restoring American confidence in British good-will had the Crown not attempted to tightly govern the colonies by Royal instructions that violated many long-standing colonial customs.[90] In April 1772, Parliament passed an act designed to better secure dockyards, ships, and goods in colonial harbors. Provisions in the bill mandated the death penalty for the destruction of any goods, and the deportation of the accused to London for trial. In Rhode Island, the colonists responded by capturing and burning the *Gaspee*, a British revenue ship. In January 1773, Parliament established a commission to investigate the incident, with the authority to send offenders to England for trial. This provision was viewed by the colonists as an attack upon their cherished right of trial by jury.

Then, in May of 1773, Parliament passed the Tea Act, which was intended to extend the monopoly of the East Indies Company in its competition with the Dutch. Americans, however, boycotted the tea. In Boston, a group of angry citizens disguised as Mohawk Indians raided several ships docked in the Boston port and dumped the tea into the harbor. Parliament, now incensed, resolved to use force against the "rebellious" colonies. Between March 31 and June 2, 1774, four bills, which were known collectively as the Coercive Acts, were passed. The Boston Port Act closed the port of Boston, and the Massachusetts Government Act essentially stripped local self-government from the citizens of Massachusetts.[91]

It was in this agitated and anxious atmosphere that the Virginia Assembly, under Henry's sagacious leadership, moved decisively and devoutly toward independence. On March 12, 1773, without Governor Dunmore's knowledge, (de Botetourt having passed away), the Assembly established "standing committees of correspondence" designed to obtain any information of Britain's movements toward the colonies and transmit the same to its sister colonies. Henry's aim was to unite the colonial Assemblies in concerted action against the Crown. After receiving the March 12 resolutions, the various colonial Assemblies unanimously agreed to appoint their own committees of correspondence. The union was advancing.

Henry understood, however, that successful opposition required more than mere human strategy. Without Divine assistance there would be no colonial resistance. Accordingly, when the Virginia Assembly convened in May 1774, having received word of the Boston Port Bill, they agreed to "boldly take an unequivocal stand" with Massachusetts.[92] Henry, Jefferson, Lee, and a few others gathered in private counsel and drew up a resolution for a day of general fasting and prayer to be appointed. The resolution entered into the Journal on May 24, 1774, shows Henry's simple faith in God's providence over human affairs and his humble reliance on God's aid for success.

> *This house being deeply impressed with apprehension of the great dangers to be derived to British America, from the hostile invasion of the City of Boston, in our sister colony of Massachusetts Bay, whose commerce and harbor are, on the first day of June next, to be stopped by an armed force, deem it highly necessary that the said first day of June next be set*

*apart by the members of this house, as a day of
fasting, humiliation, and prayer, devoutly to
implore the Divine interposition for averting
the heavy calamity which threatens destruction
to our civil rights, and the evils of civil war; to
give us one heart and one mind firmly to
oppose, by all just and proper means, every
injury to American rights; and that the minds
of his majesty and his parliament may be
inspired from above with wisdom, moderation,
and justice, to remove from the loyal people of
America all cause of danger, from a continued
pursuit of measures pregnant with their ruin.*[93]

When Governor Dunmore learned of this resolution, the
Assembly was immediately dissolved. Nevertheless, the leading members continued to meet to devise a plan to unite all
the colonies in resistance to Great Britain. George Mason,
who was in Williamsburg at this time, attests to Henry's crucial role as Virginia's leader. In a letter dated May 26, 1774, he
says: "Whatever resolves or measures are intended for the
preservation of our rights and liberties, will be reserved for
the conclusion of the session. Matters of that sort here are
conducted and prepared with a great deal of privacy, and by
very few members, of whom Patrick Henry is the principal."
Mason then went on to praise Henry's character and talents.

*He is by far the most powerful speaker I ever
heard. Every word he says not only engages, but
commands the attention; and your passions are
no longer your own when he addresses them.
But his eloquence is the smallest part of his
merits. He is in my opinion the first man upon*

*this continent, as well in abilities as public
virtues, and had he lived in Rome about the
time of the first Punic war, when the Roman
people had arrived at their meridian glory, and
their virtue not tarnished, Mr. Henry's talents
must have put him at the head of that glorious
Commonwealth.*[94]

Under Henry's guiding hand, this small group of patriots advanced the idea of state conventions, apart from royal control, designed to choose delegates for an annual Continental Congress. In this manner the colonies would, with God's help, stand united against British tyranny.

THE FIRST CONTINENTAL CONGRESS

*I*n response to the recommendation of Henry and the other leading members of the recently dissolved House, the First Virginia Convention assembled in Williamsburg on August 1, 1774, and sat for six days. After agreeing to a boycott of British imports, the Convention chose delegates to the Congress at Philadelphia in September: Randolph, R. H. Lee, Washington, Bland, Harrison, Pendleton, and, of course, Henry. The letter of instructions which was to accompany the delegates read, in part:

> *The unhappy disputes between Great Britain and her American colonies, which began about the third year of the reign of his present majesty, and since, continually increasing, have proceeded to lengths so dangerous and alarming as to excite just apprehensions in the minds of his majesty's faithful subjects of this colony that they are in danger of being deprived of their natural, ancient, constitutional, and chartered rights, have compelled them to take the*

*same into their most serious consideration; and
being deprived of their usual and accustomed
mode of making known their grievances, have
appointed us their representatives, to consider
what is proper to be done in this dangerous crisis of American affairs.*[95]

On August 30 Henry, accompanied by Edmund Pendleton, arrived at Mount Vernon, the home of George Washington. Although Pendleton had often been Henry's legal adversary, and even now had different political sentiments, he still acknowledged Henry's sterling character and lofty talents. According to Pendleton, Henry deserved "first place" as the one who "broke the influence" of the Virginia aristocracy. As to his "manners," Henry displayed "every decorum" of a "real Virginian." His "demeanor," noted Pendleton, was "inoffensive, conciliatory, and abounding in good humour." Henry's oratory was also highly praised by Pendleton, being compared to "the most renowned of British orators, the elder William Pitt." "In Henry's exordiums there was a simplicity," but "his imagina-tion, which painted to the soul, eclipsed the sparklings of art…" By this means Henry "transfused into the breast of oth-ers the emotions depicted in his own features, which ever forbade a doubt of sincerity." Even though Henry's speeches had their shortcomings for lack of division or detail, Pendleton freely confessed that "for grand impressions in the defense of liberty, the western world has not yet been able to exhibit a rival."[96]

When this tired trio of Henry, Washington, and Pendleton reached Philadelphia on September 4, most of the delegates had arrived, but none of them rivaled Henry as an orator. Among this great body of illustrious leaders, Henry shone as the "Demosthenes of the Age." Unfortunately, the records of the Congress are scanty, and provide only a few specimens of Henry's public displays.

On Monday, the fifth, the delegates assembled at the City Tavern and marched together to Carpenter's Hall, a trim, two-story brick building in the shape of a cross. After inspecting it, they took their seats. Peyton Randolph was chosen as president and Mr. Charles Townshend of Philadelphia as Secretary. Next, roll was taken and each delegate had to provide satisfactory credentials. With this routine business out of the way, Congress was confronted with its first procedural problem: was voting to proceed by individual member, by colony, or by some other "interest"? While the delegates sat in a befuddled silence, Henry rose to address the question. According to John Adams: "Mr. Henry then arose, and said this was the first General Congress which had ever happened; that no former congress could be a precedent; that we should have occasion for more general congresses, and therefore that a precedent ought to be established now; that it would be great injustice if a little colony should have the same weight in the councils of America as a great one, and therefore he was for a committee."[97] The other delegates demurred, however, and the congress adjourned for the day without a decision.

The following day, Henry startled the somewhat sedate assembly by claiming that the conflict with Britain had reduced the colonies to a state of nature.

"All government is dissolved," he said boldly, and then he drove the point home with a series of prophetic acclamations. "Fleets and armies and the present State of Things shew that Government is dissolved," he said.

"Where are your landmarks? Your Boundaries of Colonies?" Henry asked, suggesting to the delegates that the attack upon Massachusetts was an attack upon each colony.

"The distinctions between Virginians, Pennsylvanians, New Yorkers, and New Englanders are no more," he said, shaping the argument in his intensely personal way. "I am not a Virginian, but an American."[98]

Although the vote went against him, Henry elevated the tone of the debate from a mere quibbling over procedure to the loftier peak of principle. Indeed, this was always his posture. On smaller matters he was more than willing to concede, but on fundamental principles he was a stalwart, if not implacable advocate. By asserting that he was "not a Virginian, but an American," Henry succinctly showed just how keenly he understood the real meaning of the present conflict and its outcome. "That patriotic utterance was in truth a prophecy of the future United States of America."[99]

Before the second day ended, a messenger burst into the Congress with the alarming news that British ships were bombarding Boston, and that the colonists at Massachusetts and Connecticut were rising in arms against British soldiers. Alerted to the perilous circumstances–which Henry had already clearly understood–congress adjourned, but only after wisely agreeing to open the next day's session with prayer and Scripture.

The next morning, mournful bells were tolling and the streets of Philadelphia were filled with furtive cries of "war." Inside Carpenter's Hall, the Reverend Duché, an Episcopalian minister, intoned the providentially appropriate words of the thirty-fifth Psalm:

> *Plead my cause, O Lord, with them that strive*
> *with me: fight against them that fight against*
> *me. Take hold of shield and buckler, and stand*
> *up for mine help. Draw out also the spear, and*

> *stop the way against them that persecute me:*
> *say unto my soul, I am thy salvation. Let them*
> *be confounded and put to shame that seek after*
> *my soul: let them be turned back and brought*
> *to confusion that devise my hurt. Let them be*
> *as chaff before the wind: and let the angel of*
> *the Lord chase them. Let their way be dark and*
> *slippery: and let the angel of the Lord persecute*
> *them. For without cause have they hid for me*
> *their net in a pit, which without cause they*
> *have digged for my soul. Let destruction come*
> *upon him at unawares; and let his net that he*
> *hath hid catch himself: into that very destruc-*
> *tion let him fall. Let not them that are mine*
> *enemies wrongfully rejoice over me: neither let*
> *them wink with the eye that hate me without a*
> *cause. For they speak not peace: but they devise*
> *deceitful matters against them that are quiet in*
> *the land. Let them be ashamed and brought to*
> *confusion together that rejoice at mine hurt: let*
> *them be clothed with shame and dishonour*
> *that magnify themselves against me. Let them*
> *shout for joy, and be glad, that favour my right-*
> *eous cause: yea, let them say continually, Let*
> *the Lord be magnified, which hath pleasure in*
> *the prosperity of his servant. And my tongue*
> *shall speak of thy righteousness and of thy*
> *praise all the day long.*

Everyone present sensed the voice of heaven. With Henry, Washington, and others kneeling for prayer, the Reverend Duche then offered a prayer "as affectionate, as sublime, as devout, as I have ever heard offered up to Heaven," recalled Adams. "It was enough to melt a heart of stone," he said. "I saw the tears gush into the eyes of the old Pacific Quakers of Philadelphia."[100] Thus, with hearts staid on God, and without fear, the members went to work.

There were four main issues addressed by the Congress. First, they gave advice to Massachusetts on how to respond to the present conflict with Britain. Congress replied with a document known as the Suffolk Resolves which declared that the Coercive Acts were unconstitutional, that Massachusetts should form a provisional government, and that the colonists should arm themselves, yet maintain a defensive posture, "so long as it was reasonable and requisite for self-preservation."[101]

Second, Congress addressed the issue of what was, or would be, their policy position toward Britain. In other words, what was the basis of colonial rights, and what was the legitimate power of Parliament? These questions were under debate by the committee of which Patrick Henry was a member. After considerable discussion, it was agreed that colonial rights were to be based on "the immutable laws of Nature, the principles of the English Constitution, and the several [colonial] charters or compacts." The question of the power of Parliament was not satisfactorily answered, however. The members simply agreed that they would "cheerfully" consent to regulation of "external commerce...*excluding* every idea of taxation, internal or external, for raising a revenue on the subjects in America without their consent."[102]

Congress also agreed to establish a continental association to impose economic sanctions on Britain by the suspension of commerce. James Galloway, the conservative Speaker of the Pennsylvania House, objected to the non-importation plan, on the ground that many Americans would lose their jobs, and advocated in its place a plan of permanent reconciliation. His scheme, stripped of all its eloquent props, amounted to a federal legislature governed by a royal governor-general, whom Galloway called a "Resident General." Henry, however, was vehement in his opposition to such a scheme.

> *The original constitution of the colonies was*
> *founded on the broadest and most generous*
> *base. The regulation of our trade was compen-*
> *sation enough for all the protection we ever*
> *experienced from her. We shall liberate our con-*
> *stituents from a corrupt House of Commons,*
> *but throw them into the arms of an American*
> *legislature, that may be bribed by that nation*
> *which avows, in the face of the world, that*
> *bribery is a part of her system of government.*
> *Before we are obliged to pay taxes as they do,*
> *let us be as free as they; let us have our trade*
> *open with all the world. We are not to consent*
> *by the representatives of representatives.*
> *I am inclined to think the present measures*
> *lead to war.*[103]

Henry had again uttered a prophetic warning: "The present measures lead to war."

Galloway was defeated, but the other members were unwilling to face the inevitable outcome of their present crisis. Thus, when Lee, who shared Henry's sentiments, made a motion that Congress recommend to the colonies "that a militia be forthwith appointed," disciplined and "provided with ammunition and proper arms," a violent debate broke out. Rutledge and Benjamin Harrison attacked Lee's notion as a virtual declaration of war. Henry, on the other hand, favored it. "A preparation for war is necessary to obtain peace," he insisted. "America is not now in a state of peace" but "in a state of nature." "All the Bulwarks of our safety, our Constitution, are thrown down." If the planned boycott fails, he argued, then "in that case arms are necessary." And if necessary "then," they are "necessary now." But the majority so stubbornly blinded themselves to the approaching bloodshed that not even Henry's impassioned appeals could get them to open their eyes. The resolutions were accordingly watered down to such a degree that even Lee, in disgust, voted against them.[104] By October 10, the Congress had finished its work and agreed to reconvene in May of 1775, should the situation warrant.

But before departing for Hanover, Henry spent an evening with John Adams, whom he had befriended at the Congress. Both men agreed that it was necessary to "cement the union of the colonies," and that the petitions from Congress would make little or no impression on the British government. War was inevitable. As they discussed the willingness of the people to fight, Adams shared with Henry a private letter from Joseph Hawley, a Massachusetts leader who had devised a plan for military preparation. According to Adams:

> *When Congress had finished their business, as*
> *they thought, in the autumn of 1774, I had with*
> *Mr. Henry, before we took leave of each other,*
> *some familiar conversation, in which I*
> *expressed a full conviction that our resolves,*
> *declarations of rights, enumeration of wrongs,*
> *petitions, remonstrances, and addresses, associ-*
> *ations, and non-importation agreements,*
> *however they might be expected by the people*
> *in America, and however necessary to cement*

the union of the colonies would be but waste
paper in England. Mr. Henry said they might
make some impression among the people of
England, but agreed with me that they would
be totally lost upon the government. I had but
just received a short and hasty letter, written to
me by Major Hawley, of Northampton, contain-
ing "a few broken hints," as he called them, of
what he thought was proper to be done, and
concluding with these words: "After all, we
must fight." This letter I read to Mr. Henry who
listened with great attention; and as soon as I
had pronounced the words, "After all, we must
fight," he raised his head, and with an energy
and vehemence that I can never forget, broke
out with: "By God, I am of that man's mind!" [105]

Indeed he was. Of all the great men that gathered at this historic Congress, Henry was one of the few men willing to face the truth. While others talked of reconciliation, he encouraged preparation; while others imagined peace, he envisioned war. "In the Congress of 1774," John Adams later wrote, "there was not one member, except Patrick Henry, who appeared to me sensible of the precipice, or rather, the pinnacle on which we stood, and had the candor and courage enough to acknowledge it." [106]

GIVE ME LIBERTY!

W hen Henry returned to Scotchtown from Congress, his wife Sarah was extremely ill. She had been subject to serious bouts of depression and now apparently experienced a nervous breakdown. The cause of her mental problems were unknown; but her condition at the time of Henry's arrival was so serious that she had to be physically restrained from hurting herself and kept in a locked room.[107]

Meanwhile, government in Virginia had devolved upon the county committees, since Governor Dunmore had repeatedly refused to convene the House of Burgesses. The Hanover Committee, of which Henry was a member, met in February to elect delegates to the second Virginia Convention. On the eighteenth, Patrick Henry and John Syme were chosen. Henry, however, was absent because his afflicted wife had died a week or so earlier. Henry's grief was so deep that he confided to his family physician that he was "a distraught old man."[108] Thus, sorrowfully bereaved Henry was summoned to the Virginia convention at Richmond in March of 1775.

Since Richmond was at the time no more than a small trading village of approximately 600 citizens, the only building large enough to house the convention was St. John's Church in Henrico Parish. A spare wooden-framed building with a pitched roof and a squat belfry, St. John's tightly held the 120 delegates and a couple dozen spectators, who convened on March 20. Peyton Randolph presided.

After two days of discussion on the work of the Continental Congress, Henry proposed a motion that Virginia "be immediately put into a posture of defense" and that a plan be drawn up for "arming and discipling" a "well-regulated militia." Why the need for a militia? Henry asserted that "a well-regulated militia, composed of gentlemen and yeomen, is the natural strength and only security of a free government; that such a militia in this colony would forever render it unnecessary for the mother country to keep among us for the purpose of our defense any standing army of mercenary forces, always subversive of the quiet and dangerous to the liberties of the people, and would obviate the pretext of taxing us for their support." Moreover, the governor's unwillingness to call together the Virginia House had left the commonwealth "too insecure in this time of danger and distress..."[109]

Richard Henry Lee quickly seconded Henry's motion, but Pendleton, Bland, and others fought it. They insisted that the motion went "too far" and that "fortitude would be the best defense."[110] Henry's fortitude, however, had run out.

He rose to defend his motion, and gave what is now recognized as perhaps the greatest political speech in American history:

> *No man, Mr. President, thinks more highly than I do of the patriotism, as well as the abilities, of the very honorable gentlemen who have just addressed the House. But different men often see the same subject in different lights; and,*

therefore, I hope it will not be thought disrespectful to those gentlemen if, entertaining, as I do, opinions of a character very opposite to theirs, I should speak forth my sentiments freely, and without reserve. This is no time for ceremony. The question before the House is one of awful moment to this country. For my own part, I consider it as nothing less than a question of freedom or slavery. And in proportion to the magnitude of the subject ought to be the freedom of the debate. It is only in this way that we can hope to arrive at truth, and fulfill the great responsibility which we hold to God and our country. Should I keep back my opinions at such a time, through fear of giving offense, I should consider myself as guilty of treason towards my country, and of an act of disloyalty towards the majesty of Heaven, which I revere above all earthly kings.

Mr. President, it is natural to man to indulge in the illusions of Hope. We are apt to shut our eyes against a painful truth, and listen to the song of that siren till she transforms us into beasts. Is this the part of wise men, engaged in a great and arduous struggle for liberty? Are we disposed to be of the number of those who, having eyes, see not, and having ears, hear not, the things which so nearly concern their temporal salvation? For my part, whatever anguish of spirit it may cost, I am willing to know the whole truth; to know the worst, and to provide for it.

I have but one lamp by which my feet are guided, and that is the lamp of experience. I know of no way of judging the future but by the past. And, judging by the past, I wish to know what there has been in the conduct of the British ministry, for the last ten years, to justify those hopes with which gentlemen have been pleased to solace themselves and the House. Is it that insidious smile with which our petition has been lately received? Trust it not, sir; it will prove a snare to your feet. Suffer not yourselves to be betrayed with a kiss. Ask yourselves how this gracious reception of our petition comports with those warlike preparations which cover our waters and darken our land. Are fleets and armies necessary to a work of love and reconciliation? Have we shown ourselves so unwilling to be reconciled, that force must be called in to win back our love? Let us not deceive ourselves, sir. These are the implements of war and subjugation,–the last arguments to which kings resort.

I ask gentlemen, sir, what means this martial array, if its purpose be not to force us to submission? Can gentlemen assign any other possible motive for it? Has Great Britain any enemy in this quarter of the world, to call for all this accumulation of navies and armies? No, sir, she has none. They are meant for us: they can be meant for no other. They are sent over to bind and rivet upon us those chains which the British ministry have been so long forging.

And what have we to oppose to them? Shall we try argument? Sir, we have been trying that for the last ten years. Have we anything new to offer upon the subject? Nothing. We have held the subject up in every light of which it is capable; but it has been all in vain. Shall we resort to entreaty, and humble supplication? What terms shall we find which have not been already exhausted?

Let us not, I beseech you, sir, deceive ourselves longer. Sir, we have done everything that could be done to avert the storm which is now coming on. We have petitioned; we have remonstrated; we have supplicated; we have prostrated ourselves before the throne, and have implored its interposition to arrest the tyrannical hands of the ministry and Parliament. Our petitions have been slighted; our remonstrances have produced additional violence and insult; our supplications have been disregarded; and we have been spurned with contempt from the foot of the throne.

In vain, after these things, may we indulge the fond hope of peace and reconciliation. There is no longer any room for hope. If we wish to be free; if we mean to preserve inviolate those inestimable privileges for which we have been so long contending; if we mean not basely to abandon the noble struggle in which we have been so long engaged, and which we have pledged ourselves never to abandon until the glorious object of our contest be obtained,—we must fight! I repeat it, sir,—we must fight! An appeal to arms, and to the God of hosts, is all that is left us.

They tell us, sir, that we are weak,—unable to cope with so formidable an adversary. But when shall we be stronger? Will it be the next week, or the next year? Will it be when we are totally disarmed, and when a British guard shall be stationed in every house? Shall we gather strength by irresolution and inaction? Shall we acquire the means of effectual resistance by lying supinely on our backs, and hugging the delusive phantom of Hope, until our enemies shall have bound us hand and foot?

Sir, we are not weak, if we make a proper use of those means which the God of nature hath placed in our power. Three millions of people armed in the holy cause of liberty, and in such a country as that which we possess, are invincible by any force which our enemy can send against us.

Besides, sir, we shall not fight our battles alone. There is a just God who presides over the destinies of nations, and who will raise up friends to fight our battles for us. The battle, sir, is not to the strong alone: it is to the vigilant, the active, the brave. Besides, sir, we have no election. If we were base enough to desire it, it is

*now too late to retire from the contest. There is
no retreat but in submission and slavery. Our
chains are forged. Their clanking may be heard
on the plains of Boston. The war is inevitable.
And let it come! I repeat it, sir, let it come!*

*It is in vain, sir, to extenuate the matter.
Gentlemen may cry peace, peace, but there is
no peace. The war is actually begun. The next
gale that sweeps from the north will bring to
our ears the clash of resounding arms. Our
brethren are already in the field. Why stand we
here idle? What is it that gentlemen wish?
What would they have? Is life so dear, or peace
so sweet, as to be purchased at the price of
chains and slavery? Forbid it, Almighty God! I
know not what course others may take, but as
for me, give me liberty, or give me death!*[111]

The convention sat in stunned silence, as if they had
heard the voice of heaven, "for Henry had called them to the
bar of judgment."[112] Failure to move forward in preparation
would be more than cowardice. It would be treason against
God Himself, the author of those liberties now under attack.
Henry's opponents were confounded and a committee was
established to draw up a militia plan. By the convention's end
Henry was reelected to the next Continental Congress and
Virginia was preparing to arm itself for war.

TAKING UP ARMS

*P*atrick Henry's memorable and masterful speech at St. John's was anything but political bombast. He was a man of bold and honest conviction–a man of his word. When he claimed his willingness to fight, and even die, if necessary, for liberty, he meant exactly what he said. No less than six weeks later, he "appealed to arms" against Britain, in "the first overt act of war" in Virginia's history.[113]

The mobilization of the county committees and the local militias had made the British Ministry, under Lord Dartmouth, issue an order prohibiting the importation of gunpowder or munitions into the colonies. Furthermore, the colonial governors were advised to remove or destroy any ammunition already possessed by the colonies. In response, General Gage attempted to destroy the military stores at Lexington on April 19, 1775. Here was fired "the shot heard 'round the world" in the opening battle of the Revolution.

On the following day in Virginia, Governor Dunmore ordered Captain Henry Collins to remove the gunpowder stored in the public magazine at Williamsburg, and place it in the schooner Magdelen, lying on the James River. News of the theft swiftly spread throughout the colony. In Williamsburg many citizens began to arm themselves, intent upon reclaiming the stolen ammunition. The Town Council, however, restrained the crowd and appealed to Governor Dunmore for an explanation, who then concocted a story that the gunpowder was removed because of the danger posed by a slave insurrection in a neighboring county. He promised to return it, if needed.

Meanwhile, a large number of armed men, "properly accoutred as light-horsemen," had gathered at Fredericksburg, and from there were summoned by Henry to New Castle. There they joined forces with the Hanover Volunteers under Henry's leadership. Henry was "determined to strike a blow at once which would encourage the people, and would teach the Government the temper of the patriots."[114]

On May 2, Henry addressed the volunteers in an eloquent speech in which he spread before their eyes "the fields of Lexington and Concord, still floating with the blood of their countrymen." Now was the moment of decision, he claimed. They must "choose to live free and hand down the valuable inheritance to their children," or become "the tools of a corrupt and tyrannical ministry." He promised them that liberty could "be won by their valor, under the support and guidance of heaven." And he reminded them that "the same God whose power divided the Red Sea for the deliverance of Israel, still reigned in all His glory, unchanged and unchangeable." God "was still the enemy of the oppressive and the friend of the oppressed." It was to this God that they could look for protection and deliverance.[115]

The volunteers, many of them wearing shirts emblazoned with Henry's motto, "Liberty or Death," were electrified by the speech and pledged to follow Henry as their newly-elected captain. Immediately Henry sent a friend, Parke Goodall, and a contingent of sixteen men, to the home of Richard Corbin, the king's Receiver-General, to demand payment for the stolen gunpowder. Should he refuse, Henry ordered him to be taken prisoner. Henry then began to march on Williamsburg with one–hundred fifty armed men, "their rifle barrels and tomahawk blades glistening in the morning sun." As the small army stormed through neighboring towns, singing patriotic songs and shouting American slogans, new recruits fell into rank. Approximately five thousand men were now marching under Henry's command.

Governor Dunmore, now knowing that Henry was hot on his heels, called a private meeting of his council in order to justify his actions, and to denounce "the rapid recurrence to arms." He then threatened the magistrates of Williamsburg that, if they did not put a halt to the march, he would arm Indians and slaves and reduce the city to ashes.[116]

Messengers were sent to Henry, but to no avail. He was not a man to be intimidated by pompous politicians. "Liberty or Death" was his battle-cry, and Dunmore's theft of the gun-powder was a flagrant attack on Virginia's liberty to defend itself against tyrannical government. Henry prepared to march on.

The governor, in the meantime, fearing for his safety, sent his family offshore aboard the schooner Fowey. Then, learn-ing of Henry's determination to proceed, Dunmore finally backed down. He sent word via Thomas Nelson, the council president, and Braxton Carter, that restitution would be made for the gunpowder. When they arrived at Duncastle, Henry agreed to accept their "bill of exchange" and wrote a receipt to Corbin for £330 "as compensation for the gunpowder lately taken out of the public magazine by the governor's order…" Henry then promised to convey the money "to the Virginia Delegates at the General congress…"[117]

Bloodshed had been averted and the conflict won. Henry's courage and decisive action demonstrated to the royal government the "temper of the patriots." Two days later, the governor denounced Henry and the patriots as engaging in "outrageous and rebellious practices"…in open defiance of law and government."[118] But Dunmore's denunciations only enhanced Henry's heroism. As he and his company triumphantly paraded home, they were greeted with cheers and applause from the people of Virginia. In Hanover and many surrounding counties, formal resolutions of gratitude were drafted and dispatched. Thanks were "justly due to Captain Patrick Henry and the gentlemen volunteers who attended him, for their proper and spirited conduct," wrote Prince William County. "We heartily thank him," wrote Prince Edward and Frederick Counties, "for stepping forth to convince the tools of despotism that freeborn men are not to be intimidated, by any form of danger, to submit to the arbitrary acts of their rulers." In Fincastle, the citizenry assured Henry that "it would support and justify him at the risk of life and fortune."[119]

Henry was now at the height of his popular fame, saluted as "America's unalterable and unappalled great advocate and friend." And it was amidst this popular esteem and love that he headed for the Second Congress, having been entrusted by his admirers "to the gracious and wise Disposer of all human events, to guide and protect him whilst contending for a restitution of our dearest rights and liberties."[120]

THE SECOND CONTINENTAL CONGRESS

*H*enry set out on horseback on May 11 for the Second Continental Congress in Philadelphia. Escorted by a group of Hanover Volunteers, he and his good friend Parke Goodall conversed freely on the subject of the colonies. Henry confided to this associate that now was the time for a colonial confederation against Britain. He also assured Goodall that independence from the mother country was not only desirable, but inevitable–with or without foreign aid. Henry was convinced that the conflict at Lexington had irrevocably severed the bonds between America and Great Britain. The war was now to be fought for independence. But he also realized that many Americans were not yet ready for a final break with Britain, still having hope of reconciliation. "And no great leader was ever more accurate in measuring a popular movement, or wise in proposing, advanced measures at the moment when the people were ready for them."[121]

When Henry arrived in Philadelphia the same "martial spirit" that had animated him in Virginia was now alive in that city. "Scarce anything but warlike music is heard in the streets," wrote one delegate. Adams was pleased: "Uniforms and Regimentals were as thick as bees," he proudly wrote home. Henry's insistence upon armed readiness, made at the last Congress, was now the accepted course. Even the cautious Dickinson acknowledged that "the answer to our petition is written in blood."[122]

Henry took his seat on May 18. Congress, which was now meeting two blocks west of Carpenter's Hall in the Pennsylvania State House, had been in session for a week, anxiously considering the state of America. Unfortunately, we have no record of Henry's "eloquent speech" during this Congress. It is likely, however, that the "Trumpet of the Revolution" loudly blew his war-song during this critical hour. Indeed, when Congress debated Lord North's proposals for accommodation, it cannot be doubted that Henry's voice was heard.

> *The bugle call to arms, which he had sounded in the Virginia Convention only two months before, was most certainly repeated with all the energy and eloquence of which he was capable, now that he stood in the midst of the representatives of the united colonies. It is, indeed a significant fact, that the first utterance of the body after the day Mr. Henry took his seat was a unanimous determination to arm for the defense of their liberties, a determination which fixed the fate of America, and assured her political freedom.[123]*

The creation of some kind of national government was necessary, since the thirteen colonies were now virtually at war. Thus, it was also required that a national army be created; a commander-in-chief and subordinate officers be chosen; coasts, harbors, and cities be fortified; and troops supplied with clothes and ammunition. Moreover, Congress needed a plan for dealing with the Indians and the Canadians, both of whom were being recruited by Britain against the colonies.[124]

Henry served on a number of important committees to deal with these momentous issues. For instance, he served on the committee to determine ways and means for supplying the colonies with ammunition, the committee on Indian relations, and the committee for handling military questions proposed by Washington, amongst others. "The appointment of Mr. Henry on the several committees…demonstrate clearly his high standing in the body [Congress] as a working member and that he had shown himself as efficient in action as he was eloquent in speech."[125]

As a result of its deliberations, Congress appointed George Washington as the "Commander-in-Chief of the forces raised, or to be raised, in defense of America." Artemas Ward and Charles Lee were each made major-generals, and other officers were also chosen. Rules and regulations for the army were adopted, and Congress recommended to the colonies "to organize and train" their militias and provide them with ample ammunition. They also recommended that each colony appoint a "Committee of Safety, to superintend and direct all matters for the security and defense of their respective colonies," when their assemblies or conventions were in recess.[126]

Congress also issued a series of papers in which they reiterated their claim that their political rights were being violated by Britain, and declared their resolve and determination to protect them at all costs. Thus, when Congress adjourned on August 1, Henry had the gratification of knowing that his previously prophetic appeals for preparation had not been made in vain. Although it would be nearly another year before a formal announcement of independence was made, America was now fighting the War of Independence.

Colonel Henry

While the Second Continental Congress was in session, the royal governance of Virginia was deteriorating. On June 1, Governor Dunmore called together the House of Burgesses to have them consider the "Olive Branch" proposals of Lord North. The House, however, in no mood for reconciliation, confronted Dunmore about the militia he had recently called together. They also informed him that they wanted to inspect the public magazine.

Sensing the "temper of the patriots," Dunmore removed his family to the Fowey, lying at York, claiming that he and his family were not safe in Williamsburg. When he tried to have the Burgesses attend him on board the ship, they refused. Since Dunmore had essentially abandoned his post as governor, the House adjourned itself on June 24. This was the last session of the colonial legislature, and the last time a royal governor occupied Virginia's capital.

With Royal government at an end, the Third Virginia Convention met in July. It "determined at once to take up the reigns of government, and place the colony in a state of defense."[127] Accordingly, the Convention agreed to raise as many as three regiments of fifteen thousand men each, with an additional five companies for Virginia's western border. When the choice of officers was discussed, Henry's friends proposed him as colonel of the First Regiment and commander-in-chief of the Virginia army. The debate was vigorous. Several other candidates, such as Hugh Mercer and William Woodword, had fought under Braddock in the French and Indian War and were officers of experience and ability. Henry, on the other hand, lacked either training or experience in the "arts of war." Nevertheless, Henry was elected; thus showing that the majority of the convention believed that "the qualities which made Mr. Henry a great political leader would make him a great military leader also."[128]

His commission, issued on the twenty-eighth of July, constituted Henry "colonel of the first regiment of regulars, and commander-in-chief of all forces to be armed." Moreover, it required that "all officers and soldiers" were "to be obedient to him" in the execution of his commission. In a word, Henry had supreme command of the Virginia forces; he himself being answerable only to "the convention or Committee of Safety."[129] Since Royal government in Virginia was at an end, the Committee of Safety, made up of Pendleton, Mason, Page, Bland, and seven others, was now the executive authority in the colony.

Henry's supreme command was to be short-lived, however. Those in opposition to his election as commander-in-chief felt that Henry was "out of his field" when in the field–he was better fitted for Congress than camp. Accordingly, the Committee of Safety, to whom Henry was accountable, permitted his commission to be violated by insubordinate officers. Most notably, William Woodword, colonel of the third regiment, ignored Henry as his superior officer and refused to report to him. Rather, Woodword communicated directly with the Committee, thus circumventing Henry's military authority. The Committee not only tolerated this breach of protocol, but encouraged it. Moreover, although Henry had prepared his troops for battle, the Committee intentionally kept him back from seeing action. Thus, while Henry was "held in leash," Dunmore plundered the Virginia coast with impunity. To further insult Henry, Woodward was eventually sent by the Committee to attack Dunmore. And while Woodword's victory must have pleased Henry the patriot, it abused Henry the commander.[130]

When the Fourth Virginia Convention assembled in December of 1775, Henry's friends, sensible of his ill-treatment, pushed for the election of a new Committee of Safety headed by those who supported his military position. The new Committee then passed a ruling that Woodward, while acting under "separate and detached command," ought to report to Henry and accept his orders when neither the Committee or Convention was in session. This effort to restore Henry's rightful authority was, however, too little too late.

The final straw came when the Continental Congress decided to raise in Virginia six battalions for the Continental Army, two of which would be the first and third Virginia regiments. Henry was now sent a commission to retain his post as colonel instead of being offered the newly created position of "brigadier-general for Virginia." This last insult to his abilities forced Henry to resign his commission to retain his honor–which he did in February, 1776. He told his soldiers that his resignation was "from motives in which honor, alone, was concerned."[131] When news spread among the troops, they "went into mourning." His officers, who looked upon Henry as "our father and general," presented him the following loyal address:

To Patrick Henry, Junior, Esquire:
Deeply impressed with a grateful sense of the
obligations we lie under to you for the polite,
humane, and tender treatment manifested to us
throughout the whole of your conduct, while
we have had the honor of being under your
command, permit us to offer to you our sincere
thanks, as the only tribute we have in our
power to pay to your real merits.
Notwithstanding your withdrawing yourself
from service fills us with the most poignant
sorrow, as it at once deprives us of our father
and general, yet as gentlemen, we are com-
pelled to applaud your spirited resentment to
the most glaring indignity. May your merit
shine as conspicuous to the world in general as
it hath done to us, and may Heaven shower its
choicest blessings upon you.[132]

The officer's closing words were more seasonable than
they realized; for Henry's humiliation was Heaven's hand.
Like Joseph in Egypt, what men had meant for evil, God
meant for good. Now, at perhaps the lowest point of his professional career, Henry would soon be elected to the highest
office in the commonwealth of Virginia.

Independence: Virginia First

*H*enry was now out of camp and out of Congress. With wounded honor he retired in March to his beloved Scotchtown, which was shrouded in sorrow by Sarah's untimely death. Yet Henry surely returned with joy, finding great solace in the fellowship of his children and the solitude of the woods.

His recent resignation was a providential pivot in his life. Had he advanced in military rank and honor, his valuable gifts would have been missed elsewhere. Washington was undoubtedly right when he said his "countrymen made a capitol mistake when they took Henry out of the Senate to place him in the field."[133] God, however, undid the mistake. Whatever may have been the motives of Pendleton and the committee, and whatever might have come of Henry's military career, "we now see clearly that it was the hand of a gracious Providence which led him from the camp to the hall of legislation and to the office of Executive, in both of which his services…were of transcendent importance to his country."[134]

After two months of sweet seclusion, Henry was sent back to Virginia's fifth and most famous state convention.

Here were to be decided issues of "transcendent importance:" should the colony make a full determination of independence, or not? And if so, what was to be the form of the new government? Aristocratic or republican? If a new government was to be erected, who was to lead this great and newly-emancipated commonwealth?

These and similar questions were on the minds of all the delegates who convened in Williamsburg on May 6, 1776. In addition to nearly all the old delegates who returned, there were some important additions to the convention. One was the young James Madison, a graduate only a few years earlier of Witherspoon's Princeton. There also appeared for the first time Edmund Randolph, whose Tory father had sailed to England. The son had the honor of taking his father's place as the colony's attorney-general.

The burning question overshadowing all others was that of independence. Thus, after choosing Pendleton as the convention president and organizing its working committees, the assembly went into Committee of the Whole on May 14 to discuss the state of the colony. The question of independence was immediately introduced and debated for two days. That Henry favored independence is beyond dispute. However, as a sagacious statesman, he also understood that a weak confederation and an unaided cause would be vulnerable to British arms. While he eagerly supported independence, he simultaneously wished for a strong confederation of the colonies established by written articles. Moreover, Henry hoped that a foreign alliance, especially with France, would be struck in order to supply the fledgling colonies with much needed military aid.[135] During the two days of debate several resolutions were offered. The third resolution, which was Henry's, declared Virginians "absolved of our allegiance to the crown of Great Britain and obliged by the eternal laws of self-preservation to

pursue such measures as may conduce to the good and happiness of the united colonies." It further recommended that
the Virginia delgates to the next continental congress be
authorized to "exert their ability in procuring an immediate,
clear, and full Declaration of Independency."[136] As a compromise to the several resolutions, Pendleton offered the
following resolution:

> WHEREFORE, *appealing to the Searcher of*
> *Hearts for the sincerity of former declarations,*
> *expressing our desire to preserve the connexion*
> *with that nation, and that we are driven from*
> *that inclination by their wicked councils, and*
> *the eternal laws of self preservation;*
> RESOLVED, *unanimously, That the delegates*
> *appointed to represent this colony in General*
> *congress, be instructed to propose to that*
> *respectable body to declare the United Colonies*
> *free and independent states, absolved from all*
> *allegiance to, or dependence upon, the crown or*
> *parliament of Great Britain; and that they give*
> *the assent of this colony to such declaration,*
> *and to whatever measures may be thought*
> *proper and necessary by the Congress for form-*
> *ing foreign alliances, and a confederation of the*
> *colonies, at such time, and in the manner, as to*
> *them shall seem best: Provided, that the power*
> *of forming government for, and the regulations*
> *of, the internal concerns of each colony, be left*
> *to the respective colonial legislatures.*[137]

Despite not having the desirable prerequisites of a
stronger confederation and a foreign alliance, Henry boldly

advanced independence on the floor of the convention by challenging the delegates to accept Pendleton's resolution. After a slow start to his speech, (which was unusual for Henry), "he appeared in an element for which he was born." The "magnificence of his genius" rose to the occasion. "He entered into no subtlety of reasoning, but was aroused by the now apparent spirit of the people. As a pillar of fire, which notwithstanding the darkness of the prospect, would conduct to the promised land, he inflamed, and was followed by, the convention. His eloquence unlocked the secret springs of the human heart, robbed danger of all its terror, and broke the keystone in the arch of royal power."[138]

The resolution for indepenence was unanimously accepted. The knot had been cut by the sword of Henry's tongue, and when word hit Williamsburg, the Union Jack was lowered from the capitol building and replaced with the union flag. The next day independence was celebrated with a parade behind the Capitol, and patriotic toasts, interrupted by salutes of artillery, were made to the independent American states, the Grand Congress, and to General Washington.[139] Virginia was now, for all practical purposes, a free and sovereign state. Thus it was paramount for the convention to immediately prepare its bill of rights and constitution.

Virginia Bill of Rights and Constitution

$\mathcal{A}$s the Virginia declaration of independence was making its way to Philadelphia under Colonel Nelson's hand, a committee of which Henry was a member set to work on a bill of rights and constitution for the new state.

The Virginia Bill of Rights is one of those seminal works in American political and religious history which ought to be studied by every friend of freedom. As one author has noted: "the Virginia Bill of Rights...stands as an epitome of all history relating to the struggles of the human race for civil and religious liberty, and a prophecy of the future of free government. It is the matrix in which American governments have been shaped, and as long as they last they will bear testimony to the wondrous wisdom of its framers."[140] As a "compact, immense and powerful statement" of rights, the Virginia bill is without rival. In sixteen articles, it formed the basis not only of the new Virginia constitution, but also directly influenced the federal Constitution and United States Bill of Rights.[141]

Many of the principles and practices now taken for granted in America can be traced to this declaration of fundamental rights. For instance, the first article declares the equal right of all men, by nature, to freedom and independence. This truth is at the foundation of republican government. Its source, as has been properly noted, we find in Christianity, which "alone teaches the absolute, exclusive, sovereignty of God and the common origin and brotherhood of man."[142] Christianity teaches that God is not a respecter of persons, but views all men as equal before His moral law.[143] The first article also declares that men have an inalienable right to enjoy life, liberty, property, and happiness; concepts that were soon written into the federal Declaration of Independence.

Other important rights are also spelled out. For example, civil power is declared to be vested in, and derived from, the people, with civil magistrates acting as their servants. The purpose of government is the common good. Freedom of elections, the right to a speedy trial, freedom from "cruel and unusual" punishment, trial by jury, and other rights are also enumerated.[144]

The last two articles of the Bill of Rights were of particular interest to Henry, and were drafted by his own pen. The fifteenth article reads: "That no free government, or the blessings of liberty, can be preserved to any people but by a firm adherence to justice, moderation, temperance, frugality, and virtue, and by frequent recurrence to fundamental principles."[145] Henry understood that republicanism must rest on private virtue. Without individual self-government, there can be no true political freedom, for in the absence of moral restraint, anarchy will call forth tyranny to maintain order.

The sixteenth article asserts the doctrine of religious liberty, a belief very dear to Henry. Being a great friend of religious freedom, he had earlier in court championed the religious rights of the dissenting Baptists and Quakers. The original draft of the sixteenth article shows the influence of the Westminster Assembly, and stood as follows:

That religion, or the duty we owe our Creator,
and the manner of discharging it, can be
directed only by reason and conviction, and
not by force or violence; and, therefore, that all
men should enjoy the fullest toleration in the
exercise of religion, according to the dictates of
conscience, unpunished and unrestrained by
the magistrate, unless, under color of religion,
any man disturb the peace, the happiness, or
the safety of society; and that it is the mutual
duty of all to practise Christian forbearance,
love, and charity towards each other.[146]

The historical significance of this article can only be appreciated when we remember that the Church of England was the established church of Virginia, and that many other colonies also had ecclesiastical establishments. Just as Henry had "cut the knot" of political tyranny, he now cut the knot of ecclesiastical oppression. Church and state were now to be separate institutions. However, it would be a mistake to imagine that Henry desired freedom "from" religion. On the contrary, he and many of the other "founding fathers" desired the fullest expression of religious beliefs and practices. And disestablishment was the only sound way to achieve it. It is clear from Henry's entire political career that he thought Christianity was the one sure foundation of political freedom. Thus, the impetus for the sixteenth article was not a negative view of Christianity, but the hope that it would prosper in the world and provide the people with that "virtue" which is the basis of republican government.

After adopting the Bill of Rights on June 12, the committee went to work drafting the new state constitution. Though there was much agreement on broad principles, the commitee members laboriously and meticulously debated the various aspects of the proposed form of government. Henry favored what he called the "democratic" form of government outlined in John Adam's pamphlet *Thoughts on Government*, which the author had sent him. After days of debate and amending, the form of govenment adopted provided for a lower and upper house, both elected by the people–a decidedly democratic feature. Additionally, the constitution provided for a governor to be elected by joint ballot of both houses, and not to continue in office for more than three successive annual terms. After a period of four years, the same individual might again be eligible for the governor's office. Although generally pleased with the constitution, Henry argued strongly–referring to the opinions of Montesquieu and other political philosophers–that the governor be given the veto power. He failed, however, to carry the point.[147]

The new constitution was formally adopted by unanimous vote on June 29, 1776, with the convention declaring that "the government of this country, as formerly experienced under the Crown of Great Britain, is *totally dissolved*."[148] Thus, Virginia anticipated the American Declaration of Independence by five days. Virginia was the leader in declaring independence, and Henry had been the leader of Virginia. Who then was better suited to be its first governor?

EXECUTIVE AND STATESMAN

On July 5, 1776, the day that Henry took the oath of office as the first governor of Virginia, the *Virginia Gazette* published a heart-warming and congratulatory address from the First and Second Virginia Regiments:

> *Permit us, with the sincerest sentiments of respect and joy, to congratulate your Excellency upon your unsolicited promotion to the highest honours a grateful people can bestow. Uninfluenced by private ambition, regardless of sordid interest, you have uniformly pursued the general good of your country; and have taught the world, that an ingenuous love of the rights of mankind, an inflexible resolution, and a steady perseverance in the practice of every private and publick virtue, lead directly to preferment, and give the best title to the honours of an uncorrupted and vigorous state.*[149]

For the next ten years, five of which he spent as governor, Henry was the undisputed leader of the newly-formed state. From 1776 to 1779, he served three consecutive terms as governor, and from 1784 to 1786 was placed in the palace for two more terms. The intervening years he spent as the leading statesman in the Virginia Assembly.

Henry's early years as governor were a most important and critical period in Virginia's history. The newly-formed state was launched into uncharted waters. The new constitution was untried, and precedents were to be set. Moreover, it was a time of war. The new-born commonwealth was engaged in battle against the strongest earthly power, then in existence, while simultaneously fighting hostile Indian tribes on her western border. To make matters worse, Virginia was without a trained army or ready navy, and she sorely lacked the necessary munitions for war. A depreciating currency further threatened the stability of the state, and served to make the recruiting of soldiers all the more difficult.

While other men might have shirked the "honor" of being governor at this difficult period, Henry rose to the challenge and was an able, if not outstanding, wartime governor. "The Executive Journal furnishes the fullest evidence of his industry, his great executive capacity and his ardent zeal in the cause of the Revolution."[150] He strove to maintain the morale of the populace, recruited men for militia or continental service, and built a navy. He protected Virginia's western border against Indian hostilities, authorized expeditions into the Ohio, and helped supply food and clothing for the continental army. So great was the amount of work under hand, that Henry complained that "the load of business devolved on me is too great to be managed well."[151] Yet Henry did manage the state as well, or better, than his successors.

One of the most important achievements of Henry's tenure as governor was his commission, during his first term, of George Rogers Clark to explore and conquer the Northwest. Upon Clark's request, Henry granted him a letter of approval for obtaining gunpowder from the state of Virginia in order to protect Kentucky settlements against Indian and British raids. After a series of successful skirmishes, Clark was authorized, in December of 1777, to make an expedition into the Illinois territory against Kaskaskia, the center of British organization of Indian raids. By July 4, 1778, Clark had captured Kaskaskia, and in December of that year the General Assembly of Virginia created the vast virgin county of Illinois.[152]

It is also now recognized that much of the success, or perhaps it is better to say, the reason for the survival, of the continental forces under Washington was due in large part to Henry's efforts. During the conflict of 1777-1778, Washington's troops were in dire need of food and clothing. The Continental Congress was gripped with inertia and failed to provide the army with those essential items. Seeing the danger, Henry "went to work vigorously" and sent out a large supply of clothing as early as December 1777. But food was also needed. Writing to Henry in February, Washington lamented: "For several days past we have experienced little less than a famine in camp, and have had much cause to dread a general mutiny and dispersion." Henry helped avert mutiny by immediately issuing a proclamation in Virginia informing the people of the army's needs, and urging them to provide as many cattle as they could spare. Furthermore, he appointed John Hawkins as a purchasing agent, supplied him with money, and ordered him to secure and forward to the army "as much beef and bacon as their wants may require."[153]

Henry's efforts to provide for Washington's troops went beyond his call of duty as Virginia's governor. Yet, as he said: "It will indeed be unworthy the character of a zealous American to entrench himself within the strict line of official duty and there quietly behold the starving and dispersion of the American army. The genius of this country is not of that cast."[154] Indeed, had Henry stayed within the bounds of his "official duty," the American cause might have been lost. As it was, he "contributed largely to the continued existence of the American army during their bitter experience at Valley Forge, if indeed he did not prevent its disbanding."[155]

As he had promised when assuming the office of governor, Henry gave "unwearied endeavors to serve the freedom and happiness of our common country."[156] His endeavors, however, had a debilitating effect on his health. During his first term, he fell seriously ill for several weeks. And it seems that thereafter his health was never the same. After he finished his third consecutive term, Henry was nominated to the Continental Congress but declined due to "a tedious illness."[157] He even had doubts whether he might ever return to political office; yet, when the Virginia Assembly met in May, 1780, Henry was present and served there for the next four years. The records show, however, that he had to often request an absence due to his poor health.

During these brief respites, Henry found rest and comfort with his new wife, Dorothea Dandridge, whom he had married in October 1777, and who was the daughter of his old friend Colonel Nathaniel Dandridge. When Henry left the office of governor, he and Dorothea, their new daughter, and his other children by Sallie, left Scotchtown, moved south to Henry County, where they built "Leatherwood," a ten-thousand acre farm

In May of 1780, Henry became the delegate from Henry County, and made the six-day journey to the new capital of Richmond, where he attended to pressing business as the legislative leader. Between 1780 and 1784, he was placed on many important committees, and due to his popularity, controlled the legislature "with absolute sway."[158] It was during this time that he agreed to an inquiry into the official conduct of Thomas Jefferson; who, as governor, had allowed Virginia to be invaded and plundered by the British. In the flush of the victory at Yorktown in October of 1781, the inquiry was dropped, but Jefferson never forgave Henry for this "attack" on his honor. As a result, Jefferson later distorted historical facts regarding Henry's service to Virginia and even maligned Henry's character. Impartial research has shown, however, that Jefferson's judgment was beclouded by bitterness. All his slanders of Henry have been easily disproved.

The end of the war provided new challenges for the Assembly. One most pressing question was how to treat the Tories, those who had remained loyal to Britain during the war. Should they be allowed to return to Virginia and regain their citizenship? Many opposed their return, but Henry advocated forgiveness and reconciliation. "On the altar of his country's good he was willing to sacrifice all personal resentments, all past wrongs…" As far as Henry was concerned, "the quarrel is over." It was now time to "have the magnanimity…to lay aside our antipathies and prejudices…" But some feared the Tories' political principles. Henry, however, did not. "I have no fear of any mischief that they can do us. Afraid of them! What sir, shall we, who have laid the proud British lion at our feet, now be afraid of his whelps?"[159]

Henry feared the British much less than he did the French—that is, the French skepticism that was surreptitiously creeping into the country. "Mr. Henry, who was deeply pious,"…"realized as few men did the danger to the Republican institutions of his country from the undermining influence of French infidelity." As a result, he "got himself to counteracting its baneful influence by every means in his power."[160] Accordingly, Henry encouraged schools of higher learning, especially Christian schools, several of which he helped charter. Moreover, in 1784, he proposed legislation for a general tax for teachers and ministers of all Christian denominations. This general assessment for the support of a plural religious establishment reflected Henry's concern over the general morals of the people, as well as his understanding that absolute religious separation could lead to obstinate religious indifference. Henry believed that the republican form of government newly established in America would not survive without the morally elevating influence of Christianity. The French, on the other hand, "have a liberal and destructive spirit," one of "infidelity" which "under the name of philosophy" works its evil will so that "everything that ought to be done by man is covertly but successfully assailed." In contrast to American democracy, the French version was "a bloody horror."[161] Although his views on a general assessment were shared by Washington, John Marshall, and others, his bill was defeated, partially because he left the House to again become governor in 1784.

His last two terms as governor (1784-1786) were relatively quiet. He attempted to reform the death penalty, which was often imposed for very minor offenses. He also passed on to Congress, Lady Huntingdon's proposal to establish a religious settlement in the west to Christianize and civilize the Indians.[162] Of course, Indians were a continual threat, and in April 1786, Henry's own brother-in-law, Colonel Christian, was killed by a marauding band of Indians. To add sorrow upon sorrow, Henry also lost at this time his mother, his brother, William, and his only surviving aunt. During these mournful times, he found in God "a refuge that no misfortunes can take away." Writing to his bereaved sister, Anne Christian, Henry expressed his simple but profound trust in God. "I turn my eyes to heaven...and I adore with humility the unsearchable ways of that Providence which calls us off this stage of action, at such time and in such manner as its wisdom and goodness directs." [163]

A True Federalist

*T*hough nominated for a sixth term, Henry left the office of governor in 1786 and moved to Prince Edward County near Hampden-Sydney College. He was now fifty years old and in poor health. He had already lived a full life as the Trumpet of the Revolution, a constructive legislator and statesman, and as a wartime executive. He had led the colonies in resistance to tyranny, initiated independence, and aided the success of the American troops during the critical period of the war. After all these achievements and labors, Henry might have thought that now was the time to exit the public stage. But Providence had yet one more patriotic role for Henry to fulfill. As the outspoken critic of the newly-proposed federal Constitution, Patrick Henry helped to secure for all Americans those invaluable and inalienable liberties enshrined in the United States Bill of Rights.

Although the federal Convention that met in Philadelphia in May of 1787 was authorized only to revise the existing Articles of Confederation, the delegates devised an entirely new constitution that was subsequently sent to the states for ratification. Those who favored the new Constitution were named "Federalists," while their opponents were called "Anti-Federalists." These labels were apt to be misleading, however. In fact, it would be more accurate to name the pro-Constitution faction as "nationalists", and the opposing group as the true "Federalists." For it was Henry and those with similar sentiments who espoused the true principle of federalism–a federation of independent and sovereign states "whose representatives met in congress to deal with a limited range of common concerns in a system that relied heavily on voluntary cooperation."[164]

When the Virginia Ratification Convention met on June 2, 1788, the Federalists were led by Madison and Pendleton. By and large, the Federalists believed that the Articles of Confederation were too weak to provide for a strong and flourishing nation. The national government, they believed, needed the power to tax and to regulate commerce, the power to enforce its acts, the power to settle disputes between states and the national government, among others. The way to give energy to the national government was to give it power, but this required a change in its form.[165]

The Anti-Federalists (or "Federal Republicans," as they often called themselves) were led by Henry, of course. In general the Republicans were united on the principle of confederation. The current problems with the national government, they held, were more a product of post-war circumstances than defects in the Articles of Confederation. What was needed in America was not a more powerful government, but a more virtuous people. Limited government must, by definition, be locally responsive and responsible. The powers granted by the Constitution to the new national government were a tyrannical threat to the rights of the states and the liberties of the people.[166]

Although Henry was only fifty-two years old when he took the Convention floor, poor health made him appear a much older man. This fact only lent greater impressiveness to his speeches. Tradition has it that whenever he rose to speak, "a death-like silence prevailed" so that the eager listeners could catch his every word.[167] In concert with George Mason, James Monroe, Benjamin Harrison, and others, Henry's goal was to expose the weaknesses of the proposed Constitution and to offer amendments to correct these defects. Moreover, he insisted that the amendments must be adopted prior to ratification, not afterward as the Federalists suggested.

Henry's objections to the Constitution were many, but a few of the more fundamental ones are worth pointing out. First, he charged that the framers had no authority to establish a new form of government. They had been sent to Philadelphia to revise the Articles of Confederation, not to draft a constitution. "The federal convention ought to have amended the old system—for this purpose they were solely delegated: the object of their mission extended to no other consideration."[168] In effect, Henry charged the Constitutional Convention with illegal proceedings. And he was right. But since the Constitution was now before the people, and eight states had already ratified it, the point was virtually moot.

Second, Henry claimed that the Constitution established a "consolidated government" with powers drawn directly from the people and not the states. "That this is a consolidated government is demonstrably clear: …who authorized them [the framers] to speak the language of, *we the people*, instead of *we the states*?" Thus, by drawing power from the people and not the states, the principle of "federalism" was denied and the sovereignty of the states was destroyed. The existing federation of sovereign states had been transformed into a supreme national government. "States are the characteristics and the soul of the Confederation. If the states be not the agents of this compact, it must be one great, consolidated, national government of the people of all the states." Henry went so far as to call this "alarming transition" a "revolution as radical as that which separated us from Great Britain."

Furthermore, inter-regional distrust was already brewing due to the willingness of the northern states to cede the Mississippi River to Spain, and Henry believed that the balance of power between the northern and southern states would be destroyed by a national government.

More importantly, Henry protested that the Constitution did not require federal politicians to be sufficiently responsible to their constituents. Senators, for example, were not liable to recall nor bound in any legal way to obey the people's instructions. The same held true for representatives and other federal agents. Without strict and explicit accountability, Henry believed that the federal politicians would not act in the interest of the people. The individual checks and balances within the federal system were not, in Henry's opinion, sufficient to halt federal abuse. Further, the most effective checks against overreaching federal power would be the power of the state governments. The Constitution, however, had so weakened the states that they could not effectively counterbalance the federal system.

The presidency, under the new plan, Henry insisted, had such immense patronage and power entrusted to it, that he saw "an awful squint in its face, a squint toward monarchy." And what of Congress' power to establish a "strong army" or what of its "power of direct taxation"? Surely, these were the "engines of despotism" able to "execute the execrible commands of tyranny..." he warned.

Henry was relentless in pursuing these and other objections to the Constitution. Of the twenty-two days the

Convention was in session, he spoke on seventeen days. On several days he made three speeches; on one day he made five; and on another he made eight speeches. On one occasion he spoke before the assembly for seven consecutive hours! The journal of the Convention shows that Henry's addresses comprised nearly one-fourth of the entire record of speeches.[169] Nevertheless, Henry's dominance at the Convention did not weary the auditors. Neither the delegates nor the spectators tired of hearing him speak. According to Judge St. George Tucker, Henry was "sometimes as great" as when he delivered his "Give Me Liberty" speech at St. John's Church in 1775. "If he soared at times, like the eagle, and seemed like the bird of Jove to be armed with thunder, he did not disdain to stoop like the hawk to seize his prey,–but the instant that he had done it, rose in pursuit of another quarry."[170]

In spite of these rhetorical feats, Henry could not halt the drive for ratification. By a vote of eighty-nine to seventy-nine, the Convention ratified the Constitution. He did, however, gain a partial victory: at the Convention's end a majority of delegates agreed that the Constitution needed correction, and thus a committee proposed a list of forty amendments to be sent to Congress for its consideration.

Henry had vowed at the Convention that he would labor to "retrieve the loss of liberty and to remove the defects of that system in a constitutional way" rather than by force or sedition. He would be "a peaceable citizen." But he would strive to see "that government changed so as to be compatible with the safety, liberty, and happiness of the people."[171] For the next three years he backed the election of Anti-Federalist senators and zealously battled in the Virginia legislature for the adoption of amendments to the Constitution. Although Madison had been his federal foe in the Ratification Convention, Henry was able, by his control of the Virginia House, to force Madison to seek in Congress the desired changes. As Jefferson lamented: "Mr. Henry is omnipotent in Virginia." [172] Therefore, while it is true that Madison was the leader in the Congress which adopted the amendments, he was bound to do so by his constituents who were of Henry's opinion. Henry was thus the "vis a tergo" that impelled Madison to advocate the adoption of amendments. As a result, the U.S. Bill of Rights found its way into the Constitution, ratified in 1791, as the fruit of Henry's labors. And having fulfilled his promise, he retired from politics.

RETIRED BUT RECRUITED

*T*he last year that Patrick Henry graced the corridors of political power in Virginia was 1791. He retired from public service due to its exhausting demands on his health and his desire to spend time with his flourishing family. Due to financial problems, however, he continued to practice law and speculate in land. "I am obliged to be very industrious," he told his daughter Betsy, "to clear myself of debt." [173]

Over the next several years he labored at the bar in a number of cases that served to enhance his renown as a public orator. One such case, the British Debt Case, brought out the patriotic fire still smoldering in Henry's aged bones, for it harkened back to the days of the Revolution for which Henry had sacrificed so much energy and risked both reputation and life. The case involved the question of whether British merchant houses could collect pre-war debts from American debtors. Henry opposed the payment of these old British debts, and carefully prepared his case.

When he arrived at the courthouse on the day of the trial, Henry found that the legislature had been cancelled so the members could attend the trial and hear him speak. And speak he did. For three days he presented intricate legal arguments, quoted the leading legal authorities on international law, and even rehearsed for the rapt audience the grievances and deprivations of the Americans during the Revolution. The young John Randolph, who witnessed Henry's performance, said that he was like a "first-rate four-mile race horse, sometimes displaying his old power and speed for a few laps," and then slowing down again.[174] So impressive was Henry's oratory that Judge Iredell, who had never before heard Henry, and was sceptical of his talents, "sat with his mouth and eyes open in perfect wonder." And when Henry finished his rapid review of British tyranny, "there was a tumultuous burst of applause" from the crowd, and Judge Iredell exclaimed, "Gracious God! He is an orator indeed!"[175]

Henry also handled prominent criminal cases, such as the case of Richard Randolph, who, with his cousin Nancy, was accused of aborting and disposing of their bastard child. The circumstantial evidence against Henry's client was so great that a majority of the spectators and jury assumed that Randolph was guilty. However, there could be no infanticide without an infant, and it had not yet been proven that Nancy had indeed even been pregnant. The prosecution hung its case on the testimony of a Mrs. Carter Page, who testified that Nancy had most certainly been with child.

"How did she know?" the court asked. She had "satisfied her curiosity" on the question when, while visiting Nancy one day, she looked through a crack in the door while Nancy was undressing.

Henry, seeing his opportunity to discredit the witness, sarcastically quizzed Mrs. Page. "Which eye did you peep with?," Henry wryly asked. The spectators burst with laughter. Then, turning to the court, he declared, "Great God! Deliver us from eavesdroppers!" Page was discredited and the defendant was acquitted.[176]

These and other legal triumphs led to a lucrative law practice that cleared Henry's debts and provided support for his growing family. In fact, he now had several families under his care. In addition to his eleven children by Dorothea, Henry's sister, Anne Christian, had died in 1790 and left her three young children to Henry's protection. Moreover, his eldest daughter Betsy and her younger children were now also under Henry's care as the result of the death of her husband, John Fontaine. So great were Henry's domestic duties, that a visiting neighbor commented, "What a weight of worldly concerns rest upon this old man's shoulders."[177]

Henry's "worldly concerns" also included his properties. Ever the speculator, Henry continued to invest in land ventures. In 1792, he sold his estate in Prince Edward and moved to Long Island in Campbell County. In 1794, he acquired a second plantation, Red Hill, which was located eighteen miles below Long Island in the Staunton River Valley. Although Henry preferred the solitude of Long Island, with his older daughters approaching womanhood, Red Hill's more densely populated environs provided readily abundant suitors. The Long Island estate was sold and Red Hill became Henry's last residence and final resting place.[178]

Though officially retired from politics, Henry remained the dominant figure in Virginia politics and was eagerly consulted and recruited by politicians. "I no longer consider myself an actor on the stage of public life," he protested. Yet "the public" insisted on his services. Indeed, the developments then taking place in American politics made the noble patriot an attractive catch for both Federalists and Republicans. The Federalists, under the leadership of Washington and Hamilton, had alienated the "Democratic-Republican" party of

Jefferson and Madison by their "British predilections."[179] The Republicans, in opposition to Washington's administration, began to espouse a theory of states rights that justified secession and threatened the union.

As a means to bolster the Federalist party, Washington and others attempted to entice Henry back into politics. In 1794, Washington offered him an ambassadorship to Spain to negotiate a treaty concerning the Mississippi River. Henry politely declined. The following year, Washington offered him the position of secretary of state. Henry again declined. Next, Washington proffered the illustrious position of chief justice of the Supreme Court. But Henry would not budge. Lee, who was then the governor of Virginia, nominated Henry as a U.S. Senator to fill out an unexpired term, but Henry declined this honor also.

The Republicans, on the other hand, tried to induce Henry to run for a sixth term as governor in opposition to a Federalist candidate. With a strong states' rights platform, Jefferson and Madison hoped to bring Henry back into the Republican fold. Henry, however, was repulsed by the Republican sympathy for the French Revolution which had imprisoned his old friend, the patriot Lafayette. In spite of their best efforts, neither Federalist nor Republican could prevail upon Henry to reappear on the public stage. He was resolved to retire at Red Hill.

RED HILL

*H*enry retired his legal practice in 1794 and spent his final five years in repose at Red Hill. Here his "worldly concerns" were much abated by the refreshment that he found in the beauty of nature, the enjoyment of family, and the fellowship of God. According to one observer, Red Hill was "beautifully situated on an elevated ridge" dividing Campbell and Charlotte Counties.

> *From it the valley of the Staunton stretches southward about three miles, varying from a quarter to nearly a mile in width, and of an oval-like form. Through most fertile meadows waving in their golden luxuriance, slowly winds the river, overhung by mossy foliage, while on all sides gently sloping hills, rich in verdure, enclose the whole, and impart to it an air of seclusion and repose. From the brow of the hill, west of the house, is a scene of an entirely different character: the Blue Ridge, with the lofty peaks of Otter, appears in the horizon at a distance of nearly sixty miles.*[180]

Henry had always had a great love for the outdoors, and at Red Hill it was his custom to sit outside under the shady trees "in full view of the beautiful valley beneath." He would lean his chair against one of the trees, sip a can of cool spring-water, and soak in the beauty and glory of God's creation. On occasion, he could be seen walking "to and fro in the yard from one clump of trees to the other, buried in reverie, at which times he was never interrupted."[181]

He was anything but a hermit, however. When not reveling in nature he was relaxing with his family. Henry loved his young ones, and it was not beneath his patriarchal dignity to indulge in "the sports of children." Red Hill visitors often found him lying on the floor with a group of his little children climbing all over him in every direction. Or they might find Henry fiddling away as his children danced to the tune, "while the only contest seemed to be who should make the most noise." Nevertheless, Henry's playful disposition did not keep him from the serious duties of parenting. As a father "he was entirely exemplary." And beside "setting a good example of honesty, benevolence, hospitality, and every social virtue," he also actively engaged in the education of his younger children.[182]

His retirement to Red Hill also provided Henry with much desired time and solitude for religious meditation. Now, more than ever, he devoted himself to the study of the Bible. According to his daughter, Sarah, Henry's practice at Red Hill was to read his Bible every morning immediately after rising. He would sit in the drawing room meditating, and when his children rose and passed through the room, he would look up, blessing them with a "good morrow." His fondness for the Bible was not a trait that Henry concealed. Tradition has it that on one occasion a neighbor dropped in on Henry and found him reading his Bible. "This book," he said while holding the

Bible up in his hand, "is worth all the books that ever were printed, and it has been my misfortune that I have never found time to read it with the proper attention and feeling till lately. I trust in the mercy of Heaven that it is not yet too late."[183]

Besides studying his Bible, he also spent time reading the works of such English divines as Tillotson, Butler and Sherlock. He was especially fond of the last and would read portions of Sherlock's sermons to his family every Sunday evening. Then the family would join in sacred worship while Henry accompanied them on the violin. When the opportunity was available, Henry partook of Communion–an act he did not take lightly. "He approached the Communion table with the greatest reverence, after having prepared himself by fasting, and spent the day in retirement."[184]

Henry had always been a devout man–"a saint in religion" as he was called. But his studies at Red Hill increasingly convinced him of the pernicious influence of French infidelity and deism. Although he was not fond of writing, nor had any aspirations to be an author, he was so alarmed by the rising tide of deism that when Paine's *Age of Reason* was published, Henry wrote an able refutation of scepticism and defense of Christianity. According to John Fontaine, it was "the most eloquent and unanswerable argument in defense of the Bible which was ever written."[185] Unfortunately, Henry did not think so. For when Watson's *Apology for the Bible* appeared, Henry thought it was far superior to his own manuscript, and he directed his wife to destroy his apologia.[186] Thus posterity lost what would have undoubtedly proven to be a great Christian classic.

THE LAST TRUMPET

*T*he quietus of Henry's retirement at Red Hill was not only disturbed by the religious scepticism that was then becoming fashionable in the new republic, but also by the increasingly turbulent bitterness of American politics. The Republican party, which had a majority in the U.S. House, openly opposed Washington's administration and bitterly attacked him personally. When Adams became President, the United States were on the verge of war with France, and passed the Alien and Sedition Laws, which gave the president broad powers to deport or imprison dangerous aliens and to suppress unlawful conspiracies.

In response, Jefferson and the Republicans schemed to spur the state legislatures to oppose the national government. Jefferson contended that the laws were unconstitutional, violating those constitutional provisions that guaranteed personal rights. Due to his efforts both Kentucky and Virginia passed resolutions that not only condemned the Acts as unconstitutional,–"void, and of no force"–but also set forth a doctrine of state sovereignty that justified nullification.

Henry, on the other hand, had always maintained that the U.S. Constitution had transformed the federation of states into one national government. Therefore, although he strongly believed in states' rights, he did not agree with the doctrine of nullification. The *fatal change* to the American system had occurred when the Constitution was ratified. This Henry saw clearly. That is why he was so determined during the Virginia Ratification Convention to oppose its adoption without prior amendments.

Although Henry had committed himself to private life, and had refused successive offers to national office, a powerful appeal to his patriotism was sent by Washington in 1798, pleading with Henry to return to the Virginia legislature to oppose Jefferson and the Republicans. Washington was convinced that the political doctrine of the Kentucky and Virginia Resolutions was leading the Union to the brink of dissolution, with either monarchy or foreign domination soon to follow. "Infirm as he was, Mr. Henry could not resist such an appeal from the man he revered as the father of his country."[187] Accordingly, Henry immediately declared himself a candidate for the Virginia House of Delegates at the upcoming election. He sent word to the public that he would address them on the first Monday in March, which was county court day. Word spread quickly, and people came from many surrounding counties to hear the legendary oratory of Henry. When he arrived at the Charlotte Court House, he was greeted by throngs of admiring citizens. So great was the crowd's reverence for Henry, that a minister who was present felt compelled to rebuke them. "Mr. Henry is not a god!" he shouted. To which Henry agreed: "No, indeed, my friend; I am but a poor worm of the dust."[188]

When it was time for Henry to give his speech, "he arose with great difficulty and stood somewhat bowed with age and weakness. His face was almost colorless. His countenance was cavernous…" At first, he began slowly, and his voice was cracked and tremulous. But soon the old Patrick lit up as in his youthful triumphs over tyranny. As "his features glowed with the hue and fire of youth," Henry informed the multitude that the recent proceedings of the Virginia Assembly "had planted thorns upon his pillow," and drawn him from "that happy retirement which it had pleased a bountiful Providence to bestow." He reiterated his belief that Virginia and all the states had essentially given up their sovereignty by adopting the Constitution, and thus could not "pronounce upon the validity of federal laws." Resistance to the federal government would probably lead to "the enforcement of military power"– civil war! What recourse, then, do we, an oppressed people, have? "My answer is ready," he said, "overthrow the government." But do so in a constitutional way and only as a last resort.[189]

"Like Moses of old, this leader of the exodus of America from her state of bondage, used his latest breath in a prophetic warning to his people."[190] In little over a generation, Henry's prophecy came true–the last shots of the Civil War, fired at Appomattox, could be heard on the very spot where Henry uttered his last trumpet call.

Henry, of course, was elected to the House. But he was so exhausted by his trip to Charlotte and the exertion of his passionate speech, that he returned to Red Hill and was confined to bed. He never took his office in Richmond. His health quickly deteriorated, and in early June, he was considered too ill to hear the news that his own daughter, Anne Roane, had just passed away. Writing to Patsy, one of his other daughters, Henry said, "I am very unwell, and have Dr. Cabell with me."[191] The shadow of death was now upon him. Alarmed by his condition, Henry's older children and relatives rushed to

Red Hill to be with him in his last hours. When they arrived, Henry was sitting in a large old-fashioned armchair, which was more comfortable than his bed. His body was now wasted with cancer, but his mind was at peace and perfectly calm in the face of death.

On June 6, the family physician offered Henry a dose of liquid mercury as a last resort. It would bring either better health or bitter death. Taking the vial in hand, Henry paused to offer a prayer "for his family, his country and his own soul then in the presence of death."[192] He calmly downed the draft and lovingly spoke to his weeping family of the goodness of God that had blessed his life, and that was now permitting him to experience a painless death. Shortly thereafter the Trumpet of the Revolution heard the trumpet of God.

Thus, without pomp or fanfare, Patrick Henry passed on to be with his Maker in whose Son he had trusted and in whose Providence he had acted. In a quiet garden graveyard at Red Hill, Henry's body was laid to rest, covered by a plain marble slab. On it were inscribed the following words:

Patrick Henry

"His fame his best epitaph."

PART II:
THE CHARACTER OF PATRICK HENRY

ᴥ   ᴥ   ᴥ

Let us ally ourselves to virtue…without that auxiliary our appearance in the theater of nations will be fleeting…with it, fixed as the firmament.[193]

If I was permitted to add to the catalogue one other of my blessings, it should be that my countrymen should learn wisdom and virtue, and in their day to know the things that pertain to their peace.[194]

HIS FATHER

*This calls my attention back to the many precious
lessons given to me by our honored parents, whose
lives were, indeed, a constant lesson and worthy of
imitation.*[195]

*P*atrick Henry was born to neither wealth nor station. Yet he was fortunate enough to be blessed
with one of life's most important foundations–an able and
godly father. While some men–for example, a Winston
Churchill–are able to overcome the pain and emptiness of a
neglectful or absent father, it is generally true that the lack of
a strong father in the house tends toward both personal and
social disintegration.[196] It is not without reason that Proverbs
17:6 states: "the glory of children are their fathers."

It was Henry's good fortune to have a father with a
respectable heritage, an excellent education, and a godly character. Born in Aberdeen, Scotland, John Henry had a number
of relatives who were "persons of eminence as divines, orators
or men of letters..." For instance, John Henry's cousin, David
Henry, managed the "Gentlemen's Magazine," and his cousin,

William Robertson, was principal of the University of Edinburgh and author of the *History of the Reign of the Emperor Charles V.* Through his father's side, Patrick Henry was third cousin of Lord Brougham, who was an eloquent orator in his own right, and who, like Patrick, fought against parliamentary corruption.[197]

The Henry clan, then, was generally well-educated, and John Henry was a man of classical education. The Reverend Samuel Davies said of John Henry that he was "more familiar with his Homer than with his Bible," which was another way of saying that he was virtually a classical scholar. Having studied at King's College, John Henry was one of the few college-trained men in Hanover, and was highly respected in the community for his learning.[198] Since Patrick Henry was tutored by his father, he enjoyed the direct benefit of John's classical training. Thus, his father had an immediate and profound influence on young Patrick's intellectual development.

All the accounts of John Henry describe him also as a man of godly character. One author has labeled him "respectable," "plain," and "solid," while another asserts that "he led a life of irreproachable integrity and exemplary piety and won the full confidence of the community in which he lived." While he may have known his Homer better than his Bible, it is also true that John Henry was well-versed in the Scriptures. On one occasion, when he got into an argument on the subject of eternal punishment, he defended the doctrine by a critical examination of the Greek text of the New Testament.[199]

That Patrick Henry benefited as a young boy from his father's godly example is evident from his own testimony. Many years later, in 1785, his sister, Anne Christian, and her husband, William, moved to Kentucky, only to find that Indian tribes made their settlement there impossible. But in April

1786, before they could relocate, William was killed in a skirmish with the Indians. Upon hearing this sad news, Patrick Henry wrote his beloved sister Anne: "I am at a loss how to address you, my dear sister. Would to God I could say something to give relief to the dearest of women and sisters." Then, after encouraging her to "adore with humility the unsearchable ways of Providence," Henry directed her mind to the godly example set for them by their parents. "This is one of the occasions that calls your and my attention back to the many precious lessons of piety given us by our honored parents, whose lives were indeed a constant lesson and worthy of imitation."[200]

It was in the home of his parents, then, that Patrick Henry learned life's most important lessons: morality, obedience, discipline, and responsibility. In addition to his father's explicit instruction, Patrick naturally imitated what he observed. Practice is more powerful than precept, and a parent's example is more powerful than a teacher's lecture. His father, therefore, not only fashioned Patrick's mind, he also shaped his soul, and the lessons he learned at home colored his life and leadership.

His Mother

*My dear and ever honored mother died six or eight
weeks ago.... Thus is the last generation clearing
the way for us, as we must shortly do for the next.*[201]

In 1914, the United States Congress passed an historic
resolution honoring American mothers. It reads:

> *Whereas the service rendered the United States
> by the American mother is the greatest source
> of the country's strength and admiration; and
> Whereas we honor ourselves and the mothers
> of America when we do any thing to give
> emphasis to the home as the foundation head
> of the State; and Whereas the American mother
> is doing so much for good government and
> humanity, we declare that the second Sunday
> of May will henceforth be celebrated as
> Mother's Day.*[202]

The high regard for motherhood expressed in this resolution is based on a right understanding of the important

influence that a mother has on her children–a fact that has been undisputed until recently. Now, however, it is being suggested that motherhood is either a servile station in life without dignity; or worse still, that it is an obsolete role better filled by professional "caregivers." How often do we hear slogans suggesting that "society" must save "our children"? Or that the government must step into the family and take over traditional parental prerogatives?

Contrary to this anti-family trend, mothers are indispensable and irreplaceable. The bond between mother and child insures that the mother is placed in a uniquely powerful position to shape her child's character. And by molding the child, she shapes the world. Indeed, many great and influential men in American history have acknowledged their mother's impact on their lives. "All that I am," once said John Quincy Adams, "my mother made me."[203]

Henry would have heartily agreed with Adams' sentiment. From his mother, Henry undoubtedly derived his most eminent gifts of oratory. The Winstons were of Welsh stock and were well-known in Virginia as "a family marked by vitality and spirit, conversational talent, a lyric and dramatic turn" and a gift for "music and for eloquent speech..." This talent for talk ran strong in the Winston clan. Sarah's brother, William Winston, was reputed to have been a great orator himself. Tradition has it that William's "dazzling and wondrous" eloquence was unsurpassed among all the great orators of Virginia–except by Patrick Henry himself.[204]

The table talk in the Old Dominion also mentioned that the Winstons had a great fondness for country life–hunting, fishing, and the pleasures of nature. This trait certainly characterized Henry throughout his life. As a young boy he loved to hunt, fish, and roam in the wild woods. Even as a young attorney, he would at times enter court to plead a cause wearing leatherskins and carrying his hunting rifle. Although the demands of his professional and political life pulled him away from the chase, Henry never ceased to be allured by the charms of nature. Late in life, when he was finally able to retire, Henry would spend hours on end enjoying the beautiful country scenes at his Red Hill plantation.

In addition, Sarah made a major impact on Patrick's religious development, which in turn affected his professional and political career. Of his parents, Sarah was apparently the most religious. As a testimony to her Christian character, her son-in-law, Colonel Meredith wrote that "None who were acquainted with her life and conversion need wonder at her great resignation [during her last illness] to whatever might be the Divine will." During the eleven years that Sarah lived with the Merediths, her life was "one continued scene of piety and devotion, guided by such a great share of good sense as rendered her sensible and agreeable to all who were so happy as to be acquainted with her. Never did I know", said Colonel Meredith, "a Christian character equal to hers."[205]

Sarah's Christian devotion led her to seek out the more vital brand of Christianity that was being espoused by the dissenting Presbyterians in Virginia. As a result, she began to attend the Fork Church where the Reverend Samuel Davies was the preacher. Sarah's habit was to take the young Patrick to church with her and to require him after the service to reiterate the substance of the sermon. In this way, Patrick's mother drilled him in Presbyterian or Calvinistic theology, which provided the backbone for the American resistance to British tyranny. As one author has noted, Calvinism "has been able to inspire and sustain the bravest efforts ever made by man to break the yoke of unjust authority…" It has "borne ever an inflexible front to illusion and mendacity, and has preferred rather to be ground to powder, like flint, than to bend before violence, or melt under enervating temptation."[206] By the time of the American Revolution, approximately two-thirds of the colonial population had been "trained in the school of Calvin."[207] Therefore, the American historian Bancroft could claim, "He who will not honor the memory and respect the influence of Calvin knows little of the origin of American liberty."[208] Henry, through his mother, was a spiritual descendant of Calvin and represented the liberating elements of a Reformed theology and world-view.[209]

Moreover, by placing before Patrick the model of Reverend Davies' sermons, Sarah put Patrick in a school of rhetoric as well as theology. "Clearly, the evangelical rhetorical model was the dominant influence on Henry's development as a public speaker."[210] Preaching was the most common form of public communication, and Henry attended Davies' services from the age of eleven to twenty-three. According to Henry, Davies was "what an orator should be."[211] Mentored by observing the master-preacher, Henry modeled Davies' style in the public square and used it to powerfully advance American independence.

When the United States Congress, in 1914, claimed that the American mother was doing so much for good government and liberty, they wrote Sarah Henry's epitaph. Through her influence on Patrick, she helped shape one of America's greatest patriots, the man who literally led the colonies to political freedom. "Into the woman's keeping," Theodore Roosevelt once observed, "is committed the destiny of the generation to come after them."[212] Truly, "the hand that rocks the cradle, rules the world," for the children of today are the leaders of tomorrow.

SELF-EDUCATION

*Cultivate your mind by the perusal of those books
which instruct while they amuse. History, geography,
poetry, moral essays, biography, travels, sermons,
and other well-written religious productions will not
fail to enlarge your understanding, to render you a
more agreeable companion, and to exalt your
virtue.*[213]

Great leadership is seldom, if ever, the product of
natural gifts alone. History is replete with examples of talented failures: men and women whose natural gifts
were wasted on the altar of dissipation or laid dormant in the
barren soil of indolence. Heredity is not destiny. Natural gifts
must be developed by a continuous growth in knowledge and
experience.

Henry was fortunate to be raised in a stable Christian
home. His father was an educated man who passed on to him
a vast body of knowledge. His mother, as we have seen, was a
woman whose gift for conversation and heart for religion
played a large part in Henry's makeup. Nevertheless, these
facts alone do not explain Henry's later greatness as a political

leader. He grew in stature as a leader because he grew in knowledge. In other words, he learned to educate himself.

Henry's formal education by his father and uncle ended when he was fifteen years old, and it was not until the age of twenty-three that he decided to study for the bar. In the intervening nine years Henry became a farmer, a store owner, a husband, and a father. In a word, he grew up. Yet it was during these maturing years that Henry developed a taste for reading. Contrary to Jefferson's venomous assertion that Henry "was a man of very little knowledge of any sort," and that "he read nothing, and had no books," we know from Henry's letters and speeches as well as the testimony of other contemporaries, that Henry was far more educated than Jefferson wished to acknowledge. Indeed, Jefferson himself even admitted that he was "astonished" at Henry's "command of proper language."[214]

Henry not only had a "command of proper language," but he had a broad knowledge of law, history, theology, and political philosophy. When we look at Henry's speeches, we see the eloquence of an educated man. In his letters, there is also that same "nameless felicity which…is only communicable by genuine literary culture in some form."[215] In truth, Henry was more educated than his formal training can account for, and this shows that he was well-acquainted with good literature.

As a young boy he read "a few light and eloquent narratives" and then progressed to more serious books. He was fond of geography and history–especially the history of Rome and Greece. One of Henry's favorite authors was Livy, whom he read through in English "once at least in every year during the early part of his life."[216] It is also apparent from Henry's later letters and speeches that he also read English and American colonial history. When only twelve years old, Henry was introduced to evangelical theology, and one of his favorite books throughout his life was Butler's Analogy, which he may have read as a young boy. He also was familiar with other divines such as Tillotson and Sherlock. Henry was throughout his life a deeply religious person, and there is no doubt that he frequently read the English Bible, "the diction of which is stamped upon his style as unmistakably as it is upon that of the elder Pitt."[217]

The legal practice that Henry maintained for nearly forty years was one long process of self-education. While it was customary for aspiring legal students to spend years as an apprentice in a law office, or even to attend law school in England, as did John Randolph and his sons, Peyton and John, Henry took the more difficult, but cheaper course of educating himself for the bar. Although many of Henry's cases as a county lawyer were fairly simple from a legal point of view, whenever confronted with a major case, Henry would master the major legal arguments by careful and thorough study. One of the most notable examples of Henry's studiousness was when he spent several days in strict seclusion in his law office while preparing for the British Debt Case. His law office, by 1799, contained approximately two-hundred ten volumes valued at £120. A perusal of the titles "reveals an emphasis on learning and religion in the Henry household." The greatest number of books were on law (sixty-five), Greek and Roman classics (thirty), textbooks (twenty-four), and religion (thirteen).[218]

It would be wrong to suggest, however, that Henry was a "bookish" person. He did not possess the pedantic propensity of either Jefferson or Madison. And although he did not read widely, he did read well. His habit was to read a few of the best books over and over again to master their contents. Moreover, he had an excellent memory and a strong capacity for deep reflection. Whatever he read provided him material for meditation. Once, Henry commented to Judge Roane that

Montesquieu's *Spirit of the Laws* was "a good book to read on a stagecoach" because "one could read enough in half an hour to provide reflection for a day."[219] This was undoubtedly Henry's habit: read and reflect, and thereby truly master the meaning of the text.

Henry might have been more scholarly had he believed that a well-rounded education was acquired from books alone. However, he viewed all of life as an opportunity to learn, and according to historian George Williston, Henry "liked to talk with all kinds of people, no matter what their station in life." Accordingly, Henry claimed that he had never talked to anyone without learning something.[220] He had keen powers of observation, and learned from flesh and blood as well as from paper and ink. On one occasion he entered a Williamsburg store and saw the Oxford scholar, William Wormley, immersed in an ancient tome. "What, Mr. Wormley, still studying books!" he exclaimed. "Study men, Mr. Wormley, study men!"[221] And it was Henry's practice of studying men that gave him that insight into human nature which he artfully used in his rhetorical mastery over juries and assemblies.

From his youthful meditation in the Louisa woods, to his retired reflections at Red Hill, Patrick Henry was a thinking man. Whether riding the circuit or reading the Scriptures, he found food for thought. He read enough as his obligations required and time permitted; but he always observed and learned from cirumstances and people. He who would lead men, must read men. And Henry excelled in that type of self-education.

Preparation

*Be of good courage, my son, and remember that the
best men always make themselves.*[222]

$\mathcal{T}$he talents of great men create the illusion that their
success is the product of ability or fortune alone. The
inspired performance of a master musician, or the mezmeriz-
ing delivery of an impassioned orator, appears so natural and
effortless that it is easy to forget that private preparation pre-
cedes public performance. The reason that Providence places
a man on the public stage at the critical time is because the
man has prepared in private. The man and hour meet
because the man has prepared for the hour.

Henry's innate genius and native talents certainly made
his public displays of rhetoric seem natural. And they were.
But that did not exclude the necessity of careful and industrious preparation. The "forest-born Demosthenes" was as much
a product of preparation as of nature. William Wirt, Henry's
first biographer, did much to enhance the illusion that his natural genius precluded the necessity of industry and
preparation. He portrayed Henry as a lazy daydreamer who

wasted his youth wildly wandering the woods of Virginia, and then suddenly burst on the public stage with supernatural inspiration. The facts, however, are otherwise.

As we have seen, Henry's boyhood was fairly normal for his times–a mixture of school and sports, work and play. Both his father and his uncle, who had a hand in his early education, were classically trained, and they undoubtedly drilled Henry in his lessons.

When we look at Henry's legal career, it is certain that he understood the need to be well-prepared for his profession. While it is unclear just how long he prepared for the bar examination, there is no doubt that he prepared thoroughly. In a fairly brief time (some say six weeks, others say six months), Henry laboriously prepared for licensure. The legal books he studied contained legal philosophy, legal precedents, and a combination of legal French and Latin–not easy reading by any standard.[223] Instead of assuming that his natural genius would carry the day, Henry assiduously applied himself to the texts. He hit the books.

It is true that many of Henry's legal cases were minor and required little legal preparation. Nevertheless, his mind was always at work. For instance, when he was recruited for the Parson's Cause, the legal questions had already been settled, yet he had prepared a strategy to influence the outcome of the case. On the morning of the trial he asked his clergyman uncle not to attend. "Why?" he was asked. Because "I shall be obliged to say some hard things of the clergy,"[224] Henry replied. In other words, Henry had carefully considered the case and had prepared a plan to discredit the plaintiff–a clergyman. And his stratagem succeeded.

When necessity required, Henry would painfully prepare for battle, as some of his later criminal cases demonstrate. For instance, in 1793, Henry was asked to defend Richard

Randolph, the older brother of the famous John Randolph of Roanoke. The charge against him and his supposed lover, Nancy, was the murder of a newly-born infant–their own illegitimate child no less. When a messenger arrived at Henry's Long Island plantation requesting his legal services, Henry replied that he was too ill to undertake the journey to Cumberland Courthouse. The fact was, Henry believed that Nancy (Richard's cousin) was guilty; and he would only defend a client he believed to be innocent. Henry's wife, Dorothea, attempted to persuade him to take the case. But he told her he would first have to convince himself of Nancy's innocence. So, "he shut himself up in a room for two days and would not go out for meals," and Dorothea "would crack the door and leave food on a table nearby." Finally, on the third day, she heard Henry playing the violin and realized that he had convinced himself of Nancy's innocence, for he took the case and successfully defended her and Richard.[225]

In another celebrated case late in his career–the British Debt Case–Henry put himself through rigorous preparation. The suit of *Jones v. Walker*, as it was technically called, came before the United States District Court at Richmond in 1791, and revolved around the question of whether or not British merchants could collect pre-Revolutionary debts from Virginia citizens. Under the treaty of peace in 1783, the debts could be recovered; however, the state of Virginia had passed a law in 1777 permitting money due to British creditors to be paid into the state treasury with inflated currency. Those Virginians who had paid into the treasury were unwilling, of course, to pay the debt a second time. Accordingly, *Jones v. Walker* was a test case that involved intricate questions of municipal, international, and constitutional law.[226]

Henry, in league with John Marshall, Alexander Campbell, and James Innes, advocated for the defendant,

Thomas Walker. For several weeks before the trial, Henry prepared thoroughly. In seclusion from all other business, he shut himself up in his law office for days at a time, sequestered from his family, even taking his meals there from a servant who passed them through the office door. He privately pored over his law books: Vattel's *Law of Nations*, Grotius' *Delure Belle ac Pacis*, and other works of international law. From these, Henry developed his arguments and made quotations that he placed in "a manuscript volume more than an inch thick, and closely written; a book...bound with leather, and convenient for carrying in his pocket." According to his grandson, P.H. Fontaine, for several days before leaving for Richmond, Henry could be seen walking frequently in a shaded ravine in his yard, "with his notebook in his hand, which he often opened and read; and from his gestures, while promenading alone..," it appeared that Henry was committing his arguments and speech to memory.[227]

By applying all his powers of mind in preparation for this case, he "came forth, on this occasion, a perfect master of every law, natural and municipal, which touched upon the subject of investigation in the most distinct point."[228] The notion that Henry was not technically sophisticated in the law, because he was too lazy, was a product of Jefferson's embittered statements made in his old age. Yet in the British Debt Case even Jefferson was forced to admit that Henry had made himself "really learned" on the applicable law.[229]

Large crowds attended the courthouse to hear his speech, and the general opinion was that his performance was remarkable for its mastery of the law, its ingenuity of argument, and its eloquence of speech. All those who heard Henry plead this case acknowledged that it was the "most distinguished display of his professional talents."[230] Young Henry Clay, who was in the courtroom, was enthralled with Henry's "soul-stirring" speech. The Countess of Huntingdon was also present. She was so moved by Henry's performance that she declared he would have received a peerage in England for his eloquence.[231] Although it was not Henry's custom to wear jewelry, he happened to wear a diamond ring throughout this trial. And during the splendorous display of Henry's eloquence, a spectator exclaimed to one of the judges, "the diamond is blazing!"[232] And indeed it was. For, like Henry, it had been polished in private so it might shine the brighter in public.

COURAGE

Sir, it is the fortune of a free people, not to be intim-
idated by imaginary dangers. Fear is the passion of
slaves.[233]

Courage is the *sin quo non* of leadership: it is that
quality of character that will encounter danger with
firmness. Courage will stand on principle in the face of opposition and unpopularity. It will confront moral evil with the
truth, and will face physical danger with valor. While others
may falter through fear, a courageous leader will remain calm
in crisis and vigilant in action.

If there is one virtue for which Patrick Henry was known,
it is courage. When he arrived in Williamsburg as a freshman
assemblyman in May of 1765, the Virginia House of
Burgesses was dominated by men of considerable wealth,
education, and prestige. Although there was no recognized
class structure in Virginia, there certainly was a ruling aristocracy that held the reigns of power in the House–the great
Tidewater gentry, made up of Speaker Robinson, Peyton
Randolph, Nicholas Carter, and others. Robinson's political

power in the House was so great that many members privately referred to him as "the bashaw" or the "leading man." By working the rules of procedure, Robinson saw to it that "whatever he agreed to was carried and whatever he opposed was dropped."[234] Seldom was Robinson opposed in the House, and never by a neophyte assemblyman. That is, until Patrick Henry entered the House.

On Henry's third day in the House, Robinson, who also held the office of treasurer, proposed a public loan office for the use of planters suffering from the prolonged depression in the tobacco market. The real purpose of the scheme, unknown at the time, was to enable Robinson to float private loans with public money. Henry's instincts sensed the favoritism inherent in the proposal. And even though the custom in the House was for new members to be silent for the first month, Jefferson said that Henry "attacked the scheme...in that bold, grand and overwhelming eloquence for which he became so justly celebrated afterward." He courageously took the floor and vehemently denounced the plan. "What sir, is it proposed to reclaim the spendthrift from his dissipation and extravagance by filling his pockets with money?" Thus, in his very first debate in the House, only three days a member, Henry "displayed not only his great powers of eloquence, but his courage in maintaining his convictions of public duty against the united efforts of the aristocratic leaders of the body."[235] Even though the proposal passed the House, the leadership was so humiliated by Henry's bold denunciations, that the plan never took effect. When Robinson died a year later, it was discovered that he had been misusing public funds for some time.

Only six days after the public loan debate, when the Stamp Act was discussed in the House, Henry again displayed the same unfaltering courage. While all the established members of the House were willing to acquiesce in the inevitability of the stamp tax, Henry boldly ventured his now famous Resolutions defying the British power to tax the colonies. Judge Spencer Roane, who witnessed Henry's brave battle to pass the Resolutions, said that Henry "had an astonishing portion of political courage. Perhaps it is not too much to affirm that it was owing to this one quality of this single man that our Revolution took place at the time it did."[236] Amidst cries of "Treason!" Henry bravely stood for American liberty, knowing full well that his stance could lead him to the end of a rope.

Whether he was defying the inertia and fear of colonial leaders, or taking up arms against Governor Dunmore, Henry displayed a brand of courage that was indifferent to personal criticism or physical danger, and won him the admiration of the common people. The following incident, which shows the people's high respect for Henry's courage, occurred when the British marched toward Charlottesville in hope of capturing the fleeing Virginia legislators.

> *It is said that as Patrick Henry, Benjamin*
> *Harrison, Judge Tyler, and Colonel Christian*
> *were hurrying along, they saw a little hut in the*
> *forest. An old woman was chopping wood by*
> *the door. The men were hungry, and stopped to*
> *ask her for food.*
> *"Who are you?" she asked.*
> *"We are members of the legislature," said*
> *Patrick Henry; "we have just been compelled to*
> *leave Charlottesville on account of the British."*
> *"Ride on, then, ye cowardly knaves!" she said in*
> *wrath. "Here are my husband and sons just*
> *gone to Charlottesville to fight for ye, and you*
> *running away with all your might. Clear out!*

Ye shall have nothing here."

"But," replied Mr. Henry, *"we were obliged to flee. It would not do for the legislature to be broken up by the enemy. Here is Mr. Benjamin Harrison; you don't think he would have fled had it not been necessary?"*

"I always thought a great deal of Mr. Harrison till now," answered the old woman, *"but he'd no business to run from the enemy."* And she started to shut the door in their faces.

"Wait a moment, my good woman," cried Mr. Henry; *"would you believe that Judge Tyler or Colonel Christian would take to flight if there were not good cause for so doing?"*

"No, indeed that I wouldn't."

"But," he said, *"Judge Tyler and Colonel Christian are here."*

"They are? Well, I would never have thought it. I didn't suppose they would ever run from the British; but since they have, they shall have nothing to eat in my house. You may ride along."

Things were getting desperate. Then Judge Tyler stepped forward: *"What would you say, my good woman, if I were to tell you that Patrick Henry fled with the rest of us?"*

"Patrick Henry!" she answered angrily, *"I should tell you there wasn't a word of truth in it! Patrick Henry would never do such a cowardly thing."*

"But this is Patrick Henry," said Judge Tyler.

The old woman was astonished; but she stammered and pulled at her apron string, and said:

"Well, if that's Patrick Henry, it must be all right. Come in, and ye shall have the best I have in the house."[237]

Henry's flight with the legislators of 1781 might appear to contradict his general reputation for courage. But as he said to the old woman, "We were obliged to flee. It would not do for the legislature to be broken up by the enemy." It is clear from his earlier actions against Dunmore, as well as his aborted military career, that Henry was willing to face physical danger when duty required it. However, as Shakespeare said, "Discretion is the better part of valor." And as a member of the House, not of the military, Henry wisely realized that if the British captured the legislature, Virginia probably would have fallen to the enemy. Discretion, not fear, motivated his flight to safety.

When duty required, Henry would confront both friend and foe. He fearlessly opposed both colonial apathy and British tyranny. Although he was accused of treason by his own countrymen, and branded a rebel by his enemies, Henry never wavered in his devotion to what he believed to be right. He could not be intimidated by aristocratic wealth and prestige, nor would he back down to British gibbet and gun.

Henry's legendary courage was probably partly temperamental and partly experiential. Some men are by nature braver than others. And whatever Henry inherited was developed by his frontier environment. However, the hidden source of his courage lay in his profound belief in the justice of God and His providence. When he challenged the Virginia Convention at St. John's Church to see the inevitability of war, Henry swore: "Should I keep my opinions at such a time, through fear of giving offense, I should consider myself as guilty of treason towards my country, and of an act of disloyalty towards the majesty of Heaven, which I revere above all earthly kings." Henry was bold to face battle because "there is a just God who presides over the destinies of nations."[239] And that same God would raise up friends to fight in America's favor. Within a matter of days Henry again appealed to God and took up arms against Lord Dunmore's rape of the public magazine. He was confident that, "under the support and guidance of heaven," he and the Hanover military would defeat Dunmore. God was on their side–"the enemy of the oppressor and the friend of the oppressed"–and since He "still reigned in all his glory," He would fight for them.[240]

Henry's faith in God, then, was the secret spring of his public valor. Knowing that God was just, Henry had no doubt that America would be victorious if her cause was just. Providence would rule in her favor.

PROVIDENCE

*The American Revolution was the grand operation,
which seemed to be assigned by the Diety to the
men of this age in our country, over and above the
common duties of life. I ever prized at a high rate
the superior privilege of being one in that chosen
age, to which providence entrusted its favorite
work.*[241]

It is not possible to understand the actions or motives
of the leading patriots in the American Revolution
without taking into consideration their religious faith and
world-view. To a man, the founding fathers were men who
had been shaped by the morality and theology of the Bible.
Of the fifty-five men who signed the American Declaration of
Independence, only two, Franklin and Jefferson, had no
denominational affiliation. And yet even they accepted the
basic presupposition of a Christian world-view.[242]

One of the Biblical principles that had a strong influence
on Henry and his co-patriots was Providence. In the last sentence of the federal Declaration of Independence, the patriots

acknowledged their "firm reliance on the protection of divine Providence." When news arrived in the colonies that France was joining the war on the side of America, Washington proclaimed to his troops: "It having pleased the Almighty Ruler of the universe to defend the cause of the United American States and finally to raise up a powerful friend among the powers of the earth...it becomes us to set apart a day for gratefully acknowledging the divine goodness and celebrating the important event, which we owe to His divine intervention." Writing to his troops on May 2, 1778, General Washington stated their obligation to thankfully recognize God's Providence in the course of the war. "The signal instances of Providential goodness which we have experienced and which have now almost crowned our labors with complete success demand from us in a peculiar manner the warmest returns of gratitude and piety to the Supreme Author of all good."[243]

For Henry, Washington, and even Jefferson, who penned the Declaration, Providence was God's care and control of human events. According to Samuel Johnson's *Dictionary*, published in 1755, Providence was "the care of God over created beings; divine superintendence." When Noah Webster, one of the founding fathers, later penned his own *Dictionary*, he gave the following definition of Providence:

> *In theology, the care and superintendence which God exercises over his creatures. He that acknowledges a creation and denies a providence, involves himself in a palpable contradiction; for the same power which caused a thing to exist is necessary to continue its existence. Some persons admit a general providence, but deny a particular providence,*

not considering that a general providence consists of particulars. A belief in divine providence, is a source of great consolation to good men. By divine providence is often understood God himself.[244]

Providence, then, was neither an impersonal force nor a pagan fate. It was the intervention and activity of a caring and personal God who, as Franklin said, "governs in the affairs of men."

Henry's faith in God's Providence was nurtured when he was a young boy. Both the Anglicanism of his father and the Presbyterianism of his mother agreed on this point: God was the sovereign Creator and Sustainer of the world. His physical laws governed the inanimate universe, and His moral laws governed the world of men. Under the preaching of Davies, Henry heard repeated references to God's Providence. "Is the work of peace then our only business?" proclaimed Davies. "No: in such a time, even the God of Peace proclaims by his Providence, 'To Arms!'"[245]

The realization of God's Providence provided Henry with a source of comfort in sorrow and a spring of action in crisis. When his sister, Anne, lost her husband to an untimely death at the hands of marauding Indians, Patrick attempted to console both her and himself by remembering God's Providence. "My heart has felt in a manner new and strange to me; inasmuch that while I am endeavoring to comfort you, I want a comforter myself." He then turned her thoughts toward the mysterious ways of God. "I turn my eyes to heaven…and adore with humility the inscrutable ways of that Providence which calls us off this stage of action, at such time and in such a manner as its wisdom and goodness directs." Although we do not always understand why certain difficult events come to pass, "we may be assured they are directed by wisdom and mercy." Henry then attempted to cheer Anne by pointing out to her "some tokens of a kind Providence" in providing her with a good son-in-law who would take care of her.[246]

Christian Providence has often been confused with pagan fatalism, but they are as different as night and day. The latter leads to abnegation and despair, whereas the former inspires courage and action. Indeed, it was Henry's strong faith in Providence that impelled him to action in the just cause of American liberty. He sincerely believed that the American War of Independence would succeed because God would intervene on behalf of the colonies. "We shall not fight our battles alone. There is a just God who presides over the destinies of nations and who will raise up friends to fight our battles for us." This confidence in divine aid, instead of leading to acquiescence, should lead to action–to what Henry called the "proper use of those means which the God of nature hath placed in our power."[247] Henry properly understood that human action and divine Providence are not contradictory, but complimentary. Henry acted courageously because God governed providentially. "An appeal to arms, and to the God of Hosts," was his battle cry that armed the colonies for resistance and won for all Americans those inalienable rights of life, liberty, and the pursuit of happiness.

ACTION

Shall we gather strength by irresolution and inaction?…Our brethren are already in the field. Why stand we here idle?[248]

Some men lead by logic, others by action. One leader influences men by the force of his mind and arguments, while another compels men by the force of his passion and will. Madison, for instance, became the Federalist leader due to his inexorable logic and precise augmentation in debate. Henry, on the other hand, led the Anti-Federalists by the power of his passionate and eloquent speech. Words, however, are cheap. And if convictions are not backed by action, they are no better than compromise.

There is a sense in which Henry's entire pre-war political career was one long and loud call to action. From 1765, when he entered the Virginia House of Burgesses, to 1776, when independence was formally declared, Henry repeatedly challenged the colonial leaders to understand the implications of their political pronouncements–and to act on them. For instance, when Henry first became a burgess, the Stamp Act had already been under discussion for almost a year, and nearly every colonial legislature had objected to the tax and had written formal protests against it. In Virginia, the Assembly had met in November of 1764 and drafted an address to the king, a memorial to the House of Lords, and a remonstrance to the House of Commons. But no one acted. When the act formally received the royal assent on March 22, 1765, Franklin sighed that he had done everything in his power to prevent its passage. "The tide was too strong against us," he said. "We might as well have hindered the sun's setting." Although all the colonial leaders felt that "a great political right...was about to be wrested from their power," none proposed resistance. No one acted. Even the great New England patriot, James Otis, counseled submission. "It is the duty of all humbly, and silently, to acquiesce in all the decisions of the supreme legislature." John Adams, seeing clearly the effect of submission, sadly wrote in his diary on December 18, 1765: "If this authority is once acknowledged and established, the ruin of America will become inevitable."[249] Yet, no one acted.

The great majority of Americans were thoroughly convinced that the Stamp Act was a gross violation of their sacred rights, yet "no one stood forth around whom they could rally in opposition."[250] When it came time to put their protests into practice, the colonial leaders lost their nerve and failed to act. What was needed was not another remonstrance, not another theoretical argument, not another "gentlemen's agreement." What was needed was decisive action! And this, Patrick Henry provided.

Only nine days after entering the House of Burgesses, Henry assailed the apathy of the established leadership and attacked the tyranny of the accepted tax. The "men of weight" had protested the tax and felt they had done their entire duty.

But Henry was determined to act. Mere protest was useless. It was time to vigorously oppose the loathsome measure. Since the leaders felt the tax was illegal, they ought to formally declare it so by legislation, and refuse to pay it. "No taxation without representation" had been their declaration, now let it be their deed. Years later, Henry wrote that when he entered the House, "all the colonies...had remained silent," and that all "the men of weight" were "averse to opposition." And, since "no person was likely to step forth, I determined to venture and alone, unadvised, and unassisted" proposed the Stamp Act Resolutions. As a result of Henry's action, "the alarm spread throughout America with astonishing quickness," and "the great point of resistance to British taxation was universally established in the colonies."[251]

Of course, the real battle with Britain had only begun. After ten years of repeated abuses by the Crown, Henry again found himself challenging the irresolution of the colonial leadership. By the time the Second Virginia Convention met in March of 1775, a series of oppressive laws were being imposed on the colonies, and Boston was virtually under siege. As before, the colonial leaders had protested but to no avail. Yet again they refused to act. In the face of their weakness and irresolution, Henry proposed that Virginia "be immediately put into a state of defense." Pendleton and others opposed the resolution, but Henry "rose with an unearthly fire burning in his eye" to defend his proposal. He launched forth in such solemn and vehement tones that, "those who had toiled in the artifices of scholastic rhetoric" were driven to self-doubt.[252]

"This is no time for ceremony," he warned. "The question before the house...is nothing less than a question of freedom or slavery." The experience of the last ten years, claimed Henry, showed Britain's intention to enslave the colonies. "I ask gentlemen...what means this martial array if its purpose be not to force us to submission?" And with what shall Britain be opposed? "Shall we try argument?" No! "Shall we resort to entreaty, and humble supplication?" No! All such pleas "have been spurned with contempt from the foot of the throne." It is now time for action. "We must fight!" he exclaimed. "An appeal to arms and to the God of Hosts, is all that is left us."[253]

Some debated that the colonies were too weak for battle against the powerful British army. But Henry ridiculed the cowardly notion that delay would lead to strength.

> *But when shall we be stronger? Will it be the next week, or the next year? Will it be when we are totally disarmed, and when a British guard shall be stationed in every house? Shall we gather strength by irresolution and inaction? Shall we acquire the means of effectual resistance by lying supinely on our backs, and hugging the delusive phantom of Hope, until our enemies shall have bound us hand and foot?*[254]

Then, turning his piercing glance toward the party for submission, Henry thundered:

> *Our brethren are already in the field. What is it that gentlemen wish? What would they have? Is life so dear, or peace so sweet, as to be purchased at the price of chains and slavery? Forbid it, Almighty God! I know not what course others may take, but as for me, give me liberty, or give me death!*[255]

According to one observer, Henry's bold declaration– "Give me liberty"–was not a request, "but a stern demand, which would submit to no refusal or delay."[256] And Edmund Randolph, overwhelmed by Henry's power, later boasted that on that day he was proud to be a Virginian to witness "Demosthenes invigorate the timid."[257]

Henry's bold and vigorous call to arms electrified the assembly, and the torrents of his eloquence swept the colony into rapid preparation for war. The critical hour had arrived, and Henry's answer to oppression was action, not acquiescence.

As a man of action, Henry practiced what he preached. Less than two months later, when Lord Dunmore stole Virginia's gunpowder, Henry acted decisively. While the other colonial leaders negotiated, Henry took up arms and marched. It is striking to note that of all the positions that Henry either filled or was offered throughout his public career, the one he actually desired the most was the office of colonel and commander in chief of the Virginia army. The front line was appealing to Henry's active and energetic nature. "Our brethren are already in the field. So why stand we here idle?" he exhorted. And in the field was where he longed to be–the place of daring deeds and exciting exploits.

As a decisive leader, Henry resisted the all too common temptation to procrastinate in reaching a decision or to vacillate once it had been made. He realized at the brink of the war, that indecision was fatal. It was not enough to have the right principles, or even to plead the right cause. The cause demanded action, and it was Henry's great moral courage that propelled the colonial leadership to prepare for war and saved the colonies from ruin. As one historian has noted, "The moment was opportune and critical; and he seized it with a bold and felicitous energy that belonged to his ardent and passionate nature."[258] It was Henry's call to action that rescued America from inertia and ultimate tyranny.

HUMILITY

I have long learned the little value which is to be placed on popularity, acquired by any other way than virtue.[259]

*H*istory has a selective memory. There are some men of previous generations who were ignored in their own day but are now recognized for their greatness. Mozart, for instance, died in relative obscurity and dire poverty, yet today he is lauded a musical genius. On the other hand, some men achieve national or even international prominence for a short time but are later relegated to a footnote in a textbook. A rising star becomes a shooting star: burning bright but soon burned out.

In his own day, Henry was immensely popular. After his impressive performance in the Parson's Cause, Henry's name spread throughout Hanover and eventually all of Virginia. Not long after the Stamp Act Resolutions hit the newspapers, he become a recognized national figure–applauded by the colonies while detested by the Crown.

According to William Wirt Henry,

> *America was filled with Mr. Henry's fame, and
> he was recognized on both sides of the Atlantic
> as the man who rang the alarm bell which had
> aroused the continent. His wonderful powers of
> oratory engaged the attention and excited the
> admiration of men, and the more so as they
> were not considered the result of laborious
> training, but as the direct gift of Heaven. Long
> before the British poet applied the description
> to him, he was recognized as–*[the forest-born
> Demosthenes Whose thunder shook the Philip
> of the seas.][260]

In Virginia, the people were bound to Henry with an
"undying love for this champion of natural liberty," and he
was "instantly crowned with his crown of sovereignty." In a
word, Henry was "the idol" of the Virginia people.[261] And he
never did fall out of favor with the people, in spite of numerous attacks on his character. With each successive legal
victory, his reputation as an excellent defense attorney flour-
ished; and as the conflict with Britain increased, so did his
fame. Thus, in his own lifetime, Henry was a legendary figure.
So powerful was his fame, that even when he was old and
retired, politicians attempted to enhance the popularity of
their proposals by attaching to them the name of "Patrick
Henry."

Fame is dangerous, of course, because it is deceptive. At
the heels of popularity there lurks pride and all of its atten-
dant evils: arrogance, egotism, and selfishness. With every
successive victory, or every promotion in public esteem, there
is the danger of secretly congratulating oneself, thus edging

closer to a fall from the pinnacle of pride. Once a leader succumbs to pride, he disqualifies himself from holding a
position of power because he can no longer fulfill one of leadership's most important tasks: to guard and guide those under
his authority. Self-centered leadership is an oxymoron.

Fame never did corrupt Henry, however. On the contrary,
his general habit was to be very unassuming or even to depre-
ciate himself. When speaking with John Adams at the First
Continental Congress, Henry spoke so negatively of his own
education that his remarks were later used against him to
suggest that he was virtually uneducated.[262]

In his professional and public career, Henry displayed the
same humility that marked his private conversations.
According to Judge Tucker, Henry's "manner and address to
the court and jury might be deemed the excess of humility,
diffidence, and modesty."[263] And Judge Roane, who knew
Henry from 1783 on, said that in Henry's legislative labors,
"he was very unassuming as to himself, amounting almost to
humility, and very respectful towards his competitor."[264]

It is often thought that humility, especially in a leader, is
a sign of weakness and will thus lead to a loss of respect. For
instance, one popular book on leadership asserts: "In the
realm of politics and commerce, humility is a quality neither
courted nor required. There the leader needs and seeks prominence and publicity."[265] But nothing could be farther from the
truth. Humility is the ground of true leadership in every
realm–social, political, and ecclesiastical. And in Henry's case,
his humility served only to "increase his hold on the sympathy and support of the mass of the people of Virginia" because
they perceived him as "one of their own."[266] In the courtroom,
Henry's humility actually worked to his advantage. "Patrick
was a dangerous opponent because he was disarming." And
he disarmed both judge and jury "with his excess of humility,

his diffidence, and his meekness."[267] Henry's meekness and humility were anything but public posturing. If there is one sham easily discernable, it is false humility. Conceit cannot be concealed. Pride by its very nature is obtrusive, especially when placed on a stage.

Henry's fame as a lawyer was surpassed only by his popularity as a patriot. And rightly so. He set the ball of Revolution in motion. He led Virginia in the "first overt act of war" in that commonwealth. His oratory at St. John's crushed the cowardly and invigorated the timid, clothing them for war. As Virginia's first and five-term governor, Henry acted as a model executive and war-time leader, protected the coast and harbor from invasions and rescued Washington at Valley Forge. As the leading legislator, he helped frame the Virginia Bill of Rights and Constitution, which established religious liberty and political freedom. Yet, in spite of all these and other achievements, Henry remained humble and unpretentious. Judge Roane, who knew Henry later in life, says that guests often visited at Red Hill just to hear Henry talk about his own past life and brilliant achievements. Yet, whenever discussing the course of the Revolution or subsequent political developments, Henry rarely talked of his own contributions. "No man," says Roane, "ever vaunted less of his achievements than Mr. Henry. I hardly ever heard him speak of those great achievements which form the prominent part of his biography. As for boasting, he was entirely a stranger to it…"[268]

If Henry had been an ambitious man, as Jefferson later slanderously said of him, then he would have taken advantage of the many opportunities presented to him for national power and prominence. Yet, Henry declined to accept the high federal posts of ambassador, secretary of state, and chief justice of the Supreme Court. Only when his personal friend,

George Washington, pleaded with Henry that he return to Virginia politics to avert civil war, was he drawn back to the public stage from his retirement.

Henry's last appearance on that stage was a final exhibition of his deep humility. When he arrived at Charlotte Courthouse to present his election speech, the crowd was moved with admiration and reverence for the legendary patriot. A Baptist minister, observing the scene, felt obliged to rebuke the crowd for idolatry. "Mr. Henry," he said, "is not a god!" In response, Henry modestly agreed. "No, indeed, my friend: I am but a poor worm of the dust–as fleeting and unsubstantial as the shadow of the cloud that flies over yon fields, and is remembered no more."[269]

Henry has been remembered, of course, while clouds of conceited contemporaries have been forgotten. Not in spite of his humility, but because of it, Henry was able to achieve his renown as an American patriot. It made him a favorite of the people. He saw himself as no better than the common man, which led him to champion their liberties as his own. He was willing to serve the public good even though it demanded great physical danger and personal sacrifice. His wish, as he once said, was at "all times and on all occasions, to bow, with the utmost deference, to the majesty of the people."[270] And because Henry bowed to them, the people curtseyed in return, and accorded him a fame that shall never be forgotten.

CRITICISM

The most exalted virtue has ever been found to attract envy.[271]

"**N**o leader is exempt from criticism," says J. Oswald Sanders, "and his humility will nowhere be seen more clearly than in the manner in which he accepts and reacts to it."[272] Indeed, criticism is one of the hazards of leadership. Because leadership places a man in the spotlight, his flaws, which otherwise might remain unnoticed, are exposed as in the high-noon sun. Faults readily accepted in a private capacity are seldom permitted in a public one. Public men must expect public criticism.

Moreover, the prominent position of a leader inevitably annoys the envious. As Swift once quipped, "Censure is the tax a man pays to the public for being eminent." Besides, the very qualities essential to leadership are often misunderstood by those not gifted to lead. Vision is labeled as "fanaticism," planning is criticized as "control," and conviction is blasted as "stubbornness." Almost any virtue necessary for leadership can be twisted into a vice by a detractor who is ignorant of the true demands of leadership.

The great popularity that Henry enjoyed did not exempt him from criticism. On the contrary, it seems that as his fame grew, so did the number of his critics. Actually, the two were linked throughout his brilliant but tumultuous career: displays of courage and eloquence that earned him the praise of the patriots equally brought him the strictures of the loyalists. For instance, after the Parson's Cause, which launched Henry's notoriety, the Reverend May slanderously accused Henry of "demagoguery and treason." And when Henry confronted the apathy of the House of Burgesses during the Stamp Act Crisis, he later recalled that "many threats were uttered, and much abuse cast on me by the party for submission."[273] Yet he would not submit.

Henry's bold rhetoric was not the only thing that brought him criticism. He was equally criticized for some of his brave and daring actions. For example, after Henry had marched on Lord Dunmore to recover the gunpowder stolen from Williamsburg, the Governor denounced "a certain Patrick Henry, of the city of Hanover, and a number of his deluded followers" for engaging in "outrages and rebellious practices." Even the Governor's Council, made up of Americans, criticized Henry's action, expressing "abhorrence and detestation of that licentious and ungovernable spirit that is gone forth…"[274] Henry responded by writing to his friend, Francis Lightfoot Lee, that should an explanation to the House be necessary, he would gladly reply in person when he returned from the Continental Congress.

The outbreak of the war found Henry in uniform as the commander in chief of the Virginia regulars. And although his military talents were never openly criticized, it was clear that the Committee of Safety, to whom he was accountable, did not believe Henry was fit for military command–or at least that was what they communicated by not allowing him to engage in battle, and by permitting his subordinate officers to circumvent his authority. Henry's friends, however, saw the situation for what it was: envy. "From the great man's amiable disposition," an "Honest Farmer" wrote in the press, and "his invariable perseverance in the cause of liberty, we apprehend that envy strove to bury in obscurity his martial talents."[275] The treatment of Henry in the "Colonel Affair" was a striking but melancholy example of Lord Brougham's dictum: "The egotism of human nature will seldom allow us to credit a man for one excellence without detracting from him in other respects."[276] Some of the men on the committee (most notably Edmund Pendleton) saw themselves as superior to Henry, and due to envy, "wished him of less consequence that they might be of more."[277] He was left with no honorable alternative except to resign.

Henry was not a quitter, however; for even though he left the military, he did not desert the cause. While some men might have harbored resentment, and refused to serve except in the place of their own choice, Henry never let bitterness detract from his zealous pursuit of American victory. He was greatly disappointed by this missed opportunity in the military, yet he never made one recriminating remark against those who sabotaged his chance for military honor.

Far more than the "Colonel Affair," the most scurrilous attacks made against Henry resulted from his opposition to the newly proposed constitution. In the fall of 1788, after Virginia had ratified the constitution, the House was engaged in the immense battle over the question of amendments. During this time, a series of newspaper articles under the name *Decius* began to appear in the *Independent Chronicle*, published in Richmond. Among other slanders, *Decius* castigated Henry as "the cunning and deceitful Cromwell, who under the guise of amendments, seeks to destroy the constitution, break up the

Confederacy, and reign the tyrant of popularity over his own devoted Virginia." Henry's friends were outraged, and even many of his political opponents denounced the articles as little less than sacrilegious. How did Henry respond? He maintained a "dignified silence." His friend, Judge Roane, who happened to be spending some time at Henry's Prince Edward home when the attacks were their thickest, related that Henry had no interest in seeing the articles and experienced no rage at the author. Roane then observed: "It was too puny a contest for him, and he reposed upon the consciousness of his own integrity."[278]

Some months later, Henry's friend Senator Grayson wrote to him and commended him for his silence–what he called "the dignified line of conduct." To respond would have only lent credit to the accuser. This "bad digested calumny," wrote Grayson, ought to be expected. "Such kind of attacks on characters that are high in the public estimation, have been so frequent, and are so well understood, as not to deserve a moment's attention." He then reminded Henry of Addison's appropriate aphorism: "Envy and detraction is a tax which every man of merit pays for being eminent and conspicuous."[279] Indeed it is.

For the most part Henry responded to criticism by simply ignoring it. Not that he was unwilling to defend himself. It was just that many of the slanders were so outrageous as not to deserve a response. In the "Colonel Affair," the criticism was virtually covert, and provided no forum for rebuttal. Henry did, however, appeal to his superiors, and when he got little satisfaction, he moved himself to a place of usefulness. The striking thing about Henry's response to criticism–and the lesson for all leaders to learn–is that he never condescended to the level of his critics. He did not return "railing for railing" but rather, spoke highly of men who thought little of him. This fact was clear proof that Henry never permitted bitterness to lodge in his heart and poison his soul. As a great leader he understood that although criticism is inevitable, bitterness is not. A leader's reaction is always more crucial than his opponent's detraction.

Kindness

Unite liberality with a just frugality; always reserve something for the hand of charity; and never let your door be closed to the voice of suffering.[280]

A leader like Patrick Henry is often viewed as a man who possesses a few essential leadership qualities like courage, determination, and vision. A man of inflexible courage and steel-like strength–willing to die rather than suffer subjection–that is the man and those are the qualities we associate with his leadership. But such thinking is one-dimensional and does not do justice to Henry's full-orbed humanity. The secret of his power over men lay not in any of his particular gifts, but in his heart. Henry had a genuine concern for people that won him their affection. Men bowed to his authority because it was tempered with kindness. Like all great leaders, he ruled by the heart.

Henry's concern for others was apparent even in his youth. The second oldest boy in his family, he was the kind of big brother who watched out for his many little sisters. "He interested himself much in the happiness of others, particularly of his sisters," said Samuel Meredith, the husband of Henry's sister, June. Whenever the girls needed a favor from their mother, Henry would always be their "advocate."[281] Throughout his life, Henry maintained strong ties with his sisters, always looking out for their welfare. When his sister, Anne, lost her husband, for instance, Henry wrote her a tender letter expressing his love and concern for her. "I am at a loss how to address you, my dear sister. Would to God I could say something to give relief to the dearest of women and sisters…My letters are always penned as dictated by the strongest love and affection to you…For indeed, my dearest sister, you never knew how much I loved you or your husband." Henry then offered to help Anne in any way she wished. Shortly thereafter, Anne and her children became one of the families under Henry's care.[282]

Henry's kindness extended beyond his family. His defense of the dissenting Baptists, for example, was as much a labor of love as it was a sacrifice for liberty. On one occasion, when the Baptist minister John Weatherford was imprisoned for "disturbing the peace," Henry intervened to obtain an order of release. The jailer, however, would not free him until his jail fees were paid. As this was a large sum of money, much larger than the poor preacher could afford, he languished in prison. When Weatherford was later informed that an unnamed person had paid his fees and he was now free to go, he left the prison with much gratitude, and did not learn until twenty years later that his anonymous benefactor had been none other than Patrick Henry himself.[283]

As governor, Henry attempted to reform a number of British laws he considered harsh. The death penalty, for example, was imposed for many felonies, regardless of the severity of the crime. This was a practice that Henry felt was both unjust and cruel. He thus developed a plan of granting pardons, after hard labor, for lesser crimes. Writing to Charles Pearson, who was in charge of the pardoned prisoners, Henry commanded him "to observe such a degree of humanity towards these people as their condition will permit, in everything that relates to them." They are to have "plenty of wholesome food" and their clothes are to be "warm and comfortable." Their lodging, instructed Henry, should be "kept and cleaned", and they should not be overworked. And most importantly, he concluded, "You are to see that they be not restrained from attending divine worship…" Henry's concern that criminals be treated humanely and justly "shows the heart of a genuine philanthropist."[284]

His dual career as a lawyer and a politician naturally threw Henry into hostile arenas where tempers flared and hard words were uttered, yet he "was always most courteous to his opponents." During the Virginia Ratification Convention emotions ran high, and on one occasion Governor Harrison took the floor and angrily protested that Henry had attacked him "in the most illiberal manner." "His asperity is warranted by no principles of parliamentary decency," claimed Harrison, "nor compatible with the least shadow of friendship, and if our friendship must fall, let it fall like Lucifer, never to rise again!" Henry generously responded by assuring Harrison that he had "no personal intention of offending anyone, …and that he did not mean to wound the feelings of any gentleman." Henry's sympathy and kindness made him a generous opponent, "surprisingly free from the fending and bitter recriminations of so many public men…"[285]

Whether in the courtroom or the legislative hall, he "was always a good fighter, but never a good hater."

He had the brain and the temperament of an advocate; his imagination and his heart always

*kindled hotly to the side that he had espoused,
and with his imagination and his heart always
went all the rest of the man; in his advocacy of
any cause that he had thus made his own, he
hesitated at no weapon either of offense or of
defense; he struck hard blows–he spoke hard
words–and he usually triumphed; and yet, even
in the paroxysm of the combat, and still more
so when the combat was over, he showed how
possible it is to be a redoubtable antagonist
without having a particle of malice.*[286]

Not even toward America's enemies, the British, did
Henry harbor malice. During the war he advocated just and
humane treatment for British prisoners, even though the
British themselves had been extremely harsh with American
civilians.[287] After the war, he also urged the conciliatory policy of permitting Tories to return to the States. The war, of
course, had generated dark and lasting hostilities that were
not easily overcome. But Henry counselled his countrymen in
the Virginia House that "the personal feeling of a politician
ought not to be permitted to enter" the Assembly. For himself,
instead of harboring bitterness for the war, Henry said that
"on the altar of his country's good he was willing to sacrifice
all personal resentments, all private wrongs." Since American
independence has been acknowledged, "the quarrel is over–
peace has returned…" Therefore, "let us have the magnanimity…to lay aside our antipathies…"[288]

Public professions of compassion are commonplace political ploys. But in Henry's case, his professions were backed by
action. Besides his attempts to reform harsh penalties and to
limit taxes on the poor–services he rendered as a public
man–Henry also spent his own time and money as a private

citizen alleviating the needs of the disadvantaged. In his retirement, Henry showed his kindness to the poor by furnishing them with food and possessions from his farm, and in loaning them money. The loans, of course, were seldom collected.

It was Henry's kindness as much as his eloquence that made him Virginia's favorite son. He won the affections of the people because they sensed in him a man who sympathized with their wants and who was willing to give voice to their desires. In a sense, his great career as the champion of liberty was one long crusade of compassion. The liberty that he so jealously guarded was not simply his own, but the people's. His role as the guardian of liberty, then, was more than a commitment to principle. It was a concern for people–the ultimate test of true leadership.

Religion

*That religion, or the duty we owe our Creator, and
the manner of discharging it, can be directed only by
reason and conviction, and not by force or violence;
and, therefore, that all men should enjoy the fullest
toleration in the exercise of religion, according to
the dictates of conscience, unpunished and unrestrained by the magistrate, unless, under color of
religion, any man disturb the peace, the happiness,
or the safety of society; and that it is the mutual
duty of all to practise Christian forbearance, love,
and charity towards each other.*[289]

The highest form of leadership is based on deep conviction. Providing a compass in times of storm, and
a shield against the shafts of criticism, conviction strengthens
and inspires both the leader and those following him. Like
Jeremiah's "burning," true conviction must burst forth in
either eloquent speech or noble action. In Henry's case, his
deepest convictions were rooted in his religious faith. And
although he spent the greater part of his life in politics, he

readily acknowledged that religion was "infinitely more important than politics."[290] Indeed, both Henry's private and political life rested on the Christian faith he learned as a child and professed at his death.

As a child, Henry was raised in a Christian home with two rich religious traditions. His father was a devoted Anglican and vestryman at St. Paul's Parish, who was noted for his "irreproachable integrity and exemplary piety." His father's brother, the Reverend Patrick Henry, helped to educate young Patrick and taught him the Anglican catechism. As a result, he was baptized into the Anglican Church and remained a member throughout his life. His mother, Sarah, was a devout woman who won the admiration of those who knew her. "Never have I known," said Henry's son-in-law Meredith, "a Christian character equal to hers." But instead of worshipping with her husband, Sarah Henry became a Scottish Presbyterian–a "new light" who came under the influence of the renowned Samuel Davies.[291] At age eleven, young Henry began to attend services with his mother and heard the dissenting ministers at Morris's reading house and Hanover Church.[292] Henry never did convert to Presbyterianism, but continued throughout his life to attend both Presbyterian and Anglican services when possible.

There is a certain irony in the fact that Henry acquired public notoriety in the Parson's Cause, a case in which he vehemently attacked the established clergy. The truth is, Henry had a high regard for the religion they represented– "the mild and benevolent precepts of the gospel of Jesus"[293]–and after his victory in the case, Henry sought out the plaintiff, Reverend Maury, to reassure him that his remarks did not reflect any personal ill-will.

Those who were familiar with Henry readily recognized his religious character. Roger Atkins, one of his contemporaries, described Henry as "modest and mild, and in religious matters a saint."[294] Contrary to many of the Virginia elite, Henry did not indulge in gambling or strong drink, and even attempted to reform the abuse of alcohol by developing and promoting his own brand of low-alcohol beer. Another aspect of his behavior noted by his contemporaries was Henry's "abstinence from swearing."[295] Whenever Henry invoked the name of God in one of his speeches, it was always accepted as a solemn oath. Unlike some of his colleagues, Henry was also exempt from any rumors of illicit sexual behavior with his servants. A leader's authority to command the respect of others is directly related to his moral authority. And Henry's power over men was primarily due to their recognition of his Christian character.

Not only on Sunday, but every day, Henry was a witness for Christ. He was just as bold in his defense of the faith as he was in his defense of his liberty. "As regards his religious faith, Patrick Henry, while never ostentatious of it, was always ready to avow it, and to defend it."[296] Indeed, when Henry became alarmed at the spread of Deism in the colonies, he wrote to his daughter avowing his deep conviction that Christianity would survive the French onslaught.

> *The view which the rising greatness of our*
> *country presents to my eye is greatly tarnished*
> *by the general prevalence of deism; which with*
> *me, is but another name for vice and depravity.*
> *I am, however, much consoled by reflecting,*
> *that the religion of Christ has, from its first*
> *appearance in the world, been attacked in vain*
> *by all the wits, philosophers, and wise ones*
> *aided by every power of man, and its triumph*
> *has been complete. What is there in the wit*
> *or wisdom of the present deistic writers or*

> *professors, that can compare them with Hume,*
> *Shaftsbury, Bolingbroke, and others? And yet*
> *these have been confuted, and their fame decay-*
> *ing; insomuch that the puny efforts of Paine are*
> *thrown in to prop their tottering fabric, whose*
> *foundations cannot stand the test of time.*[297]

Henry's confidence in Christianity's ultimate triumph, however, did not keep him from actively promoting the faith. Never a passive spectator in a great conflict, Henry enlisted in the battle against scepticism. On a private level, he often encouraged young men that he met to study religion, and he helped found a number of Christian colleges.[298] He also underwrote, at his own expense, a private printing of Butler's *Analogy* and Jenning's *Internal Evidence of Christianity*, which he freely distributed. On one occasion, he gave copies of Jenning's work to some judges at the courthouse and wryly asked them not to mistake him for a "traveling monk."[299]

Henry rightly understood that the moral condition of the American people was a direct product of their religious faith, and that politics and morality were inevitably intertwined. Thus, the political structure ultimately rested on a religious foundation. The "great pillars of all government and of social life," Henry once observed, are "virtue, morality, and religion." "This is the armor...that renders us invincible" to all our enemies. But "if we lose these, we are conquered, fallen indeed."[300] It is not surprising, then, that as a politician Henry advocated a number of measures that aided the spread of Christianity. Early in his political career, he was the champion of religious toleration. In 1766, he favored the exemption of Quakers from military service on religious grounds, and in 1768, he proposed toleration toward dissenting Baptists. His argument for toleration was that it made the clergy independent and thus more likely to attend to their duty of reproving immorality. "It is the business of a virtuous clergy to censure vice in every appearance of it," he said. "Therefore, under a general toleration this duty will be commonly attended to."[301] When Virginia formally claimed independence from England and drafted her own Bill of Rights, Henry helped frame the fifteenth and sixteenth articles, which state that liberty rests on virtue, and that men should enjoy the fullest toleration in the exercise of religion.

After the war, the disestablishment of the Anglican Church meant that the churches and ministers were no longer paid by the state, but had to depend on voluntary contributions. With the hardship of the war, and the depreciation of the currency, many families were unable to make financial contributions, and, as a result, church buildings fell into disrepair, Sunday worship was held infrequently, and a general decline in morals occurred. In addition, Deism and French scepticism were breaking down the traditional religious restraints on public vice. Colleges were becoming, one author said, "hotbeds of infidelity," and taverns the source of "licentious and profane" behavior by unsavory war veterans.[302] The decay in religion and morals was so bad, that public-minded men such as Henry's friend George Mason, who had planned republican government on the basis of the virtue of the people, became greatly alarmed. Writing to Henry in May, 1783, Mason lamented that "Justice and virtue are the vital principles of Republican Government; but among us a depravity of manners and morals prevails, to the destruction of all confidence between man and man."[303] Dr. William Hall, who was a student at Hampden Sydney at the time, said "the demoralizing effects of the war left religion and the church in a most deplorable condition. The Sabbath had been almost forgotten and public morals sadly deteriorated." As one historian aptly summarized the moral situation: "Iniquity greatly abounded."[304]

To stem the tide, Henry not only personally spread the gospel, but he proposed a measure in the Virginia Assembly in 1784, calling for a moderate assessment for the support of the Christian religion.[305] The small tax was to apply equally to any Christian denominations of the taxpayer's choice, and those who wished not to do so, could apply the tax to the maintenance of a school. "This was in effect a tax for the support of secular education, with the privilege to each taxpayer of devoting his tax to the support of the religious teachers of his own denomination."[306]

In tandem with Washington, Marshall, Lee, and others, Henry championed the assessment bill against Madison and Jefferson, who opposed it. In order to become law, the bill had to pass the legislative House three times, and Henry successfully carried the bill through the first and second reading. Madison, however, strategically delayed the third reading, and Henry was in the meantime elected governor. Without Henry's leadership and eloquent support, the bill failed to pass the third reading, but only by a margin of three votes. Shortly thereafter, in 1786, Jefferson's "Bill for establishing Religious Freedom" was offered as a countermeasure and passed.[307] Consequently, many clergy left Virginia for want of support, and the decline in religion and morality continued unabated for some time.[308]

Soon after taking the governorship (his fourth term), Henry received a letter from the famous Countess of Huntingdon, a strong follower and supporter of George Whitefield. She presented to Henry a well-designed plan to "Christianize and civilize the North American Indians." Her plan called for small colonies of "pious, industrious people from Great Britain" to be settled near or among the Indian tribes to win the Indians to the Christian faith. Lady Huntingdon's goal, she said, was to make the Indians "good Christians and useful citizens" by preaching "the glad tidings of Salvation in the wilderness, to bring the inhabitants of those benighted regions from darkness to light, to the knowledge of the true God and of Jesus Christ." In addition, education was to accompany religion.

> *Schools will also be established. Children will be educated in them to religion and virtue, in a liberal manner agreeably to that great principle of Christianity, Love to God, universal charity and good-will to all mankind. They will also be instructed in useful knowledge so that they may become good Christians and useful members of the Community.*[309]

Lady Huntingdon then requested from Henry grants of land to establish her missionary communities, closing with a pathetic appeal: "with humble submission to the divine will, let us do our duty. Let us endeavor to obey his divine precepts and to follow his precious example of benignity to mankind."[310]

Henry heartily approved of the countess' plan, but since the Northwest territory had been ceded to Congress, he had no authority to grant her the land she requested. He did, however, forward the plan to the Virginian delegates, encouraging them to support it in the United States Congress. "The civilization and Christianizing of the Indians," he wrote, "if indeed they are two things, are matters of high moral and political concern." If it depended solely on him, he said, "to give the necessary assistance to the views of this worthy Lady, a moment would not be lost."[311] Unfortunately, the plan was rejected by Congress for fear of British influence. Had the proposal been adopted, there is no doubt that much of the blood and treasure spent on the cruel wars against the Indians would have been saved.

In spite of these disappointments, Henry's own faith grew stronger as he grew older. When he retired from politics, he had more time for reading the Scriptures and theological works, and even composed his own refutation of Thomas Paine's *Age of Reason.* Even on his deathbed, Henry continued to witness for Christ. Just moments before he died, Henry, fixing his eyes with much tenderness on his dear friend, Dr. Cabell, with whom he had formerly held many arguments respecting the Christian religion, "asked the doctor to observe how great a reality and benefit that religion was to a man about to die."[312] Henry then passed away, his wife said, "in full confidence that through the merits of a bleeding Savior that his sins would be pardoned."[313] Henry's will, dated March 20, 1798, divided his estate between his wife and children. After disposing of his estate, Henry added his final witness for Christ:

> *This is all the inheritance I can give to my dear family. The religion of Christ can give them one which will make them rich indeed.*[314]

Duty

I shall act as I think my duty requires.[315]

Duty is one of those old-fashioned concepts which would, if revived, benefit our increasingly hedonistic society. Duty assumes there is a moral order in the universe that demands recognition. "The eternal difference between right and wrong does not fluctuate," said Henry. "It is immutable."[316] And if the moral order does not change, then it imposes on us obligations toward God and man. Duty, then, requires the willingness to accept responsibility and to sacrifice one's desires to a higher law.

In Henry's day there was a ready recognition of the duty one had toward both God and society. It is striking that in the Sixteenth Article of the Virginia Bill of Rights, penned by Henry himself, religion is defined as "the *duty* which we owe our Creator." This principle was at the foundation of Henry's entire approach to life. As he learned from his uncle, Henry's calling was to "do my duty in that state of life unto which it shall please God to call me." Henry accepted this dictum early in life and his father often commented that he "was one of the most dutiful sons that lived..."[317]

Henry submitted to the claims of God and was throughout his life distinguished for his sincerity, honesty, and integrity. Spencer Roane commented that Henry's character "had many sublime virtues," and that "he had no vice that I knew or ever heard of, and scarcely a foible."[318] Henry's success as a political leader was the result of his "honesty and integrity," said one historian. "Everybody saw that he was sincere...."[319]

Like many of America's founders, Henry had a strong sense of duty toward society.[320] The French called it *noblesse oblige*–"privilege entails responsibility"–the obligation of the noble. This notion of public stewardship was at the heart of Henry's devotion to his country and his willingness to sacrifice for American liberty. As one historian has noted, "the Virginian gentry," of which Henry was a member, "labored tirelessly at the routine and tedious business of governing...not primarily to secure the relatively small tangible economic rewards they derived from their efforts but rather to fulfill the deep sense of public responsibility thrust upon them by their position in society."[321] As a politician, he recognized, and even enshrined into the Virginia Bill of Rights, the idea that government is instituted for the benefit of the people, and that magistrates are the trustees and servants of the community.

Throughout his political career, Henry responded to the call of duty, sacrificing time, energy, and even his health. As the wartime governor of Virginia, he was overwhelmed with onerous work. In addition to a great number of routine tasks, Henry had to repeatedly raise troops for the war to fill Virginia's quota. This task was all the more difficult due to the depreciation of currency. Thus, he labored to stabilize the economy of Virginia. Hostilities were also taking place on the western border, and Henry himself organized a number of expeditions against the Indians. With enemies on both land and sea, it devolved on Henry to secure the necessary munitions for war. He sent troops to Jamaica to acquire salt, built a lead factory at Fredericksburg, sent emissaries to Europe for medicines and munitions, and simultaneously built a navy. Henry even went beyond the call of duty when he helped rally public donations of food and clothing for Washington's army at Valley Forge.

Henry was naturally an affable and urbane gentleman, but the responsibilities of his public duty wore upon him heavily. On one occasion during the early part of the war, the patriot St. George Tucker, who was acting as an agent for Virginia, took £500 out of his own pocket in order to purchase and ship indigo to be exchanged for arms. When he called upon the Governor's Council to request reimbursement, Tucker relates that Henry did not thank him for his "zeal or expedition, or for advancing my money." On the contrary, says Tucker, Henry hinted that Tucker may have paid too high a price for the indigo. "I felt indignation flash from my eyes," said Tucker, and he held a grudge against Henry for years. Henry's conduct in this case was uncharacteristically insensitive, and shows not only a strained and burdened wartime leader, but also "a faithful servant of the State" who "must look sharply in her behalf." It is clear that when he was focused on the execution of public duties, "he hardened much in manner."[322] This fact explains why Henry could be such a passionate and vehement legal or political opponent while simultaneously holding no personal animosity toward his adversaries. Duty demanded his utmost efficiency and sharpest performance.

After his retirement from politics, Henry was repeatedly recruited to serve in a national capacity. In October 1795, Washington tendered to Henry the office of secretary of state.

In his reply, Henry stated, "I should be unworthy the character of an honest man if I withheld from the government my best and most zealous efforts..." Yet Henry declined. Why? As he went on to explain to Washington, "my domestic situation pleads strongly against a removal to Philadelphia, having no less than eight children by my present marriage," not to mention "Mrs. Henry's situation" (pregnancy) as he called it. "Permit me to add," he said, "that having devoted many years of the prime of my life to public service and thereby injured my circumstances, I have been obliged to resume my profession and go again to the Bar, at a time of life too advanced to support the fatigues of it. By this means my health has been injured." Henry admitted the solemn duty he had to his country, saying that he did "execrate the conduct of those men who lose sight of the public interest from personal motives." [323] Yet his duty to his family was equally sacred. As one historian has noted: "We expect a great deal of our heroes, but it is hardly fair to insist that they shall throw their families out of the window." [324] This, Henry would not do. So, feeling old and infirm, he continued to practice law and engage in land speculation in order to provide for his children's education and inheritance.

Only a few months before Henry's death, Washington finally wooed him out of retirement. Believing Washington's fear that the Union was near dissolution and the horrors of anarchy were imminent, Henry dutifully stood for election to the Virginia Assembly. He was then in very poor health and desired only the tranquillity of retirement. "My present views are to spend my days in privacy," he said. "If, however, it shall please God during my life, so to order the course of events as to render my feeble efforts necessary for the safety of my country...that little which I can do shall be done." [325] The "little" that Henry did, was to make one last brave and valiant sacrifice to duty. His eloquent speech at Charlotte Court House, in which he warned his countrymen against the threat of civil war, was too taxing on his broken health. "It forced the gallant warrior to his bed and to his death," only three months later.[326]

Henry's sense of duty inspired him to sacrifice the prime years of his life for the welfare of others and the liberty of his country. Unlike many so-called leaders who use political office to greedily line their pockets or selfishly secure professional connections, Henry believed politics was a sacred duty. Authority means service for the common good. And the greater the authority, the greater the sacrifice. "Uneasy lies the head that wears a crown," said Shakespeare. And those who wear the crown of power and privilege must feel its gilded weight–the demands of duty.

FAMILY

A difference with your husband ought to be considered as the greatest calamity–as one that is to be most studiously guarded against; it is a demon which must never be permitted to enter a habitation where all should be peace, unimpaired confidence and heartfelt devotion.[327]

L ord Bacon's cynical remark that "the care of posterity is most in them that have no posterity," surely did not apply to Henry. He was the proud father of seventeen children–six by his first wife, Sarah, and eleven by his second wife, Dorothea. "The cradle began to rock in his house in his eighteenth year," said his sister, "and was rocking at his death in his sixty-third year."[328] His children bore him more than seventy grandchildren, a fact that humorously suggested to some that Henry, not Washington, ought to be called "the father of his country."[329]

Indeed, Henry was a dutiful, loving, and affectionate father, who took great pleasure in his children. When he lived at Scotchtown with his first wife, Sarah, he was frequently absent due to his involvement in the growing crisis with Britain, and his young children reportedly "were as wild as young colts." According to his brother-in-law, the young Henry boys ran "bareheaded, barefooted, hallooing and whooping about the plantation in every direction, and as rough as nature left them." Not considering their behavior the result of neglect, it seems that Henry actually thought the rowdiness was healthy. "In the management of his children," says Colonel Meredith, "Mr. Henry seemed to think the most important thing is in the first place to give them good [physical] constitutions." Treating his children "like companions and friends," Henry's love for them was evident.[330] He generally called them by their pet names: for instance, Dorothea was "Dolly," Martha Catherina was called "Kitty," and Edward was "Neddy." The girls born to Henry by his second wife were called "little stair steps" as a term of endearment.[331]

When Henry retired from politics in 1791, he gladly devoted much more time to enjoying and training his children. At Red Hill, entertainment in the Henry household was a family affair. Henry's love of music had revived, and he entertained himself and his family by improvising on the violin or flute. His wife, Dorothea, and several of his daughters also had musical talent, and often joined Henry on the lute or pianoforte. It was not uncommon for a visitor at Red Hill to find Henry's children dancing around him to the tune of his violin, or to discover him lying on the floor covered with affectionate, noisy little ones.

The Henry musical talent was also put to sacred use in their home. Henry's habit was to devote Sunday evenings to a time of family worship when he read to his family portions of Scripture and some of his favorite sermons. After the readings, the family "joined in sacred music while he accompanied them on the violin."[332]

When his children reached school age, Henry devoted himself to their education. At one point, he contracted the soon-to-be famous poet Thomas Campbell to come to America from Scotland to tutor his children. Campbell's brother opposed the idea, however, and the plan fell through. Thus, Henry became their primary school master. According to several of his daughters, he had a great interest in poetry–which explains why he would have picked a poet as a tutor for his children–and he himself wrote poetry beautifully. Henry's daughter told the Reverend Fontaine that their father's poems were "gems of poetic beauty," and that he "often composed with much facility little sonnets adopted to old Scotch songs which he admired for his daughters to sing and play." [333] Unfortunately, he carefully destroyed his sonnets soon after composition because he seemed to fear that "such compositions, if published, would injure his reputation as a Statesman and lessen his influence with the people of Virginia." Since some of Henry's political opponents had called him all tongue and no substance, the fear was somewhat warranted.

Yet Henry used poetry as a didactic tool in his tutoring. One of the surviving poems by Martha Catherina (Kitty) reflects the moral values that Henry strove to inculcate in his children:

> *Through each event of this inconsistent State*
> *Preserve my Temper equal and sedate*
> *Give me a mind that nobly can despise*
> *The low designs and little arts and Vice*
> *Be my Religion such as taught by Thee*
> *Alike from pride and superstition free*
> *Inform my Judgement regulate my Will*
> *My reason strengthen and my passion still.* [334]

Henry's sons enjoyed the benefit of having their father tutor them in the law. Both William and Edward, along with Henry's nephews, John Christian and Nathanial West Dandridge, studied under Henry. Edward followed in his father's footsteps as a lawyer, while William served as a county sheriff his entire adult life.[335]

As a dutiful father, Henry continued to practice law and purchase lands in order to provide each of his children with an earthly inheritance. He also helped arrange his daughters' marriages to successful men who could maintain a secure living for them. Both Anne and Betsy married at Red Hill, and Henry wrote to his sister that "the matches are agreeable to me, the gentlemen having good fortunes and good characters."[336] His solicitude for his daughters' happiness, as well as his own views on the marital relationship, permeates a letter he wrote to Anne shortly after her marriage to Spencer Roane.

> *My Dear Daughter: You have just entered into that state which is replete with happiness or misery. The issue depends upon that prudent, amiable, uniform conduct which wisdom and virtue so strongly recommend on the one hand, or on that imprudence which a want of reflection or passion may prompt on the other.*
>
> *The first maxim which you should impress upon your mind is never to attempt to control your husband, by opposition, by displeasure, or any other mark of anger. A man of sense, of prudence, of warm feelings, cannot, and will not bear an opposition of any kind which is attended with an angry look or expression. The current of his affections is suddenly stopped;*

his attachment is weakened; he begins to feel a mortification the most pungent; he is belittled in his own eyes; and be assured that the wife who once excites those sentiments in the breast of a husband will never regain the high ground which she might and ought to have retained. When he marries her, if he be a good man, he expects from her smiles, not frowns; he expects to find her one who is not to control him—not to take from him the freedom of acting as his own judgment shall direct, but one who will place such confidence in him as to believe that his prudence is his best guide. Little things, that in reality are mere trifles in themselves, often produce bickerings and even quarrels. Never permit them to be a subject of dispute; yield them with pleasure, with a smile of affection. Be assured, one difference outweighs them all a thousand, or ten thousand, times. A difference with your husband ought to be considered as the greatest calamity—as one that is to be studiously guarded against; it is a demon which must never be permitted to enter a habitation where all should be peace, unimpaired confidence, and heartfelt affection. Besides, what can a woman gain by her opposition or her indifference? Nothing. But she loses everything; she loses her husband's respect for her virtues, she loses his love, and with that, all prospect of future happiness. She creates her own misery, and then utters idle and silly complaints, but utters them in vain.

Mutual politeness between the most intimate friends is essential to that harmony which should never be broken or interrupted. How important, then, it is between man and wife!...I will add that matrimonial happiness does not depend upon wealth; no, it is not to be found in wealth, but in minds properly tempered and united to our respective situations. Competency is necessary. All beyond that is ideal.[337]

Henry was equally concerned for the successes of his sons, and sought to provide them resources to become self-made men like himself. Of his sons, "Neddy" showed the most promise of being an outstanding lawyer like his father, and was probably Henry's favorite. In 1792, Edward paid court to Sally Campbell, daughter of a wealthy planter, but Henry did not approve because he feared that by marrying into wealth Neddy would jeopardize his need to become a self-made man. "I shall be better pleased," Henry wrote, "to see him independent by his own industry than ever so rich by the favor of any person he might marry."[338] Quite tragically, Sally married another, and Neddy fell ill and was dead two years later.

Patrick Henry is today remembered as a great patriot and a great politician–which he was. But he was also a great father. He understood that the home was the foundation of a stable society and that the authority a man "exercised within the larger society was rooted in the authority exercised at home."[339] If a man cannot rule his children, how shall he govern a country? Thus the measure of a man's character can be seen in his home, and the training ground for all sound leadership is the family.

VISION

Are we disposed to be of the number of those who,
having eyes, see not, and having ears, hear not,
the things which so nearly concern their temporal
solution?[340]

A leader is a man who has one eye on the present and one eye on the future. He is not a dreamer who eschews the mundane facts of the present while weaving a hypothetical future from the thread of his own brain. Rather, his firm grasp on the present enables him to envision the future outcome of his policies and actions. He is not bound by the past, but neither does he ignore it. The true inspirational leader so thoroughly grasps the lessons of history and the facts of the present that he can accurately paint the face of the future.

It was Henry who foresaw most clearly that the brewing trouble with Britain must inevitably explode into a full-scale war. Shortly before going to the Continental Congress in 1774, Henry held a conversation with Colonel Overton and others, and was asked whether "Great Britain would drive her colonies to extremities." And if so, what "would be the issue of the war?" According to Overton, Henry answered confidently: "She *shall* drive us to extremities–no accommodations will take place–hostilities will *soon* commence–and a desperate and bloody touch it will be." When Overton questioned whether the feeble colonies could alone defeat Britain, Henry responded: "I doubt whether we *shall* be able, *alone*, to cope with so powerful a nation. But where is France? Where is Spain? Where is Holland?… Will Louis the XVI be asleep all this time? Believe me, no!" Henry then emphatically stated the future outcome: "Our independence will be established, and we shall take our stand among the nations of the earth!"[341]

When Henry attended the first Congress, he insisted that war was fast approaching. Indeed, he acted as if war were a foregone conclusion. "I go on the supposition," he said, "that government is at an end. The present measures lead to war." According to John Adams, Henry was the only delegate who had the clearness of political vision to foresee the future bloody conflict. Writing to Jefferson in 1813, Adams said, "In the Congress of 1774, there was not one member, except Patrick Henry, who appeared to me sensible of the precipice, or rather, pinnacle, on which he stood, and had the candor and courage enough to acknowledge it."[342]

Up until the outbreak of open hostilities, Henry repeatedly predicted the coming contest. During his speech at St. John's, he boldly and prophetically announced, "We must fight! The war is inevitable. And let it come!" Indeed, said Henry, "the war is actually begun," and "the next gale that sweeps from the north will bring to our ears the clash of resounding arms." And as Henry had previously confided to Overton, he stated his belief that foreign aid would assist the colonies in their struggle for liberty. "There is a just God who presides over the destinies of nations," said Henry, "who will raise up friends to fight our battles for us."[343] His predictions came to pass, of course. The war came, and God raised up France just as Henry had foreseen.

Henry's political sagacity is most readily seen in his objections to the newly-proposed Constitution. Throughout the Ratification Convention of 1788, he warned that the new federal government which was to be established under the Constitution would jeopardize personal liberty and state sovereignty. Why? Because the federal government would not confine itself to the powers enumerated in the Constitution, but would claim implied powers and then abuse them. Henry prophetically warned that Congress would construe clauses empowering it "to lay and collect taxes," or "to provide for the common defense" and "to make all laws necessary for carrying into execution the powers invested..."–Congress would construe these clauses so as to transcend the enumerated power. In only a brief time after ratification, in 1798, Madison admitted that "a spirit has been manifested by the federal government to enlarge its powers by forced constructions" of the Constitution. The effect, said Madison, who had previously disagreed with Henry, was "to consolidate the states by degrees into one sovereignty" and thereby "transform the present republican system of the United States into an absolute, or at least a mixed, monarchy."[344] This, of course, was Henry's position ten years earlier when Madison opposed him in the Virginia Convention.

Henry also predicted that the balance of power between northern and southern states would be changed under the Constitution, creating a sectional rivalry based on different interests–the north being industrial while the south was more agricultural. As early as April, 1790, Henry Lee wrote to Madison that "Henry is already considered a prophet" because "his predictions are daily verified–his declarations with respect to the divisions of interest which would exist under the Constitution and predominate on all the doings of the government already have been undeniably proved."[345]

The sectional tension between north and south prompted Henry to predict the possibility that the U.S. Government might exercise its implied power to abolish slavery.

> *Among ten thousand implied powers which they may assume, they may, if we be engaged in war, liberate every one of your slaves if they please. And this must and will be done by men, a majority of whom have not a common interest with you…Have they not power to provide for the general defense and welfare? May they not think that these call for the abolition of slavery? May they not pronounce all slaves free, and will they not be warranted by that power?*[346]

The fulfillment of Henry's prophecy came to pass, just as he said, when President Lincoln issued the Emancipation Proclamation during the Civil War. Indeed, even that war itself had been foreseen by Henry as the unavoidable result of the doctrine of nullification expressed in the Kentucky and Virginia Resolutions. "Opposition on the part of Virginia to the acts of the General government," he presaged, "must beget their enforcement by military power," and "this would probably produce civil war."[347] The civil war came with a vengeance, and the federal government oppressed the states, using a "standing army to execute the execrable commands of tyranny," as Henry had forewarned the Virginia Convention. Regarding the future effect of adopting the Constitution,

Henry "understood the nature of the new government more thoroughly, and foresaw its practical working more clearly, than any of his contemporaries. In truth, he seemed endowed with something akin to prophetic vision in regard to its future."[348]

Henry's faculty of vision indeed bordered on prophetic foresight. But his foresight was built on his insight. He understood human nature and was a careful observer of current events. In many cases, his predictions were nothing more than a statement of the logical outcome of common sense laws of human nature and the simple lessons of history. The past, the present, and the future are all of a thread; and the leader with vision must remember the past, regard the present, and relate both to the future.

FUTURE

*I venture to prophecy there are those now living
who will see this favored land among the most powerful on earth... They will see her great in arms and
arts–her golden harvest waving over fields of
immeasurable extent–her commerce penetrating the
most distant seas, and her cannon silencing the
vain boasts of those who now proudly affect to rule
the waves.*[349]

*A*leader must lead. Where others see obstacles, he
must see opportunities. When others see prob-
lems, he must see possibilities. It is not enough to envision the
drastic consequences of a proposed policy; a leader must foresee the proper course and initiate constructive action. "We all
know what not to do," Henry once said. "But knowing what
we ought to do is another matter altogether." Civilization is
not built on a negation but on an affirmation–an affirmation
of the bright and promising possibilities that the future holds
for those who are enterprising enough to pursue them. "The
negative is no replacement for the positive."[350]

In many respects, Henry was ahead of his time. He was one of the first assemblymen in Virginia to advocate religious toleration. Yet his views on toleration were not solely based on his notions of liberty; rather, toleration was also seen by Henry as the wisest course for inviting industrious immigrants into Virginia, and thereby developing commerce and strengthening the colony's independence. "A general toleration for religion appears to me the best means of peopling our country and enabling our people to procure those necessarys among themselves, the purchase of which from abroad has so nearly ruined a colony, enjoying, from nature and time, the means of becoming the most prosperous on the continent."[351] Henry's early advocacy of toleration, then, was strongly influenced by his vision of Virginia's future independence.

Besides his enlightened views on religion, Henry's views on race were well in advance of his era. It is clear that he foresaw, and even desired, the eventual abolition of slavery. Moreover, he hoped to ameliorate, if not end, the continual hostility between the Indians and the whites on the western borders. Treaties were temporary, and presents were perishable. What was needed was a permanent solution based on mutual affection. Therefore, in 1784, Henry introduced a resolution in the Virginia House for the encouragement of interracial marriages between whites and Indians. Inducements to be offered were "pecuniary bounties at marriage, and at the birth of each child," exemption from taxes and provision of education for the children. The bill passed two readings, but failed the third since Henry had left the legislature for the governor's chair, and was not present to support it by his earnestness and eloquence. Whatever may be thought of the particulars of Henry's bill, it is evident that he was remarkably free from the racial prejudice of his age, and sought tolerant, long-term solutions.[352]

It was undoubtedly Henry's vision of America's rising prosperity–auguring future greatness–as well as his tolerance, that caused him to champion the return of post-war Tories to Virginia. Again, agents of prejudice and hostility opposed him. Yet he appealed to his countrymen to lay aside their animosities and envision the future greatness of their country.

> *Cast your eye, sir, over this extensive country–observe the salubrity of your climate, the variety and fertility of your soil–and see that soil intersected in every quarter by bold, navigable streams, flowing to the east and to the west as if the finger of heaven were marking out the course of your settlements, inviting you to enterprise, and pointing the way to wealth. Sir, you are destined at some time or other, to become a great agricultural and commercial people… I venture to prophesy there are those now living who will see this favored land among the most powerful on earth–able, sir, to take care of herself, without resorting to that policy which is always so dangerous, though sometimes unavoidable, of calling in foreign aid. Yes, sir, they will see her great in arts and in arms–her golden harvests waving over fields of immeasurable extent–her commerce penetrating the most distant seas, and her cannon silencing the vain boasts of those who now proudly affect to rule the waves.*[353]

As governor, Henry was a far-seeing statesman who wisely anticipated later generations. He not only reformed capital punishment and pioneered the improvement of the waterway system in Virginia, but he also played an important role in securing the Northwest Territory, including the Mississippi River, for the United States. He also duly appreciated the implications of the rapidly developing industrial revolution. During 1785, he was visited by the eccentric genius John Fitch, who that spring had conceived the idea of the steamboat. In order to raise money for his experiments, Fitch was selling copies of a map he had drawn of the Northwest Territory. On his visit to Governor Henry, Fitch unveiled his plan of steamboat navigation. Henry immediately saw the future prospect of the steamboat and contracted for Fitch "to exhibit a full proof of the practicality of rowing a vessel by the force of a steam engine in the commonwealth of Virginia..." On August 22, 1787, Fitch made a successful trip with his steamboat on the Delaware at Philadelphia. Robert Fulton, who is usually credited with the invention of the steamboat, actually obtained Fitch's drawings and perfected them.[354]

Henry's vision was much more than the ability to predict disaster and thus issue monitory warnings, as he had done before the war. He also viewed the future with a compelling confidence that led him to inaugurate innovative and bold plans. "Will anyone censure me as an innovator?" he once quipped. "I care not."[355] What Henry cared about was the future of his country. And if a policy was in the best interest of America, then he would introduce it in spite of its apparent novelty. A country such as America, with an expansive and unexplored frontier needed a leader who lived on the frontier of his time. And Patrick Henry was that leader.

REALISM

It is natural to man to indulge in illusions of hope. We are apt to shut our eyes against a painful truth and listen to the song of that siren till she transforms us into beasts... For my part, whatever anguish of spirit it may cost, I am willing to know the whole truth; to know the worst and provide for it.[356]

The truth has never been popular, especially in an age like our own where people feed on fantasy and run from reality. A leader, however, has no choice but to face the cold hard truth, brutal as it may be. For if he succumbs to illusions, his plans will be miscalculated and his policies misguided. Ignorance may be bliss, but only temporarily, since ignorance can result in apathy and lead to tragedy.

Since the truth is often painful, a leader must possess courage in order to face reality. He must be willing to know the entire truth, "whatever anguish of spirit it may cost," as Henry said. Problems do not pass away; they must be solved. And crises do not calm themselves; they must be conquered.

A leader knows this, and is willing to know the facts accurately in order to act appropriately. For a true leader, opinions and feelings, whether his own or others', are always subservient to the truth.

Henry's success as a leader was largely due to his desire to fearlessly face the truth. When his colleagues in the Virginia Assembly shuddered at the thought of resistance, Henry pushed them to see the ineluctable conclusion of their protests to the Stamp Act. Indeed, from the time of the Stamp Act crisis to the declaration of independence, Henry repeatedly challenged his fellow patriots to face the cruel reality that British policy must be met with resistance, or tyranny would follow.

As early as 1774, Henry warned the Continental Congress that Britain's "present measures lead to war." Yet his friends were obdurate. They fooled themselves with false hopes of reconciliation. Thus, when Henry arrived at the Virginia Convention in March of 1775, he had the unpleasant task of shattering the deluded dreams of the party for appeasement. It was clear to Henry that Britain was bent on war. "Ask yourselves how this gracious reception of our petitions comports with those warlike preparations which cover our waters and darken our land," he said. "Are fleets and armies necessary to a work of love and reconciliation! No!" They are "the implements of war and subjugation. So why should men continue to indulge the fond hope of peace and reconciliation?" It is foolish to "deceive ourselves," he warned. All the facts point to war. It is vain, to cry "peace, peace." "The war is actually begun." The bloody handwriting was on the wall, and Henry was brave enough to read it. The bitter letters spelled war. Being a realist, he refused "to indulge in the illusions of hope"; but rather sought to prepare for war.[357]

Henry's realistic approach to the questions of his age is most clearly seen in his opposition to the new federal Constitution. Though he agreed with the Federalists that the Union needed to be strengthened, he was plainly cautious of the Constitution because the arguments advanced in its favor contradicted Henry's "realistic versus theoretical" approach to politics. Throughout the Ratification Convention of 1788, he consistently defended his arguments by appealling to the obvious lessons of history and the common sense maxims of experience. Being a realist, he was not willing to venture the fate of Virginia or the Union on mere speculation, assumption, or opinion. What he wanted was not elaborate arguments for discarding the Articles of Confederation and adopting the new Constitution, but compelling evidence.

> *If it be demonstrated that the adoption of the new plan is a little or a trifling evil, then, sir, I acknowledge that adoption ought to follow: but sir, if this be a truth, that its adoption may entail misery on the free people of this country, I then insist, that rejection ought to follow. Gentlemen strongly urge its adoption will be a mighty benefit to us: but, sir, I am made of such incredulous materials that assertions and declarations, do not satisfy me.*[358]

One of the leading arguments advanced in favor of adoption was that the Union was in danger of dissolution without a stronger central authority. But was the danger real? That was Henry's question, and he demanded a substantial, not theoretical, answer.

> *Unless there be great and awful dangers, the change is dangerous, and the experiment ought*

> *not to be made. In estimating the magnitude of*
> *these dangers, we are obliged to take a most*
> *serious view of them, to feel them, to handle*
> *them, and to be familiar with them. It is not*
> *sufficient to feign mere imaginary dangers;*
> *there must be a dreadful reality. The great ques-*
> *tion between us is, does that reality exist?*[359]

In the great debate over the Constitution, Madison and others claimed that adoption of the new system would relieve America of its post bellum debts. But Henry, in his character-istic attitude of realism, demanded proof.

> *Will this new system promote manufactures,*
> *industry and frugality? If instead of this, your*
> *hopes and designs will be disappointed; you*
> *relinquish a great deal, and hazard infinitely*
> *more, for nothing. Will it enhance the value of*
> *your lands? Will it lessen your burthens? Will*
> *your looms and wheels go to work by the act of*
> *adoption? If it will in its consequence produce*
> *these things, it will consequently produce a*
> *reform, and enable you to pay your debts.*
> *Gentlemen must prove it. I am a sceptic–an*
> *infidel on this point. I cannot conceive that it*
> *will have these happy consequences. I cannot*
> *confide in assertions and allegations.*

Henry's stubborn refusal to be swayed by high-sounding assertions kept him from an unrealistic political theory and, hence, from being seduced by erroneous views of human nature and society. As a careful observer of men, he was not about to be fooled by speculations that contradicted his experience. His practice, as he told Mr. Wormsly, was to "study men." And he realized that human nature could not be trusted with unchecked power. "Human nature will never part with power," he asserted. "Look for an example of a voluntary relinquishment of power from one end of the globe to another—you will find none."

Besides his careful observation of human nature, Henry's realism was born of an intimate knowledge of history. For him, historical precedent was always more convincing than abstract argument. "I have but one lamp by which my feet are guided," he said, "and that is the lamp of experience."[360] Throughout the Ratification Convention, Henry demanded that his Federalist foes produce historical examples to buttress their arguments. "I call for an example," he continually shouted. "Show me an instance," he repeatedly demanded. As a practical politician—a realistic politician—Henry scorned the "visionary projects" of modern politicians. "Tell me not of imaginary means," he chided, "but of reality." And for Henry, history was a lesson book in reality. It was the "experiences of the ages"—the "experience of the world"—which could be neglected only with great peril.

Whether he was calling the colonies to arms, or issuing caveats against the Constitution, Henry's approach to politics can be summed up in the realist's motto: "Experience is the best teacher"—an aphorism he publicly endorsed. Theory and argument alone are no match for observation and history. And one of the requirements of leadership is the ability to remember the past while gazing at the future. "To comprehend the history of a thing," said Hilaire Belloc, "is to unlock the mysteries of its present and more, to disclose the profundities of its future."[361]

When Henry viewed the future, he saw it through the lens of the past. If experience told him of positive precedents, then he was optimistic; if not, he was pessimistic. Yet that is exactly what realism means: neither a fatuous optimism nor a paralyzing pessimism; rather, a balanced view based on the truth. A man who has the courage to accept the claims of truth, even if painful, will always be a superior leader to a man who finds solace in falsehood, ever so peaceful.

ADVERSITY

Adversity toughens manhood and the characteristic
of the good or the great man is not that he has been
exempt from the evils of life, but that he has sur-
mounted them.[362]

*P*atrick Henry's realistic view of life was a product
of his acquaintance with the Scriptures, his knowledge of human history, and his experience of real life. As a
realist, he knew that anyone who expected the easy life–to be
"exempt from the evils of life"–was no better than a foolish
dreamer. Life is hard because we live in a fallen world. And
anyone who aspires to leadership must accept the hard reality that adversity is essential to maturity, and that without a
crucifixion there is no coronation. Greatness is not served up
on a platter.

As a young man, Henry experienced a series of hardships
and setbacks that would have crushed a man of less resolve
and faith. By the time he was only twenty-three, his first business had collapsed, bad weather had ruined his farm, a fire
had destroyed his home, and a second business had gone

bankrupt. Moreover, to add to his burden, Henry was by then a married man responsible for a wife and several young children. Yet instead of giving in to despair, Henry maintained a "self-reliant spirit," and when Jefferson met Henry during this time, he commented that there was no trace of his trials "either in his countenance or conduct."[363]

At this juncture, Henry benefited from the lessons of adversity and turned to the legal profession. He applied himself assiduously to his legal texts, labored at his practice, and climbed out of debt. But his encounter with adversity was far from over.

Once he established himself as an attorney and legislator, adversity struck again at the point nearest Henry's heart–his wife. Sallie had been Henry's childhood sweetheart, and he was so eager to marry her that they wed when he was only eighteen and possessed very little means of support. Always his close friend and companion, Sallie had been a source of encouragement through Henry's previous adversity, but now it was she who was struck by adversity. For some unknown reason, perhaps a stint with malaria, Sallie began to experience a severe depression that ultimately led to a nervous breakdown. Shortly thereafter, in February of 1775, Sallie died, leaving Henry "a distraught old man" at the age of forty. Yet, instead of giving in to despair, Henry consoled himself in his Christian faith. "Providence has ordered to all a portion of suffering and uneasiness in this world," he later told his daughter, "that we may think of preparing for a better."[364] Being strengthened by his faith in God, he continued to advance the cause of American independence even while carrying a deep wound in his heart. Only six weeks after Sallie's death, he gave his most famous speech at St. John's Church.

Henry also suffered the loss of several other loved ones. He lost his parents, his brother, William, and several of his children. Richard died in 1793, at about eighteen months of age, and Jane Robertson survived birth, in 1798, by only a few days. More painfully, Henry lost two adult sons. John, who had been a captain in the Revolutionary War, died in 1791, and "Neddy," Henry's favorite, passed away in 1794.[365]

In addition to these heart-rending personal trials, Henry was subject to much adversity as a public man. Even though he was immensely popular with the people–or perhaps because of it–Henry was subject to repeated criticism throughout his career. Perhaps some of the worst attacks on Henry's character occurred when he opposed the Constitution. According to its supporters, Henry was guilty of "blowing the trumpet of discord" and of feeding "poison" throughout the Union. By these means, his opponents alleged, Henry "artfully prejudiced the people's mind against the Constitution." And although Henry had publicly stated that his motive for opposing the Constitution was his fear that the new government threatened the people's liberties, his opponents said his "real design" was to dismember the Union. Even Henry's friend, George Washington, suspected that Henry had "no great objection to the introduction of anarchy and confusion" into the Union.[366]

In spite of all the adversity and sorrow that he experienced throughout his life, Henry maintained a steady course of fortitude and faith. He knew that adversity was to be expected in a fallen world. "Experience will teach you," he once counseled his daughter, Betsy, "that this world is not made for complete happiness."[367] This sentiment, instead of being a declaration of despair, was actually a statement of hope. If we have a realistic acceptance of life's hardships, we will fortify ourselves against false hope and disillusionment. To be forewarned is to be forearmed.

Failure never stopped Henry either, for he knew that as long as a man persevered, no failure need be final. His knowledge of the Bible and his study of history taught him that "those who made history were men who failed at some point and some of them drastically, but who refused to continue lying in the dust."[368] Because of Henry's faith and fortitude, none of his failures were final, and adversity only served to ennoble his character.

VIGILANCE

*But, sir, suspicion is a virtue, as long as its object is
the preservation of the public good and as long as it
stays within proper bounds…Guard with jealous
attention the public liberty. Suspect everyone who
approaches that jewel.*[369]

The notion that the purpose of leadership is to provide
inspiration or vision is only partially true. For in
addition to direction, a good leader also provides protection.
He is a guardian. Like a sentry at his post, a leader will be
alert to an enemy's movements, sense approaching danger,
and sound the alarm when attacked. In a word, a strong
leader will be vigilant. He will watch out for persons or influences which might destroy the institution or harm the people
under his charge.

When Henry assumed the office of governor of the newly-
formed Commonwealth of Virginia, he realized that the infant
government would be exposed to "numberless hazards and
perils," and that, in order to survive, it "must be guarded by
an affectionate assiduity and managed by great abilities."[370]

Throughout his five terms as governor, Henry was vigilant to protect Virginia from internal and external foes and guard her eastern and western borders. He armed the colony, fortified the Chesapeake Bay, and policed the western border. To "prevent mischief and to do good" was Henry's motto as governor. And he was so successful that one historian asserts that Henry's "zeal and vigor in this business entitled him to the highest honor as a guardian of America in her time of trial."[371]

Perhaps the clearest demonstration of his vigilant attitude can be seen in his opposition to the proposed federal Constitution. While he and other Anti-Federalists were (and still are) often misunderstood, Henry's objection to the Constitution was motivated by a zealous and vigilant concern for the liberties of the people. Long before Lord Acton penned his now-famous aphorism–"Power corrupts and absolute power corrupts absolutely"–Henry was suspicious of any concentration of power that might endanger the rights and liberties of his countrymen. "Nothing is more perilous than constructive power," he warned the Ratification Convention.[372]

Henry's assertion that when it comes to human power, "suspicion is a virtue," was based upon his understanding of human nature and human history. Throughout the course of the Convention, he made the point that since human nature is defective, or fallen, it cannot be trusted with too much power. "Human nature never will part from power," he claimed. That is a simple fact of man's fallen condition. "Notwithstanding what gentlemen say of the probable virtue of our representatives, I dread the depravity of human nature…I will never depend on so slender a protection as the possibility of being represented by virtuous men." But were not the American patriots virtuous men themselves? Yes. But they were fallen men like the rest of us, and therefore, could not be naively trusted. "Will you be safe when you trust men at Philadelphia with power to make any law that will enable them to carry their acts into execution? Will not the members of Congress have the same passions which other rulers have had?" Indeed they will; for "they will not be superior to the frailties of human nature." Therefore, "however cautious you may be in the selection of your representatives, it will be dangerous to trust them with such unbounded power."

The notion that human nature was depraved and inclined to abuse power was more than a theological assertion. According to Henry it was an historical fact. The "experience of the ages" unquestionably shows a pattern of the tyrannical abuse of power. "I have reason," he said, "to suspect ambitious grasps of power." Why? Because "the experience of the world teaches me the jeopardy of giving enormous power." Will human nature part with power? Never–not if history be our guide. "Look for an example of a voluntary relinquishment of power, from one end of the globe to another–you will find none." For Henry, historical precedent conclusively confirmed his suspicion of human power. "Look at the use which has been made in all parts of the world," he intoned, "at that human thing called power. Look at the predominant thrift of dominion which has invariably and uniformly prompted rulers to abuse their power."

Both theological theory and human history shaped Henry's view of human nature and made him a vigilant protector of human liberty. Had he possessed a more optimistic or sentimental view of human nature, or had he been less knowledgeable of history, he might never have secured for himself and his country those valuable liberties enshrined in the Bill of Rights. But because he was a realistic and practical politician, he was ever on guard against the "depravity of human nature." He saw himself as a guardian of the people's interests. I consider myself as the servant of the people of this commonwealth," he once said, "as a sentinel over their rights, liberty and happiness."[373]

Every leader, like Henry, must be vigilant to protect those under him. Authority, by its very definition, places a man in the unenviable position of having the responsibility to guard those he leads. A father must care for his children, a minister must pastor his flock, and a politician must protect his citizens. Vigilance, then, is an essential element of leadership; for a true leader must safeguard his followers. As Jesus said, "The good shepherd lays down his life for his sheep."[374]

Virtue

No free government or the blessings of liberty can be preserved to any people but by a firm adherence to justice, moderation, temperance, frugality, and virtue.[375]

*P*atrick Henry and the men who led the colonies through the revolutionary period and founded the new republic of America governed their lives by a value system that seems increasingly foreign to the modern mind. That system, derived partially from the Bible and partially from the ancient classics, inculcated and highly esteemed a quality coined "virtue." More than mere goodness, virtue encapsulated all those qualities essential to private and public self-government. According to historian Forrest McDonald, "Public virtue entailed firmness, courage, endurance, industry, frugal living, strength, and above all unremitting devotion to the weal of the public's corporate self, the community of virtuous men." Virtue was both individualistic and communal: "individualistic in that no member of the public could be dependent upon any other...communal in that everyone gave himself totally to the good of the public as a whole."[376]

Henry was a powerful leader because he embodied the prevailing notion of virtue. Both in his private and public life he demonstrated endurance, industry, frugality–as well as devotion to the public good.

Throughout his life he experienced adversity, first as a young entrepreneur and farmer, and then later as a bereaved husband and father. Yet during all of his trials, he displayed a manly courage and endurance. He labored diligently to overcome financial difficulties and worked hard at his legal practice and land speculation–with the result that he died a fairly wealthy landowner.[377] In spite of his personal sorrows, Henry never gave in to despair. He was a fighter. He endured.

Henry also exercised a high degree of personal discipline, always maintaining a simple lifestyle. "In his habits of living," said one author, "he was remarkably temperate and frugal."[378] Although his position as a leading statesman and governor might have excused a more luxuriant lifestyle, "Henry was a plain man who preferred a plain style of living, plain clothing, a plain diet, and plain words."[379]

Henry's courage–another aspect of virtue–was legendary, as we have seen. As a neophyte legislator he boldly stood up to the Virginia elite, and as a freeborn Virginian he bravely defied British tyranny. He was the first Virginian leader to literally take up arms against Britain and would have gladly and courageously faced combat had he not been forced to resign from the military in order to retain his honor.

A virtuous man is more than an industrious or brave man, however. He is also a public-spirited man. He lives not only for his own success but equally for the good of the community. Henry, of course, was a model of public virtue. The best years of his life were devoted to public service at great expense to his own family and health. He sincerely believed that public service was a moral obligation placed on every man. "I should be unworthy the character of an honest man," he told Washington, "if I withheld from the government my best and most zealous efforts....And I do most cordially execrate the conduct of those men who lose sight of the public interest from personal motives."[380]

Like his fellow-patriots, Henry was convinced that the American experiment in republicanism would only succeed with a virtuous citizenry. Political liberty is incompatible with personal iniquity. Therefore, he was greatly alarmed by the corruption of morals and the decline of religion that was taking place in America due to the ravages of the war and the influence of Deism and scepticism. Writing to his friend, Archibald Blair, Henry expressed his apprehension at the pernicious effect of the French infidelity on the American people. "And while I see the dangers that threaten ours from her intrigues and her arms, I am not so much alarmed as at the apprehensions of her destroying the great pillars of all government and of social life; I mean virtue, morality, and religion. This is the armor, my friend, and this alone that renders us invincible. These are the tactics we should study. If we lose these, we are conquered, fallen indeed. In vain may France show and vaunt her diplomatic skill, and brave troops; so long as our manners and principles remain sound, there is no danger."[381] The danger, however, was very real; that is why Henry sought to bolster public virtue by supporting Christian schools and proposing a general assessment for the support of Christian ministers.

To his dying day, Henry fully believed that American liberty depended on virtue, and he vehemently hoped that his labor as a patriot would prove a blessing to future generations. Among the papers found after his death, was a copy of the Stamp Act Resolutions, written in his own hand, with a letter explaining the events surrounding their passage, and how they brought on the war that established American liberty. He concluded the letter with a warning to all American citizens and an exhortation to all future leaders:

> *Whether this [liberty] will prove a blessing or a curse, will depend upon the use our people make of the blessings which a gracious God hath bestowed on us. If they are wise, they will be great and happy. If they are of a contrary character, they will be miserable. Righteousness alone can exalt them as a nation. Reader! Whoever thou art, remember this; and in thy sphere practice virtue thyself, and encourage it in others.*[382]

ORATORY

Should I keep back my opinions through fear of giving offense, I should consider myself as guilty of treason towards my country and an act of disloyalty toward the majesty of Heaven, which I revere above all earthly kings.[383]

*I*f there is one thing for which Patrick Henry has been remembered, it is his spellbinding and moving oratory. More than anything else, his fame has come to rest on his spoken words, most notably his well-known exclamation "Give me liberty or give me death!" which is still memorized by thousands of American school children. Yet even in his own lifetime Henry's commanding eloquence was legendary, earning him such epithets as the "Forest-Born Demosthenes," the "Trumpet of the Revolution," and the "Son of Thunder."

All those who heard Henry deliver a public speech agreed that he was the most eloquent speaker in the Colonies, and probably the greatest orator in the Western world. Thomas Jefferson, for instance, said that Henry "spoke as Homer wrote," and that he was "the greatest orator that ever lived."[384]

Edmund Randolph, another of Henry's contemporaries and political foes, gave Henry the highest tribute when he stated his belief that "for grand impressions in the defense of liberty, the Western world has not yet been able to exhibit a rival."[385] Coming from his political opponents, these are very high compliments indeed.

Even men who were themselves recognized as excellent orators "accorded to Mr. Henry the palm of oratory over all other men." For instance, John Randolph of Roanoke, who heard Henry in the British Debt Case, and who later earned the reputation as being one of the most eloquent speakers of his day, said that Henry was "the greatest orator that ever lived." On one occasion, when Randolph was asked to describe Henry's oratory, he picked up a piece of charcoal from a fireplace, pointed to a white wall and said:

> But it is in vain for me to attempt to describe
> the oratory of that wonderful man. Sir, it would
> be as vain for me to try, with this black coal, to
> paint correctly the brilliant flash of the vivid
> lightning, or to attempt, with my feeble voice,
> to echo the thunder, as to convey, by any power
> I possess, a proper idea of the eloquence of
> Patrick Henry!

Randolph declared that Henry, in sum, "was a Shakespeare and Garrick combined, and spake as never man spake."[386]

Considering these glowing testimonies, it is unfortunate that we do not have more records of Henry's excellent speeches. But one of the reasons that so few of his speeches have survived intact is that his eloquence was so spellbinding that often the House recorder forgot to take notes because he was enthralled with Henry's speech–he was too captivated to write it down! According to the Reverend Conrad Speece, who witnessed Henry plead a criminal trial, when Henry spoke "my feelings underwent an instant change." Amongst the gallery there was an unusual "bowing of the soul." "The spell of the magician was upon us," said Speece, "and we stood like statues around him."[387]

Indeed, when Henry spoke, it was not uncommon for his listeners to be so enraptured by his rhetoric that they would forget their surroundings. For instance, Judge Roane tells of a humorous incident involving his father.

> *It is among the first things I can remember, that my father paid the expenses of a Scotch tutor residing in his family, named Bradfute, a man of learning, to go with him to Williamsburg to hear Patrick Henry speak; and that he laughed at Bradfute, on his return, for having been so much enchanted with his eloquence as to have unconsciously spirited tobacco juice from the gallery on the heads of the members, and to have nearly fallen from the gallery into the House.*[388]

How do we account for the almost magical power of Henry's eloquence? First, he was a naturally gifted speaker, although this was not apparent when he was a young boy. Not until he pled the Parson's Cause did anyone who knew him– even his father–realize Henry's latent powers as an orator. Secondly, Henry had the good fortune to sit under the preaching of Samuel Davies, who many considered the best preacher in the Colonies next to Whitefield. "It indeed seemed that God had given Patrick a superlative tutor and mentor in oratory during his formative years."[389]

Henry's natural gifts and early experiences were enhanced, moreover, by his keen powers of observation and deep reflection. As a boy, he was really not much of a talker; rather, he liked to listen to others. Colonel Meredith once observed that Henry's habit in his boyhood was to attentively observe everything that occurred near him. "Nothing escaped his notice." This penchant for observation gave Henry deep insight into human nature. "He knew well all the springs and motives of human action." Thus, when he addressed a jury or assembly, "he measured and gauged them by a discriminating judgment," knowing how to produce the desired effect on their minds and hearts.[390]

But most importantly, Henry had power as an orator because he was sincere and earnest in his delivery. He meant what he said. And when he believed something deeply, he spoke it vehemently. While the written word can never do justice to the power of the spoken word, the following eyewitness account of Henry's delivery of his Liberty Speech gives us a glimpse into the secret of his power:

> *Henry arose with an unearthly fire burning in his eye. He commenced somewhat calmly–but the smothered excitement began more and more to play upon his features and thrill in the tones of his voice. The tendons of his neck stood out white and rigid like whipcords. His voice rose louder and louder, until the walls of the building and all within them seemed to shake and rock in its tremendous vibrations. Finally his pale face and glaring eyes became terrible to look upon. Men leaned forward in their seats with their heads strained forward, their faces pale and their eyes glaring like the*

speaker's. His last exclamation– "give me liberty
or give me death"–was like the shout of the
leader which turns back the rout of battle![391]

Dr. Archibald Alexander, the president of Princeton Theological Seminary, once related that he went to hear Henry speak in order to "ascertain the true secret of his power." His conclusion? "The power of Henry's eloquence was due, first, to the greatness of his emotion and passion…"[392]

Like all great leaders, Henry was a man of profound conviction, and because he was also a man of courage, he was not afraid to speak his mind. To "keep back my opinions," he said at St. John's, "through fear of giving offense," would be treason to his country and disloyalty to God. Henry's courage and conviction, therefore, were the true keys to his oratorical power over men. And though few leaders will be able to imitate Henry's natural gifts as an orator, all may emulate the passion and conviction which set them ablaze.

POWER

The experience of the world teaches me the jeopardy of giving enormous power.[393]

The measure of a man's character can be gauged by how he handles success and power. While there are trials peculiar to adversity, there are temptations perilous in prosperity. Some amount of failure and adversity is the lot of every man–as it was to Henry. But not every man experiences the heights of popularity and power that he achieved. And how a man uses his position of influence says as much, if not more, about his character, than how he responds to struggles and setbacks. If he overcomes the trials of adversity, he must face the even greater trials of success.

After enduring a series of business and financial disappointments as a young man, Henry persevered and became a successful lawyer, businessman, and politician. With his successful and eloquent performance in the Parson's Cause, he began a long and lucrative career as a defense attorney. As a general rule, he successfully defended most of his clients, and he never lacked customers eager for his services. His legal practice, however, was interrupted by his service in the Virginia Assembly, especially with the onset of the war.

As a result, Henry augmented his income by engaging in land speculation. Henry had a shrewd business sense–probably the product of his earlier financial failures–and throughout his life invested in promising land ventures. From 1768 to 1799, he was involved in land investments and plantation acquisitions, all made with an acute business intuition. Throughout this period of thirty-two years, Henry "owned at one time or another about one-hundred thousand acres, and from 1789 to 1795 was a partner in a western land investment company that claimed what one author estimated to be fifteen and one-half million acres!" As an owner, speculator, and trader, Henry turned the soil into profits, and before his death, he was one of the wealthiest landowners in Virginia.[394]

His greatest success, of course, was as a political orator and statesman. Due to his spellbinding and splendorous eloquence, Henry was immensely popular with the people of Virginia. He was virtually their "idol"–a celebrity before the cult of celebrities became a phenomenon. And after his Stamp Act Resolutions were published throughout the Colonies, America was filled with his fame.

But Henry's power and influence extended beyond that of the average citizen. For virtually his entire political career, he was the undisputed leader of the Virginia legislature. This fact is all the more striking when we remember that his colleagues numbered such men as George Washington, Thomas Jefferson, James Monroe, James Madison, and John Marshall– just to name a few. "But whatever might be the individual or combined talents of his colleagues, Mr. Henry was easily the leader..."[395] For instance, after the Constitution was ratified, Henry returned to the Virginia Assembly sworn to see that it was amended to protect the people's liberty. Amidst the great legislative battle, he used his power and influence to essentially force Madison, then a United States representative in Congress, to propose those amendments we now know as the Bill of Rights. Washington, who was then president, feared Henry's "anti-Federal" disposition and wrote to Madison lamenting Henry's power over the Virginian House: "In one word it is said that the edicts of Mr. H are enregistered with less opposition in the Virginia Assembly than those of the grand monarch by his parliaments. He has only to say, 'Let this be law, and it is law.'"[396] While perhaps an overstatement, it is nevertheless true that Henry was recognized by both political friend and foe as the unchallenged leader of Virginia, and for many years the most powerful man in the state.

Ironically, Henry himself had a deep distrust of human power. Knowing the frailties of human nature, he well knew that power corrupts. Yet, surprisingly, Henry was remarkably free from abusing his own power and using his fame for personal advantage. On the contrary, he responded to popularity with humility and exercised power responsibly. Unlike so many leaders who become dizzy in the heights of prominence and power, Henry always kept his feet squarely planted on the ground. He was basically a modest man who could not be touched by fame. His character was his armor. Archibald Blair, a close friend of Henry, said of him: "I never saw anything tyrannical in his disposition, or otherwise ambitious than to be serviceable to mankind."[397] Moreover, Henry understood that power, especially political power, was a sacred trust to be used for the benefit of society. As one author said of Henry: "No man ever knew men better, singly or in mass; none ever better knew how to sway them; but none ever less abused that power; for he seems ever to have felt, with a religious force, the solemnity of all those public functions which so few now regard."[398]

We confuse the shadow for the substance when we imagine that fame and power are traits of a great leader. Fame has been given to fools, and power to tyrants. Rather, the real test of greatness is not whether a man possesses fame or power, but how he employs them. Henry was great, not because of power, but in spite of it. Being the great leader he was, he avoided the pitfalls of popularity–pride, egotism, and ingratitude–and did not fall from the pinnacle of power. He passed not only the test of failure, but the more trying test of success. And for that reason especially, he serves as a model for all those who aspire not to the shadow, but to the substance, of true leadership.

PROPERTY

*For if our present system grows into a tyranny, is
not a frontier possession most eligible? and a central one most to be dreaded?…A comfortable
prospect of the issue of the new system would fix me
here for life. A contrary one sends me southwest-
ward.*[399]

*F*rom the moment the first settlers came to America,
they ever cast their eyes westward to the frontier
that lay waiting to be subdued. If there was one resource that
America possessed in abundance, it was land. And those who
were enterprising developed the land–building homes, establishing towns, and acquiring wealth. For Henry, the frontier
was both a school and a haven, and the land a source of pleasure and profit.

Henry's fascination with the frontier began in his boyhood. Like so many other Virginian boys, the woods, streams,
and hills were his playground. Hunting, fishing, canoeing,
climbing trees, skipping rocks on a pond, or taking a swim–
these were his favorite frontier pastimes. But they were also

experiences that helped shape his character. Tradition has it that when Henry was an old man retired at Red Hill, a half-Indian scout named Jack White asked him about his boyhood pleasures on the South Anna. Henry replied that his purpose in roaming the woods was to "learn the language of the birds."[400] Those early lessons in rhetoric were apparently well-learned, since Henry grew to be one of America's greatest orators.

During the busy years of professional development and political turmoil, Henry never lost his affection for the frontier. That is one reason he never really settled in any one residence until he fully retired. "He had a great deal of the pioneer and pathfinder in him," says historian George Morgan. Thus, throughout his life, Henry had as many as fifteen personal residences, if we include the Governor's Palace. While we associate Washington with Mount Vernon and Jefferson with Monticello, Henry's "adventurous spirit and roaming disposition" kept him moving "until we find him, in his declining years at Red Hill. There it was that the gypsy spirit left him; and there he lingered."[401]

At Red Hill, Henry continued to enjoy the pleasures of the land; but more importantly, he now had more time to turn it into profit. Although he began to speculate in land as early as 1768, from 1778 until his death in 1799, Henry invested large amounts of time and capital into various land ventures. In addition to purchasing properties in several Virginia counties, he also acquired acreage in Kentucky, North Carolina, Mississippi, and Georgia. His most ambitious project was the Virginia Yazoo Company, which he formed in 1789 with eight investors. Its aim was to acquire and develop land along the Mississippi River between the thirty-first parallel and the Yazoo River that Georgia had obtained from the Cherokee Indians. In the fall of 1789, Henry petitioned the Georgia legislature to sell his company a portion of the land,

and the Yazoo Act of December 21, 1789, granted Henry's company a tract of land comprising an astounding eleven-million four-hundred thousand acres for the modest price of $93,741. Unfortunately for Henry, Washington's efforts to make peace with the warring Indians devastated his Yazoo Company. On August 7, 1790, the United States signed a treaty with a number of Indian chiefs, returning three million acres of western Georgia to the Indians, with the remainder of the property returning to the state of Georgia. Then, due to a series of frauds in the Georgia legislature, much of Henry's land was sold off to newly-formed companies that had bribed many of the legislators.[402]

Burned by the Yazoo adventure, Henry now began to liquidate many of his holdings and concentrate on the acquisition of choice plantations. In 1797, he purchased Seven Islands (one-thousand four-hundred acres), and in 1798, Saura Town (six-thousand three-hundred fourteen acres) in North Carolina. These and other Henry plantations were farmed for profit and eventually provided an inheritance for his children.

For Henry, as well as many colonists, the land provided more than pleasure and profit. According to Edmund Morgan, the "widespread ownership of property is perhaps the most important single fact about the Americans of the Revolutionary period."[403] Why was property ownership so important? Because it provided economic and political independence. The average American was not a peasant worker who had to bow to a titled lord, but a free-man property holder with the right of suffrage. And the right to vote gave the average, landholding American a political power and independence unknown in aristocratic Europe.

Born and bred in an agricultural society of independent land-owners, Herny imbibed the notion that liberty and property are inseparable. With the book of nature open before his eyes, Henry saw her truths, her laws, and her beauties; and this schooling made him appreciate the pleasures of freedom that he would faithfully champion. According to historian Robert Meade,

> *Few of the great Americans of this and subsequent eras–not Thomas Jefferson or even Abraham Lincoln–seem to have got more beneficial results from their frontier environment. It was a broadening, toughening, and almost wholly enjoyable experience. The frontier, its distinctive customs and people, helped to make Patrick Henry a flaming apostle of American democracy.*[404]

HUMOR

But gentlemen of the jury, this plaintiff tells you that he had nothing to do with the turkey. I dare say, gentlemen,–not until it was roasted![405]

*H*enry was known for his plain dress and serious manner. Undistinguished when in a crowd, he looked like "a common planter who cared very little for his personal appearance." Dressed in a homespun suit of black or "parson's gray," Henry was often mistaken for a minister. When in a rostrum or before an assembly, he looked "gloomy as a preacher"–dark eyes hidden behind sallow cheeks and bushy brows; a long face with an habitual scowl of intensity. Indeed Henry's general appearance was so grave and serious that someone said, "you would swear that he had never laughed at a joke."[406]

But not only did Henry enjoy laughing at a good joke, he was a master at telling one. His humor was one of his most endearing qualities–disarming his enemies and entertaining his friends. His wit was so natural and spontaneous that he attempted to curb it in the Assembly because he thought it unbecoming to a statesman. He did resort to it on several occasions, however, with hilarious effect.

For instance, during the 1788-1789 Assembly, Henry put forth a resolution calling for amendments to the Constitution. Public sentiment required it, he argued. And for his part "he was ready and willing *at all times* and *on all occasions,* "to *bow,* with the *utmost deference* to the *majesty of the people.*"[407]

Francis Corbin, a youthful Tidewater delegate, and son of the aristocratic Colonel Richard Corbin (whom Henry confronted during the Gunpowder Episode) ventured a rebuttal. But instead of relying solely on argument, Corbin indiscreetly attacked Henry's character, challenging the sincerity of Henry's motives for opposing the Constitution. "Whether a country was ruled by a despot, with a tiara on his head, or by a demagogue in a red cloak" and "a caul-bare wig" (clearly implying Henry), was of little importance, said Corbin. Adding, with a deep and graceful bow, "although he should *profess on all occasions to bow to the majesty of the people.*"

Henry's friends were shocked at the breach of convention that forbade abusing a person of Henry's distinction. The insult was aggravated, moreover, by the difference in experience and politics between Corbin and Henry. Corbin's family was loyalist, and he had spent the Revolutionary years being reared and educated in England. Henry, on the other hand, had been the leading patriot in Virginia, enduring the toils and hardships of the war. The contrast–indeed, the ludicrous difference between them–was not lost on Henry.

Awkwardly raising himself to reply, Henry addressed the speaker:

> *I am a plain man, and have been educated*
> *altogether in Virginia. My whole life has been*
> *spent among planters, and other plain men of*

> *similar education, who have never had the*
> *advantage of that polish which a court alone*
> *can give, and which the gentleman over the*
> *way has so happily acquired; indeed, sir, the*
> *gentleman's employments and mine (in com-*
> *mon with the great mass of his countrymen)*
> *have been as widely different as our fortunes;*
> *for while that gentleman was availing himself*
> *of the opportunity which a splendid fortune*
> *afforded him, of acquiring a foreign education,*
> *mixing among the great, attending levees and*
> *courts, basking in the beams of royal favour at*
> *St. James', and exchanging courtesies with*
> *crowned heads, I was engaged in the arduous*
> *toils of the revolution; and was probably as far*
> *from thinking of acquiring those polite accom-*
> *plishments which the gentleman has so*
> *successfully cultivated, as that gentleman then*
> *was from sharing in the toils and dangers in*
> *which his unpolished countrymen were*
> *engaged.*
> *I will not, therefore, presume to vie with the*
> *gentleman in those courtly accomplishments, of*
> *which he has just given the house so agreeable*
> *a specimen; yet such a bow as I can make shall*
> *be ever at the service of the people.*[408]

Then, without warning, Henry surprised the assembly with a "ludicrously awkward and clownish" bow that sent the house into an uproar of laughter. Upon straightening, Henry sarcastically apologized: "The gentleman, I hope, will commiserate the disadvantages of education under which I have labored, and will be pleased to remember that I have never been a favorite with that monarch, whose gracious smile he has had the happiness to enjoy."[409] For nearly twenty minutes Henry treated the House to his satirical display of humility, to the continual laughter of all–except Corbin. Judge Roane, who witnessed the scene, says, "It exceeded anything of the kind I ever heard. He spoke and acted his reply, and Corbin sank at least a foot in his seat."[410]

Henry's performance was undoubtedly one of the occasions referred to by Judge Tyler, when he said that he had seen Henry reply to various members of the Assembly "with such a volume of wit and humor that the House would be in an uproar of laughter and even set his opponents altogether in a perfect convulsion."[411]

Doubtless, Henry's sense of humor was born of his keen insight and observation. He could draw a ludicrous image in the minds of his auditors because he so clearly saw it himself. Besides, Henry was a deeply humble man, and as such, he did not take himself too seriously. Therefore, he could find the humor in a situation even when he himself was being criticized. Although he spent the greater part of his life grappling with serious issues of grave importance, Henry never lost his sense of balance, nor his sense of humor. Life is serious, yes. But it can be hilariously funny also. And a leader who maintains his wit without losing his dignity will always attract followers in need of the refreshment that comes from a hearty laugh.

HOSPITALITY

Mutual politeness between the most intimate friends is essential to that harmony which should never be broken or interrupted.[412]

*H*e was a man who fought in the courtroom, battled in the legislature, and warred at the Convention–a gladiator in the political arena, and a warrior in the struggle for American independence. Yet, despite his passionate and sometimes ferocious public rhetoric, Henry was a man who always retained a simple, almost child-like appreciation for people. He was affable and hospitable, always enjoying the fun and entertainment provided by friends, relatives, and even strangers. Like all great leaders, Henry had a large heart, capable of appreciating the many facets of life and warmly welcoming people regardless of their station.

Those who knew Henry as a youth remarked that his "disposition was very mild, benevolent and humane," and that he "indulged much in innocent amusements."[413] In other words, Henry was good-natured and liked to have a good time. As a youth, he was even somewhat of a prankster.

Charles Dabney, Henry's cousin, used to relate that when he and Henry canoed down the South Anna River, it seems that whenever the canoe would "accidentally" tip over, Dabney and his brother were always fully clothed, while Patrick was "coincidentally" prepared for the plunge.

Henry's playfulness struck Jefferson when the two met in the winter of 1759. Jefferson was on his way to college, and passed the Christmas holidays at Colonel Dandridge's, a neighbor of Henry. During the holiday festivities, the two men became acquainted, and Jefferson later remarked that Henry's "passion was music, dancing and pleasantry. He excelled in the last, and it attracted everyone to him." He was, said Jefferson, "the best humored man in society I almost ever knew."[414]

Henry's "good humor" was noticed by those who knew him well. Judge Spencer Roane, for instance, stated that Henry's disposition was "the best imaginable"–always calm and collected. He had a "remarkable facility for adapting himself to his company." And company, according to Roane, was one of Henry's favorite pastimes. "His great delight was in conversation, and in the society of his friends and family..."[415]

Even while a wartime governor, Henry found time to entertain friends and important guests at the Governor's Palace. Indeed, his penchant for hospitality caused Henry to overspend his budget, so when he left the Palace he was in debt and had to revive his law practice.

After retiring from political life, Henry had more time to spend on hospitality and entertainment, his favorite leisure activities. According to one nineteenth century author, Henry always maintained an open door at Red Hill and welcomed all to enjoy the fruits of his labor.

> *...Those who lived near always came to break-*
> *fast, where all were welcomed and made full.*
> *The larder never seemed to get lean. Breakfast*

*over, creature comforts, such as might console
the belated for its loss, were set forth on side-
tables in the wide entrance-hall. All further
comers helped themselves as the day or their
appetites advanced.*

*The master saw and welcomed all with kind-
liest attention. At noon, for the early dinner,
from twenty to thirty often sat down. It was
always, according to the wont of such houses
in that well fed land, a meal beneath which the
table groaned. Every thing was excellent at
these lavish feasts. There were no luxuries save
such as were home grown. There was also at
Governor Henry's interesting conversation,
which at times grew gay and even, it is said,
"gamesome."*[416]

Henry's affability and hospitality demonstrated his genuine appreciation for people from all walks of life. Not like so
many modern politicians who make perfunctory professions
of their concern for "humanity," Henry actually liked people–
a much more difficult task. Men beat a path to his door
because his door was always open, as was his heart. Like all
great leaders, Henry was a lover of men with a large capacity
for friendship and fellowship. As A. W. Tozer once said of all
true leaders, "Nothing can take the place of affection. Those
who have it in generous measure have a magic power over
men."[417] Henry, of course, had that magic because he was a
man of great affection.

WORK

The whole economy of this lower world proves that it is by labor and perseverance only that good is obtained and evil is avoided.[418]

*P*atrick Henry inherited and exemplified what has come to be known as the Protestant work ethic. Derived from the Scriptures, this ethic taught that man was created in the image of God for the purpose of subduing the earth and exercising dominion over it. The first man, Adam, was accordingly given a garden to cultivate. According to the Biblical view, then, work is not a curse to be endured but a calling to be fulfilled. Every job or vocation, except one that is explicitly sinful, is a divine calling from God that deserves our best effort.

The modern view of work has, to a great degree, undermined the older Protestant ethic. According to the modern view, the primary goal of work is to acquire money for the purposes of consumption. By making a hard and fast distinction between the secular and the sacred (something that Henry and the other founders never did) modern work no longer has any spiritual or eternal significance in the eyes of the worker. Except for the desire to get a raise or promotion, there is no longer any motivation to excel at one's work. The result is an increasingly bored employee and increasingly inferior work.

Henry learned the Biblical view of work as a child, being taught "to learn and labor truly to get my own living, and to do my duty in that state of life into which it shall please God to call me."[419] Here the Biblical view of work is aptly summarized: it is a divine calling that demands our utmost labor.

At fifteen, Henry went to work as a store owner, and though he worked hard, the economy ruined his business. Next he tried his hand at tobacco farming, a task that required demanding physical labor and constant oversight. According to one historian:

> *Tobacco was produced on a fifteen-month cycle requiring performance of a sequence of steps at periodic intervals, each of which demanded painstaking care and judgment. About two weeks after Christmas, the tobacco seed was planted in specially prepared beds. In late March or April, when the planter judged the seedlings sufficiently large and hardy, they were replanted in the main fields. Throughout the summer the planter and his laborers weeded and "topped" the plants until, sometime in early fall, the plant was cut and the leaves moved to curing barns. After curing, the leaves were "stripped" and "stemmed," then "prized" into large wood hogsheads. Finally, sometime in early spring, the hogsheads were shipped (sometimes rolled) to market. Tobacco was hard*

> *on the land, for it utilized soil nutrients at a*
> *voracious rate, and new acreage had to be*
> *cleared every few years. Since each step in pro-*
> *duction was equally important there was no*
> *end of the cycle; planters were already working*
> *on the next crop as they prepared that of the*
> *previous season for shipment.*[420]

Unlike many of his fellow legislators who enjoyed an aristocratic upbringing, Henry learned as a young man the value and demands of hard work. "Sunburnt, sweaty, hard-handed," he was learning by experience to sympathize with the common worker whom one day he would rally to independence. As historian George Morgan has noted, "Much of the sound common-sense characteristic of Patrick Henry was in all likelihood developed under stress of hard work at Pine Slash. Much of his subsequent popularity with the plain people of Virginia was due to the fact that he was their spokesman, and he was their voice because he had learned to enter into their feelings. He had been one of them, and continued to be one of them."[421]

After three years of farming, Henry ceased to labor with his hands and began to labor with his mind. Although he was already a hard worker, the spur of necessity only served to quicken him: in a brief time he prepared for, and passed, the bar examination, and began to build a successful law practice. His success as a lawyer then opened the door to politics where he spent the majority of his years laboring for the welfare of his native Virginia. As a legislator and governor, Henry was known for his zeal and industry. The House Journals show that he was more than an armchair politician. In every session, he served on numerous committees and attended to the mundane details of drafting legislation. When George Mason first met Henry, he wrote home that Henry "was the most powerful speaker I ever heard..." However, "his eloquence is the smallest part of his merit. He is, in my opinion, the first man upon this continent, as well in abilities, as public virtues."[422]

As the wartime governor, the burden of work was so great that Henry groaned to his friend, R. H. Lee that he doubted if he would be able to hold up under the strain. "I am really so harassed by the great load of continental business thrown on me lately," he told Lee, "that I am ready to sink under my burden...For my strength will not suffice."[423] Of course, Henry maintained his strength, and continued to serve as governor (five times), a leading legislator, a practicing attorney, a land investor, a plantation owner, and father of fifteen surviving children.

In spite of the heavy work load that he carried throughout his life, Henry believed that work was not a curse but a positive good. During the Ratification Convention, for instance, he voiced his belief that if America were to be great, her citizens must be industrious. "The want of money is the source of all our misfortunes," he said, "and only hard work and frugality will remedy the problem. You will never pay your debts but by a radical change of domestic economy," not by a change of government. "At present you buy too much and work too little to pay for it. The evils that attend us lie in extravagance and want of industry, and can only be removed by assiduity and economy."[424]

Greatness–whether individual or national–is never the result of talent or natural resources alone. Henry knew this and was willing to pay the price that always accompanies any great accomplishment: hard work. And those who aspire to emulate his leadership abilities must do the same.

Tradition

> *I call upon every gentleman here to declare, whether the king of England had any subjects so attached to his family and government–so loyal as we were…We retained from our earliest infancy, the most sincere regard and reverence for the mother country. Our partiality extended to a predilection for her customs, habits, manners and laws.*[425]

A leader is a builder. Whether he is developing the character of his children or expanding the markets of his business, he is building for the future. But instead of discarding the contribution of previous generations, a wise leader will always employ the resources and tools provided by the past as he constructs the future. In this sense, every great leader will be a traditionalist, a conservative.

Surprising as it may sound, Patrick Henry was at heart a conservative, in spite of the fact that his ardent nature and bold speech earned him such labels as "radical" or "rebel," and that his early speeches were often met with shocked cries of "Treason!" His "radicalism," if it may be called that, "was radical only within the context of Virginia politics." Whereas Pendleton, Randolph, and others sought to maintain a long-standing working accommodation with royal authority, Henry pressed the Virginia leadership to take more decisive action against the increasing royal interference. Nevertheless, Henry's political stance throughout the growing crisis with Britain was not a rejection of the English Constitution per se, but rather a desire to see it "restored by purging it of corrupting influences."[426] The American "revolution," then was really a conservative movement aimed at preserving the existing social order from the external threat of British corruption.

If we take Russell Kirk's description of conservatism as our starting point,[427] it is clear that the "radical" Henry was a dyed-in-the-wool conservative. For instance, Henry believed in a transcendent moral order, which he referred to as "the law of nature." Being well acquainted with Vottel, Grotius, Montesquieu, and others, Henry accepted the notion that the law of nature and the law of God were essentially the same: the former recognized by reason and the latter perceived by faith. Henry's moral postulates were derived from the King James Version of the Bible and the Anglican catechism.

Second, Henry adhered to the conservative principle of "preservation"–that is, "of things established by immemorial usage."[428] Although Henry was willing to propose, on occasion, novel legislation, he had a great respect for the long-standing British Constitution, charters, and customs. More importantly, he had a profound respect for "the experience of the world" and thus constantly consulted history as a guide. When reading Henry's speeches, one is impressed with the large number of historical allusions. For instance, in his "Ratification" speech, Henry repeatedly appealed to British history, Swedish history, colonial history, and the history of other countries to defend his views.

Also, Henry was conservative in that he had a realistic view of human nature. As Kirk put it, "conservatives are chastened by their principle of imperfectability."[429] Henry believed that human nature was seriously flawed: it was fallen. And human depravity poses a very real threat to political liberty. "I dread the depravity of human nature," he told the Ratification Convention. "I will never depend on so slender a protector as the possibility of being represented by virtuous men."[430] Likewise, Henry's view of human nature led him to disavow any utopian social schemes. He did not believe in, nor attempt, simple and sweeping changes to society in order to usher in a humanist's paradise. He was a practical and prudent politician who had little faith in the theoretical psychology or abstract politics then seeping out of France. Thus, he criticized French scepticism and ultimately repudiated the French Revolution, which had as its object the destruction of everything that had gone before, whether sacred or profane. "The spirit it developed was that of indiscriminate warfare on the past." The American Revolution, on the other hand, was a conservative, and even religious, movement. "The whole movement" of the Revolution, one author has said, "had been eminently conservative and wise, following the suggestion of Bacon who says, 'It were good that men in their innovations, would follow the example of time, which indeed innovateth greatly, but quietly and by degrees.'"[431]

While Henry was a visionary and prophetic leader, he was rooted in what Kirk calls "the Great Tradition"–the classical and Christian intellectual heritage that formed the curriculum of the schools and undergirded the existing social order.[432] As a patriot, Henry's passion was preservation. He sought to protect the long-standing rights and liberties that he and his countrymen had enjoyed for decades–indeed, for centuries. Being rooted in the Great Tradition, Henry then hoped to build a future reflecting that tradition. As a wise leader, he was a builder erecting his edifice on the foundation of the Great Tradition. And every sound leader-builder must do the same, or he will build on sinking sand.

CHRISTIANITY

*It cannot be emphasized too strongly or too often
that this great nation was founded, not by religion-
ists, but by Christians; not on religions, but on the
gospel of Jesus Christ. For this very reason peoples of
other faiths have been afforded asylum, prosperity,
and freedom of worship here.*[433]

The Christianity of Patrick Henry was more than the
pocketful of precepts he learned from his Anglican
uncle. It was a comprehensive world-view that shaped his perspective on every area of his life, including his politics. The
modern notion that "religion and politics don't mix" was an
idea completely foreign to Henry and many of his co-patriots.
On the contrary, their religion–the Christianity of the Bible–
was the foundation of their political and social philosophy.
When one looks at the letters, speeches, and public papers
produced by the Founding Fathers, the influence of Biblical
Christianity is undeniable. For instance, a recent study of their
political writings has demonstrated that the "source most
often cited by the Founding Fathers was the Bible…"[434]

This fact should not surprise us when we recall that North America was originally colonized by Christian peoples. For instance, Jamestown was settled by Anglican adventurers, and thirty years later the Pilgrims landed at Plymouth. In 1630, the Puritans began to build Boston and eventually populated most of New England. Elsewhere, Lord Baltimore's Catholics settled in Maryland in 1634, the Quakers established themselves in Pennsylvania and New Jersey in 1682, and thousands of Scots-Calvinists poured into the colonies in the early 1700's–one of whom was Patrick Henry's father.[435]

Although there was a multitude of sects in colonial America, they all agreed "concerning the duties of men to one another," and all preached the same morality in the name of God.[436] One reason for their unanimity of world-view was that, except for the Catholics in Maryland, all the Christian groups in America were the offspring of the Reformation. Thus, the majority of colonial Americans came from Calvinist backgrounds. As the Reformed scholar Lorraine Boettner has noted:

> It is estimated that of the 3,000,000 Americans
> at the time of the American Revolution,
> 900,000 were of Scotch or Scotch-Irish origin,
> 600,000 were Puritan English, and 400,000
> were German or Dutch Reformed. In addition
> to this the Episcopalians had a Calvinistic con-
> fession in their Thirty-nine Articles; and many
> French Huguenots also had come to this west-
> ern world. Thus we see that about two-thirds of
> the colonial population had been trained in the
> school of Calvin.[437]

Henry was himself a direct spiritual descendant of Calvin. On his father's side, he inherited the more moderate Calvinist theology encapsulated in the Thirty-nine Articles, and on his mother's side he was taught the more pure form of Calvinism espoused by American Presbyterians. From ages eleven to twenty-three, he regularly heard the Calvinistic sermons that issued forth from the pulpit of Samuel Davies, the greatest Presbyterian of his day.

What did Henry learn from Calvin that shaped his politics–indeed, his entire world-view? First and foremost among Calvinist doctrines is the sovereignty of God, a fact that Henry readily and publicly acknowledged. In his long struggle against British tyranny, Henry believed that God governed in the affairs of men and would intervene on the behalf of the Colonies. Because "God presides over the destinies of nations," Henry knew that the American cause, if just, would ultimately triumph. God's Providence, which is merely another name for his sovereignty, was the foundation of Henry's political courage.

In Calvin's theology, the corollary to God's sovereignty is man's depravity, a fact that Henry thought was self-evident. As a result, he had a great distrust of concentrating political power in the hands of "virtuous" leaders. "I dread the depravity of human nature," he warned the Virginia Ratification Convention, and had no faith in "being represented by virtuous men."[438] Therefore, he advocated not only a federal governmental system with internal checks and balances, but also a written Bill of Rights and constitutional provisions that recognized the authority of state governments. Since rulers are themselves sinners, they must be effectively restrained by checks and balances, and be directly accountable to their constituents. Accordingly, Henry supported limited government with clearly delegated powers.

Henry also believed that the moral law of the Bible was absolute and unchanging. "The eternal difference between right and wrong does not fluctuate," he once thundered. "It is immutable."[439] As a result, Henry held that the morality of the Bible was essential to a thriving republicanism; therefore, he saw no contradiction between advocating religious toleration while at the same time pressing for a general assessment to support Christian ministers and teachers. Morality matters. And Henry held that the eternal law reflected in nature and written in the Bible was the surest foundation of social and political life.

Moreover, since the law of God is eternal and immutable, the civil ruler does not have the authority to violate this law. Civil magistrates who presume to ignore or contradict God's law or the law of nature–for they are essentially the same–are acting without legitimate authority, and according to Henry, should be resisted. The "justness of revolution," as it has been called, was a political doctrine developed by Calvinist theologians and advocated by Henry.[440]

Calvinist theorists also took the covenant concept and applied it to civil government. The practical application was that although rulers derive their authority from God (Romans 13), that authority is mediated through the people who form a covenant or compact with the ruler. Thus, from a practical point of view, "power is vested in, and consequently derived from the people," and magistrates are not lords, but servants of the people.[441]

According to historian Rhys Isaac, Henry's overriding passion was for "a world reshaped in a truly moral order."[442] And that moral order, both personal and political, was derived from the Bible and mediated to Henry through the teachings of Calvinism. The revolutionary principles of republicanism, liberty, and self-government, inherent in Calvinism, were brought to America when the first settlers arrived from Europe. Thus, the German historian Ranke could say that "John Calvin is the virtual founder of America."[443] But if

Calvin is the virtual founder, Henry was the actual founder. For it was his faith, courage, and passion that led the colonies to defend Calvin's principles against tyranny and establish America as an independent republic.

Patriotism

As individuals professing a holy religion, it is our
bounden duty to forgive injuries done us as individ-
uals. But when to the character of Christian you add
the character of patriot, you are in a different situa-
tion. If your enemy smite one cheek, turn the other
to him. But you must stop there. You must not apply
this to your country.[444]

*P*atrick Henry will be forever remembered in the
annals of American history as one of our bravest
and most passionate patriots. Yet while being lauded as a
patriot, the very notion of patriotism is seldom clearly
explained. Does patriotism simply mean "love for my country" just because it is "mine"? Or is patriotism a nobler virtue?
Moreover, where does patriotism fit in our hierarchy of values? Are love of God and love of country compatible? Can a
political leader be both a good Christian and a true patriot?

Properly understood, patriotism is more than pride in
one's country or state. Rather, it entails love for one's ancestry,
culture, or homeland. Derived from the Greek *patrios* ("of

one's fathers") or *patris* ("one's fatherland") the *Oxford English Dictionary* defines a patriot as "one who disinterestedly or self-sacrificingly exerts himself to promote the well-being of "his country." A patriot is "one who maintains and defends his country's freedom or rights."

While we tend to think of a patriot as a person who puts his country first in opposition to another country, originally the term meant one who supported the rights of "country" or "land" against the King and his court. In other words, a patriot stood for the rights of local self-government and was opposed to tyrannical rule–even by his own King. Thus, true patriotism is the impulse to defend one's land, country, or way of life against unjust governmental oppression.

This understanding of patriotism was exemplified by Henry and America's founding fathers. To a man, the founders admired and imitated British culture; therefore, American society and government were intentionally patterned after the British model.[445] Even as political tensions with Britain increased during the critical years of 1765-1776, loyalty to the Crown was a virtue much insisted on by American colonial leaders. Though they tried to reconcile their differences with Great Britain, the breach between colonies and Crown only widened, and the founders were eventually forced to break away from their fatherland.

The Declaration of Independence was then penned as a statement to the world of the colonies' reasons for being so bold to separate from England. Not only did the Declaration catalog the offenses of King George, but it also claimed that the American colonies were defending "the laws of nature and of nature's God." That eight word phrase–"the laws of nature and of nature's God"–encapsulated the principle upon which the Founders stood.

According to Blackstone's *Commentaries on the Law*, the laws of nature were nothing less than the will of God for man as revealed to reason. However, because man's reason is fallible and does not always perceive this law, God reiterated His law in the Holy Scriptures. Blackstone explained it like this:

> *And if our reason were always…clear and perfect…the task would be pleasant and easy; we should need no other guide but this [law of nature]. But every man now finds the contrary in his own experience; that his reason is corrupt, and his understanding full of ignorance and error. This has given manifold occasion for the benign interposition of divine providence; which…hath been pleased…to discover [reveal] and enforce its laws by an immediate and direct revelation. The doctrines thus delivered we call the revealed or divine law, and they are to be found only in the holy scriptures.*[446]

Blackstone then concluded his discussion on the law of nature by saying that "Upon these two foundations, the law of nature and the law of revelation, depend all human laws: that is to say, no human laws should be suffered to contradict these."[447]

As an American patriot, Henry stood in the long tradition of Christian political theory, as exemplified by Blackstone, Vattel, and others, that sanctioned the right to resist unjust human laws. While it was recognized that the Scriptures placed great emphasis on due submission to civil authorities,[448] other scriptural passages approved resistance to ungodly authority. For instance, when the apostles were commanded by the Sanhedrin (which was both a religious and civil tribunal) to cease preaching the gospel, the apostle Peter boldly asserted: "We ought to obey God rather than men."[449]

Thus, the Founding Fathers, contrary to the modern notion of revolution, were not rebelling against law and order. They were not anarchists or revolutionaries. Rather, they were attempting to uphold the law of God against the unjust and oppressive laws of men. They had a profound respect for the "laws of nature and of nature's God." So instead of being "rebels without a cause" they were "patriots under the law"– the law of Almighty God.

It is noteworthy that Henry, who is now recognized as a great patriot, stood on higher ground than a simple or selfish love for his own country. He stood on the pinnacle of the principles that are reflected in God's Word and transcend loyalty to one's own country. Real patriotism, then, is not simply the exaltation of one's country over someone else's simply because it is "mine." Rather, it is the courage to stand on God's Word in the face of unjust human authority, whether in one's own country or abroad. Like Henry, it means appealing to the God of Heaven for justice on earth. And most importantly, it means that we live out our lives, even in the political realm, with our primary allegiance to God. Those who live in this manner, like Henry, are the real patriots in the eyes of God.

Rest

I live much retired amidst a multiplicity of blessings from that Gracious Ruler of all things.[450]

*P*atrick Henry's Christian world-view shaped his attitude toward both work and rest. He believed that honest labor was a divine calling and that neither he nor anyone else could expect an easy solution to life's demands. Both personal and social success had to be the result of old-fashioned industry. Yet he also appreciated the value of rest. Indeed, just as he had learned from the Bible that man was created to work, he learned that man was commanded to rest. The Genesis account of man's creation, a passage that he undoubtedly knew well, teaches us that man's first day of existence was a day of rest, or a Sabbath. What does this tell us? At least this much: while work is important, it is not our highest purpose in life. Rather, our highest duty as well as our greatest joy is to delight in our Creator and his creation.

Henry never had a problem relaxing. Unlike some leaders who seem obsessed with their work, much to the detriment of their family, Henry learned as a young boy the pleasures of God's creation as he roamed the Virginia woods. Moreover, his mother, a devout Christian, regularly took him to church on Sundays and taught him the importance of the Sabbath. According to the Reverend Charles Dresser, Henry's widow informed him that her husband used to receive "the communion as often as an opportunity was offered, and on such occasions, always fasted until after he had communicated, and spent the day in the greatest retirement. This he did both while governor and afterward."[451]

After leaving politics, Henry continued to work as a lawyer, land speculator, and plantation owner; yet he also continued to observe the Sabbath with his family. These occasions were not spent in somber idleness, however, but in active rejoicing. They were times of refreshment and recreation–times of joyous celebration. In the evening, Henry would read sermons and Scripture to his family, and then they would sing sacred music together. At this time in his life he also made it a habit to spend "one hour every day…in private devotion," a practice that provided spiritual refreshment and deep rest.[452]

Henry was not a man of incessant activity. His energy was more like the force of a volcano that releases great power after internal pressure builds up. When circumstances demanded it, Henry could exhibit tremendous energy and strength, but it seems that his natural tendency was to take a more relaxed approach to life. When he finally retired to Red Hill, he found no greater pleasure than simply enjoying God's handiwork in what he called "the garden-spot" of Virginia. He would often sit under the trees that shaded his lawn "with his chair leaning against one of the trunks, and a can of cool spring water by his side, from which he took frequent draughts."[453] The idyllic serenity of Henry's retirement days is aptly drawn by his great granddaughter, Elizabeth Henry

Lyons. "Towards the close of the day, in summer-time," she wrote, "he took the breeze on the lawn. Around him played his children, to whom he was greatly attached, and whom he treated as companions and friends. He was very fond of music, and oftentimes the sweet notes of his flute or violin, echoing on the evening air, broke the stillness of the valley."[454]

In his retirement, Henry mastered the art of holy leisure. He could rest because he had paid his debt to society and enjoyed the fellowship of his family. Moreover, he was not, as Jefferson had said, an "ambitious" man. Although Henry was offered numerous prestigious and powerful federal posts, he declined them all. He was content with the contribution he had already made to the American cause; and being a humble man, he left his future reputation in the hands of historians. Most importantly, Henry could truly rest because he had made his peace with God. Thus, his retirement was a joyous preparation for his coming eternal rest.

Death

Oh, how wretched should I be at this moment, if I had not made my peace with God.[455]

*H*enry was no stranger to death. Living in an age unsustained by modern medicine and scientific sanitation, he buried both his parents, his brother, William, his brother-in-law, Colonel Christian, his beloved first wife, and four of his own children. He literally walked in the shadow of death, the War having soaked the Virginia countryside with patriotic blood, leaving many a widow and orphan in its wake.

Since Henry was a man of profound religious conviction who acknowledged the veracity of the Scriptures, he consequently accepted the Christian view of death and the after-life. He therefore readily confessed his own mortality: "I am but a poor worm of the dust," he told a Baptist minister, "as fleeting and insubstantial as the shadow of the cloud that flies over yon fields."[456] Viewing life from the vantage of the grave, Henry was mindful of his duty to provide an inheritance for his children. In the last years of his life he devoted himself to clearing his estate of debt and providing equitable provisions for his wife and children.

Knowing that this life was but a prelude to life everlasting, Henry did not expect to find unalloyed joy in this vale of tears. "This world," he once told his daughter Betsy, "is not made for complete happiness."[457] Rather, Henry looked forward to a better world in heaven where there are no more tears or sorrow. Writing to his sister, Anne, shortly after she lost her husband, Henry reminded her to turn her eyes to heaven where her husband had gone. And if perchance Henry and Anne did not see each other again in this world, he hoped to be reunited with her some day in heaven–"oh, may we meet in that heaven to which the merits of Jesus will carry those who love and serve him."[458] Henry knew, as did his friends, that his own days were numbered. Around the time that Anne lost her husband, one of Henry's legal associates, Richard Venable, noted in his diary that Henry would possibly soon depart the world. "His head now blossoms for the grave," wrote Venable, "his body bends to mingle with its kindred dust…"[459]

Henry lived for several more years, but ill health wasted his strength and his body. After the exhausting trip to Charlotte Courthouse in 1799 to deliver his final prophetic and patriotic warning to his countrymen, he was confined to his chamber in preparation for death. His grandson, Patrick Henry Fontaine, who was present during Henry's final moments, gives a graphic yet touching account of Henry's Christian confidence in the face of his own death.

> *On June 6, all other remedies having failed Dr. Cabell proceeded to administer to him a dose of liquid mercury. Taking the vial in his hand, and looking at it for a moment, the dying man*

said: "I suppose, doctor, this is your last resort."
The doctor replied: "I am sorry to say, governor,
that it is. Acute inflammation of the intestines
has already taken place; and unless it is
removed mortification will ensue, if it has not
already commenced, which I fear." "What will
be the effect of his medicine?" said the old man.
"It will give you immediate relief, or–" the
kind-hearted doctor could not finish the sentence. His patient took up the word: "You mean,
doctor, that it will give relief or will prove fatal
immediately?" The doctor answered: "You can
only live a very short time without it, and it
may possibly relieve you." Then Patrick Henry
said, "Excuse me, doctor, for a few minutes;"
and drawing over his eyes a silken cap which
he usually wore, and still holding the vial in
his hand, he prayed, in clear words, a simple
child-like prayer for his family, for his country,
and for his own soul then in the presence of
death. Afterward, in perfect calmness, he swal-
lowed the medicine. Meanwhile Dr. Cabell, who
greatly loved him, went out upon the lawn, and
in his grief threw himself down upon the earth
under one of the trees weeping bitterly. Soon,
when he had sufficiently mastered himself, the
doctor came back to his patient, whom he
found calmly watching the congealing of the
blood under his fingernails, and speaking
words of love and peace to his family, who
were weeping around his chair. Among other
things, he told them that he was thankful for
that goodness of God, which, having blessed

*him all his life, was then permitting him to die
without any pain. Finally, fixing his eyes with
much tenderness on his dear friend, Dr. Cabell,
with whom he had formerly held many arguments respecting the Christian religion, he
asked the doctor to observe how great a reality
and benefit that religion was to a man about
to die. And after Patrick Henry had spoken to
his beloved physician those few words in praise
of something which, having never failed him in
all his life before, did not then fail him in his
very last need of it, he continued to breath very
softly for some moments; after which they who
were looking upon him, saw that his life had
departed.*[460]

Patrick Henry died with the full conviction that the religion of Christ was the only hope for his country, his family,
and his own soul.

PART III:
THE LEGACY OF PATRICK HENRY

✧   ✧   ✧

The voice of tradition, I trust, will inform posterity of our struggles for freedom: if our descendants be worthy the name of Americans, they will preserve and hand down to their latest posterity, the transactions of the present times; and though, I confess, my exclamations are not worthy the hearing, they will see that I have done my utmost to preserve their liberty![461]

It is impiously irritating the avenging hand of heaven, when a people who are in the full enjoyment of freedom, launch out into the wide ocean of human affairs, and desert those maxims which alone can preserve liberty![462]

THE GREAT ADVERSARY

*A*t the time of his death, Henry was the most famous figure–after George Washington–of the Revolutionary period; thus it is not surprising that when news of his decease spread, it was met with a mixture of distress and dismay. General Henry Lee, who was dining with some friends when the sad report arrived, asked for a piece of paper, and in a few moments wrote a striking, Shakespearean eulogy to Henry.

> *Hung be the heavens with black,*
> > *yield day to night!*
> *Comets, importing change of times and states,*
> *Brandish your crystal tresses in the sky,*
> *And with them scourge the bad revolting stars,*
> *That have consented unto Henry's death!*[463]

When word reached John Marshal on June 12, 1799, he lamented that "Virginia has sustained a very heavy loss, which all good men will long deplore…"[464]

Yet "all good men" did not equally deplore Henry's departure. In fact, some of his political opponents undoubtedly secretly rejoiced that their "great adversary" was no longer alive to battle them in the legislature. Indeed, when the Virginia Assembly convened in its next session, a resolution was put forward for the execution of a marble bust in tribute of Henry, which was to be placed in the hall of the House of Delegates. Considering Henry's many patriotic contributions to American independence, the vote should have been an unanimous "Aye!" Yet the bitter acrimony of party politics eclipsed Henry's honor: the Republican majority defeated the measure. Thus the man to whom "the proudest monuments of national gratitude" should have been erected, was denied, at least for a time, the honor of his indebted countrymen.[465]

Thus spirit of ingratitude that animated the newly-formed Republican party had been festering a decade earlier when Henry opposed the federal Constitution. It was then that Madison dubbed him "the great adversary" who, he feared, would render the outcome of the ratification debate "precarious."[466] Ironically that appellation–"the great adversary"–was a fitting description of Henry's entire political career. He was certainly the great adversary of British tyranny against the colonies; and even within Virginia he was the great adversary against religious persecution. Perhaps Madison should not have been surprised then that Henry would once again appear as "the great adversary" to a scheme that forebode the loss of state sovereignty and personal liberty. Yet, by opposing the Constitution, Henry has suffered in the estimation of many, both past and present. Those who have learned to venerate the construction of the Constitution as a "miracle at Philadelphia" and who are not familiar with the arguments he advanced in its opposition, fail to appreciate that without his persistent protests and unflinching efforts, the United States

Bill of Rights might never have been attached to the Constitution. Moreover, from an historical vantage point, it appears that Henry stood against the grain of our nation's subsequent development; thus, he could be viewed as "a loser" in history. But Henry's caveats at the Ratification Convention have, more than not, proven prophetic; and his critique of the Constitution has made a lasting contribution to America's civil freedom and political discourse.[467]

It was Madison's Republican cohort, Thomas Jefferson, however, who did most to tarnish Henry's fame and obscure his place in history. Upon the request of William Wirt, who was gathering information for the first biography of Henry, Jefferson wrote to him reminiscences that were tainted by both political and personal animosity. According to Jefferson, Henry's legal knowledge "was not worth a copper." Worse still, Jefferson presumed to judge Henry's heart: he was "avaricious and rotten hearted," spewed Jefferson. "His two great passions were love of money and of fame."[468] Over time, these and other dark pictures of Henry found their way into several books on the revolutionary period. Jefferson's opinion, however, has never been independently corroborated, and his hostility toward Henry was probably the result of Henry's support, in 1781, of an inquiry into Jefferson's conduct as governor during the British invasion. From that time forward, Jefferson's private letters show a dislike and distrust of Henry's character and politics.[469]

Moreover, when Henry opposed Jefferson's Kentucky and Virginia Resolutions, he was labeled by Jefferson as "the great apostate" who betrayed the Anti-Federalist position. Henry was merely being consistent, however, for he had warned the Ratification Convention that, should they adopt the Constitution, their state sovereignty would be lost forever. Once the Constitution was ratified, the respective states could no longer judge the validity of federal laws; and should they believe the federal government was acting contrary to the constitution and the principles of liberty, their only recourse was "to overthrow the government."[470] It was the Republican leaders, Madison chief among them, who had altered their earlier support for the Constitution.

In spite of the party strife that then troubled the American political scene, the "good men" of Virginia who stood above bitter partisanship eventually came to remember their "favorite son." Twenty years after his death, Henry's marble bust was belatedly placed in the Virginia House. Then, in 1858, when proud Virginians unveiled Thomas Crawford's statue of Washington on his steed, he was flanked by none other than Thomas Jefferson and Patrick Henry, a fitting testimony to Henry's achievements and a tacit reproof of Jefferson's slanders. The God of history has a way of vindicating the memory of the righteous. And Henry, who cared little for fame, will always be remembered as a noble patriot because he was "the great adversary" of injustice and oppression both at home and abroad.

THE LEGACY OF LIBERTY

*H*enry's overriding passion as a statesman and patriot was liberty. It was the motive for all his political acts, and the keynote of all his patriotic utterances. "The time has been when every pulse of my heart beat for American liberty," he told the Ratification delegates, "and which, I believe, had a counterpart in the breast of every true American." Liberty is not merely one object of good government, argued Henry, it is the government's ultimate end. "The great and direct end of government is liberty. Secure our liberty and privileges, and the end of government is answered."[471] Life without liberty is not worth living, thought Henry. Thus, the choice of any noble man must be "liberty or death"–there is no third alternative.

Accordingly, it was Henry's passion for liberty that inspired him to "venture alone and unassisted" in proposing his famous Stamp Act Resolutions; that inflamed him to deliver his moving "liberty or death" speech; that emboldened him to take up arms against Lord Dunmore in the first overt act of war in Virginia; and that sustained him as a burdened wartime leader. Indeed, it was Henry's love for liberty that moved him, near the end of his political career, to hazard his reputation by opposing the newly-proposed Constitution. "The thing I have at heart," he confided in the Convention, "is American liberty."

Henry was equally the champion of religious liberty, which he considered just as important as civil or political liberty. In fact, the two are twin freedoms, and Henry was, throughout his career, a stalwart defender of persecuted Christians. For instance, in the late 1760's, another revival, not unlike the previous Presbyterian one, was sweeping across Virginia. Only this time the main "dissidents" were Baptists and Quakers. Of the two groups, the Baptists were the more vocal, with their itinerant preachers spreading the gospel home to home and in larger outdoor gatherings. Not always respectful of the established clergy, the Baptist preachers further alarmed the established "gentry" by drawing swelling crowds of "commoners" and even allowing slaves into their communion. The "specter of peasant uprisings and religious revolt" loomed before the minds of those "gentlemen" affiliated with the established church.[472]

As a result, a general persecution spread throughout twenty-eight counties. Itinerants were either jailed by the authorities, or abused by the public with legal impunity. In June 1768, the sheriff of Spotsylvania jailed four preachers for no fewer than forty days. In the neighboring county of Culpepper, John Ireland, an itinerant preacher who had been jailed there, tried to preach to a crowd outside his cell window. As he did so, "ruffians" rode up "at a gallop" and violently attacked the crowd, with the "poor Negroes" being stripped and beaten.[473]

Ever the friend of freedom, Henry responded to the itinerant preachers' appeals for help. On one occasion, he rode fifty miles out of his way to defend–free of charge–the jailed itinerants in Spotsylvania. Arriving on the day of trial, he entered the courtroom just as the charge of "disturbing the peace" was being read aloud. He asked to see the indictment. Then, looking toward the bench, he said: "Did I hear it distinctly, or was it a mistake of my own?" he queried. "Did I hear an expression, as of a *crime*, that these men whom your worships are about to try for misdemeanor, are charged with,–with–*what?*, preaching the Gospel of the Son of God?!"

Then, after a long pause, Henry held the indictment papers high in the air, slowly waving them three times above his head. Then, with his face and arms raised toward heaven, as if in reverential supplication, Henry bellowed, "Great God!" and again "Great God!" And once more, with the force of mixed disbelief and sarcasm: "Preaching the Gospel of the Son of God–Great God!" The prosecution was shamed to silence, and the case dropped.[474]

In the legislature, Henry was no less in favor of toleration. He supported the exemption from military service for Quakers, and the right of Virginia dissidents to "enjoy the full and free exercise of their religion without molestation or danger of incurring any penalty whatsoever."[475]

On the question of slavery, Henry and other founding fathers have been unjustly charged with duplicity. But this is to misunderstand both the men and the times in which they lived. The fact is, the Virginia Assembly of February, 1772, strongly addressed the King in protest against the slave trade. Moreover, Henry privately lamented that slavery was a clear violation of Biblical morality and civilized society. In response to a book on the slave trade sent to him by Robert Pheasants, a wealthy Quaker planter, Henry wrote the following:

> *Dear Sir: I take this opportunity to acknowl-*
> *edge the receipt of Anthony Benezet's book*

*against the slave trade. I thank you for it. It is
not a little surprising that the professors of
Christianity whose chief excellence consists in
softening the human heart, and in cherishing
and improving its finer feelings, should encourage a practice so totally repugnant to the first
impressions of right and wrong. What adds to
the wonder is that this abominable practice has
been introduced in the most enlightened
ages... Is it not amazing, that at a time, when
the rights of humanity are defined and understood with precision, in a country, above all
others, fond of liberty, that in such an age and
in such a country, we find men professing a
religion the most humane, mild, gentle and
generous, adopting a principle as repugnant to
humanity, as it is inconsistent with the [B]ible,
and destructive to liberty? Every thinking, honest man rejects it in speculation, how few in
practice from conscientious motives!*[476]

Henry then went on to rebuke his own practice of holding slaves. "Would anyone believe I am the master of slaves
of my own purchase!...I will not, I cannot justify it." Yet Henry
hoped that an opportunity would be offered "to abolish this
lamentable evil." In the meantime, however, his duty was to
"improve it" and "treat the unhappy victims with lenity." This
was the least that a Christian ought to do in showing "the
purity of our religion" which "is at variance with that law
which warrants slavery."[477]

Why then, did he himself own slaves? Much for the same
reason that a modern American drives an automobile to work
every day while lamenting pollution or the depletion of natural

resources: it is seen as an unhappy yet inevitable fact of life. Thus it was with slavery. It was not so much hypocrisy, but a perceived necessity, which caused Henry and his contemporaries to contradict their principles by their practice. For instance, Jefferson, in his original draft of the *Declaration of Independence*, had included a denunciation of slavery and the slave trade, even though he was a slaveholder himself. The reference was deleted, however, in deference to the Southern delegates in whose states slavery "seemed essential to the economy."[478] Moreover, as McDonald has pointed out, American slavery was "a comparatively mild institution" when contrasted with European "serfdom." "Travelers to colonial Virginia from the North and from Europe, expecting to see horrors, repeatedly reported that they saw none and that slaves appeared to live easy and easygoing lives. Americans who had traveled in Europe knew that 'free' European peasants suffered considerably greater oppression and misery than did American bondsmen."[479] This fact made it easier for the Founders to overlook the inherent contradiction between their republican professions and their social customs.

Henry had a keen sense of popular sentiments; and he knew that the time was not yet ripe for emancipation. To advocate emancipation contrary to the will of his constituents, would have been violation of republicanism or representative government. He did hope and believe, however, that a day would soon come when this "lamentable evil" would be abolished.

On the whole, Henry held a consistent position on liberty. He championed the freedom of the colonies from oppression, defended the freedom of dissent against persecution, and acknowledged the violation of freedom inherent in chattel slavery. And to him, more than any other colonial leader, we are indebted for the many civil and religious liberties we now take for granted. He was the recognized leader in Virginia, and it was that state which had the predominant influence on the direction of the colonies. "After all," confessed Jefferson, "it must be allowed that he was our leader in the measures of the Revolution in Virginia, and in that respect more is due to him than to any other person." It was owing to Henry's love of liberty and political courage that the American Revolution "took place at the time it did," said Judge Roane.[480] And the outcome of the Revolution affected not only the rights of Americans but also the liberties of mankind. By halting British tyranny in the colonies, and establishing republicanism in the United States, free institutions were advanced throughout the entire western world. Thus, Fox was not overstating the case when he said on the floor of Parliament that, "The resistance of the Americans to the oppressions of the mother country has undoubtedly preserved the liberties of mankind."[481]

Liberty, then, was not only Henry's passion, it was also his legacy. And the legacy is still unfolding. As his biographer, William Wirt Henry, has rightly claimed, "The beneficent influence of the American Revolution, therefore, on the governments of the world is a thing as yet incalculable."[482] Thanks to Henry's wise and courageous leadership, the legacy of liberty lives on.

"IMITATE MY HENRY"

The legacy of Patrick Henry lives on not only in his monumental achievement of American independence and western liberty, but also in the example he set for future generations of leaders. In fact, his legacy of liberty is inseparable from his legacy of character. As the Scripture says, a tree shall be known by its fruit. What, then, can one generation of aspiring leaders learn from the life and character of Patrick Henry? What were the fundamental characteristics of his leadership?

First, Henry was a man of persistence. The advantages he received in life were a godly family and a native genius. The rest was up to him. His destiny, like that of every leader, was in his hands. So, Henry learned the hard way that life is neither fair nor easy, and that the path to success and greatness was perseverance. He faced many obstacles as a young man, and might have lived and died in obscurity had he not determined to succeed. When chastened by adversity, he matured; and when humbled by failure, he endured. When one door of opportunity closed, he knocked on another–and then another–until one opened. When death robbed him of his first love, he never gave in to sullenness, and when his political opponents desecrated his character, he never succumbed to bitterness. Throughout his sixty-three years, he faced both personal trials and political turmoil with a persistent faith and determination.

Secondly, Henry was a man of passion. He truly believed in the principles he advanced in public. Unlike modern political profiteers and bureaucratic hirelings, Henry did not utter sweet slogans in order to secure a vote. His integrity would not permit such prostitution. Rather, he passionately advocated measures that he sincerely held to be in the best interest of his country. While some might differ with his policies, none debated his sincerity. He spoke and acted from the heart, and by doing so, he moved the hearts of others. His flaming oratory spread fire throughout the colonies because it erupted from a burning passion. Men were overawed by his oratory, not because of its nice rhetorical devices, but because it was a torrent of truth. It was honest conviction fired from the cannon of a courageous spirit.

Thirdly, Henry was a man of perception. His political sagacity was such that he foresaw the coming War of Independence long before his confused colleagues. Thus, his vision alerted him to the approaching danger and placed him in the position to be a watchman who issued monitory warnings to his slumbering brethren. Due to his continual caveats, both in the Continental Congress and in the Virginia Convention, the colonies awoke from their dream of reconciliation with Britain and escaped the chains of tyranny. Moreover, Henry understood the actual workings of the Constitution and foresaw its dangers more than any other man in Virginia. His predictions of federal abuse have, to a surprising degree, come true. Thus, his critique of the Constitution, a stance that has lowered his reputation in the eyes of many historians, was evidence of his almost prophetic perception. Yet, his foresight was built on his insight. And Henry had an astounding knowledge of the human heart. "Study men," was one of his mottoes, and by mastering this study, he became a master of multitudes.

Fourthly, Henry was a man of patriotism. Yes, he loved his native Virginia, and even the united colonies; but his patriotism was rooted in his love for liberty first. For Henry, patriotism was more than a narrow self-interest, it was a principled position rooted in the immutable laws of nature and God. To be a patriot meant standing on the firm foundation of God's justice in the face of oppression, injustice, and obloquy. A patriot was one who stood with his country because his country stood for right. But should his country turn toward the wrong, as did King George in his policy toward the colonies, then a patriot must stand against his country. A true patriot as well as a genuine leader must always take the higher ground of God's law when confronted with the evils of man's law.

Lastly, Henry was a man of piety. His Christian faith was the hidden well-spring that nourished his "many sublime virtues." It sustained him during adversity, comforted him during loss, and energized him during conflict. It determined his presuppositions, shaped his character, and governed his politics. In a word, Henry's entire career is inexplicable apart from his Christian faith–secular historians notwithstanding.[483] When Henry marshaled Virginians to prepare for war, he did so by reminding them that there was a just God in heaven who, through his Providence, would intervene on their behalf. Confident that God was still the friend of the oppressed–the same God who interposed on behalf of the Israelites and made a way for them through the Red Sea–Henry bravely marched the Hanover militia against Lord Dunmore. Henry was confident that God was on his side, because Henry was defending the higher law of God. His long and arduous contest for liberty was not a struggle for "liberation" from law but a quest for moral order under the laws of God and nature. His view of liberty–that "jewel" he strove to protect–was rooted in his Christian world-view. Government is not the enemy, for it is ordained of God. The enemy to freedom is tyrannical government that presumes to take the place of God. And the only God to which Henry would bow was the God of the Bible. His patriotic valor was an expression of his religious faith, and his defiance toward man was an act of submission to God. Therefore, Henry continues to serve succeeding generations of leaders as a model of Christian patriotism, and uncompromising statesmanship.

ℐ   ℐ   ℐ

On June 14, 1799, the *Virginia Gazette* printed Patrick Henry's obituary notice,[484] an enduring testimony to his character and an inspiring and relevant challenge to our own generation of leaders.

> *Mourn, Virginia, mourn! Your Henry is gone! Ye*
> *   friends to liberty in every clime, drop a tear.*
> *No more will his social feelings spread delight*
> *   through his happy house.*
> *No more will his edifying example dictate to his*
> *   numerous offspring the sweetness of virtue,*
> *   and the majesty of patriotism.*
> *No more will his sage advice, guided by zeal for the*
> *   common happiness, impart light and utility to*
> *   his caressing neighbors.*

No more will he illuminate the public councils
with sentiments drawn from the cabinet of his
own mind, ever directed to his country's good,
and clothed in eloquence sublime, delightful,
and commanding.
Farewell, first-rate patriot, farewell!
As long as our rivers flow, or mountains stand–so
long will your excellence and worth be the
theme of homage and endearment, and
Virginia, bearing in mind her loss, will say to
rising generations,
imitate my Henry.

THE LESSONS OF LEADERSHIP

- A leader is indebted to the legacy of his parents.
- Providence chooses the leader who has prepared to be chosen.
- Great leadership is never the product of natural gifts alone.
- The best leaders always educate themselves.
- A leader knows that adversity is the handmaiden to maturity; therefore, he will not shrink from difficulties.
- The unseen source of a leader's courage is faith in God and His justice.
- A leader acts courageously because God governs providentially.
- Conviction is worthless unless converted into conduct.
- Humility is essential to leadership because it makes a leader a servant.
- A leader knows that criticism is inevitable, and thus will not allow himself to be poisoned by bitterness.
- All great leaders rule by the heart.
- A concern for people is the ultimate test of true leadership.
- The highest form of leadership is based on the bedrock of religious conviction.
- A leader's source of duty will move him to lay aside personal comfort for the interest of others.
- A man who cannot rule his family cannot govern his country.
- The home is the testing ground for all sound leadership.
- A leader's vision is rooted in his knowledge of the past.
- A leader faces the future with a sober confidence.

- Leadership requires the courage to face the truth, even if painful.
- The difference between vision and fanaticism is realism.
- Every great leader fails; no great leader accepts failure as final.
- A leader is a guardian of his followers.
- Inspiring oratory is the result of courageous conviction.
- The character of a leader is revealed by the manner in which he handles success and power.
- A healthy sense of humor reflects a leader's insight, humility, and sense of balance.
- A charlatan loves humanity; a leader loves people.
- A leader knows that hard work is a calling, not a curse, and the only sure path to greatness.
- Patriotic leadership means standing on divine principle in the face of human injustice.
- Every great leader will be a conservative who builds the future on the tried foundation of the past.
- A leader must be active but not driven. He knows the value of rest.
- A leader of men must be a reader of men.
- A leader's courage is most clearly seen in how he faces death.

Bibliography

On Patrick Henry

Arnold, S. G. *The Life of Patrick Henry of Virginia.* New York: Hurst & Company Publishers, 1845.

Beem, Richard. *Patrick Henry: A Biography.* New York: McGraw Hill, 1974.

Bennett, Michael Jesse. *Patrick Henry's Comment on Life, Liberty and the Pursuit of Happiness.* Brookneal, VA: Patrick Henry Memorial Foundation, 1991.

Bradford, M.E. *The Trumpet Voice of Freedom: Patrick Henry of Virginia.* Marlborough, NH: The Plymouth Rock Foundation, 1991.

Campbell, Norine Dickson. *Patrick Henry: Patriot and Statesman.* Old Greenwich: Devin-Adair, 1969.

Carson, Jane. *Patrick Henry, Prophet of the Revolution.* Brookneal, VA: Patrick Henry Memorial Foundation, 1992 [1979].

Daily, Patrick. *Patrick Henry–The Last Years–1789-1799.* Bedford, VA: Patrick Henry Memorial Foundation, 1986.

Elson, James M., ed. *Patrick Henry Essays: In Celebration of the Fiftieth Anniversary of the Patrick Henry Memorial Foundation.* Brookneal, VA: Patrick Henry Memorial Foundation, 1994.

Hardwick, Kevin R. *Patrick Henry: Economic, Domestic and Political Life in Eighteenth-Century Virginia.* Brookneal, VA: Patrick Henry Memorial Foundation, 1991.

Henry, William Wirt. *Patrick Henry: Life, Correspondence and Speeches.* Harrisonburg, VA: Sprinkle Publications, 1993 [1891].

McCants, David. *Patrick Henry: The Orator.* New York: Greenwood Press, 1990.

Mayer, Henry. *A Son of Thunder: Patrick Henry and the American Republic.* New York: Franklin Watts, 1986.

Mayo, Bernard. *Myths and Men: Patrick Henry, George Washington and Thomas Jefferson.* Athens, GA: University of Georgia Press, 1959.

Meade, Robert D. *Patrick Henry: Patriot in the Making.* Philadelphia: J.B. Lippincott, 1957.

Patrick Henry: Practical Revolutionary. Philadelphia: J.B. Lippincott, 1969.

Morgan, George. *The True Patrick Henry.* Philadelphia: J. B. Lippincott Company, 1929 [1907].

Tyler, Moses Coit. *Patrick Henry.* Boston: Houghton Mifflin and Co., 1887.

Wirt, William. *Sketches of the Life and Character of Patrick Henry.* Philadelphia: J. Webster, 1818.

Supplemental

Adler, Bill. *Motherhood: A Celebration.* New York: Carroll & Graf Publishers, Inc., 1987.

Ahlstrom, Sydney E. *A Religious History of the American People.* New Haven and London: Yale University Press, [1972] 1973.

Barton, David. *The Myth of Separation.* Aledo, Texas: WallBuilders Press, 1992.

The Spirit of the American Revolution. Aledo, TX.: WallBuilders Press, 1994.

Blackstone, William. *Blackstone's Commentaries on the Laws of England.* Philadelphia: Robert Bell, 1771.

Boettner, Loraine. *The Reformed Doctrine of Predestination.* Grand Rapids: Eerdmans Publishing Company, 1932.

Boorstin, Daniel J. *The Americans: The Colonial Experience.* New York: Random House, 1958.

Bowen, Catherine Drinker. *Miracle at Philadelphia: The Story of the Constitutional Convention, May to September 1787.* New York: Book of the Month Club, Inc., 1966.

Bradford, M.E. *A Worthy Company: The Dramatic Story of the Men Who Founded Our Country*. Westchester, Illinois: Crossway Books, 1992.

Burns, James MacGregor. *Leadership*. New York: Harper & Row Publishers, 1978.

Calvin, John. *On God and Political Duty*. Indianapolis: Bobbs-Merrill Company, Inc., 1956.

Carson, Clarence, B. *The Colonial Experience, 1607-1774*. Wadly, Alabama: American Textbook Committee, 1992.

The Beginning of the Republic 1775-1825. Wadly, Alabama: American Textbook Committee, 1992.

Curtis, George Ticknor. *History of the Origin, Formation, and Adoption of the Constitution of the United States; With Notices of Its Principal Framers*. New York: Harper and Brothers, 1854.

Demar, Gary. *America's Christian History: The Untold Story*. Atlanta: American Vision, Inc., 1993 [1995].

God and Government: A Biblical and Historical Study. Brentwood: Wolgemuth and Hyatt, Publishers, Inc., 1989.

God and Government: Issues in Biblical Perspective. Brentwood: Wolgemuth and Hyatt, Publishers, Inc., 1984.

God and Government: The Restoration of the Republic. Brentwood: Wolgemuth and Hyatt, Publishers, Inc., 1986.

De Tocqueville, Alexis. *Democracy in America*. New York: Alfred A. Knopf, [1840] 1945.

Eidsmoe, John. *Christianity and the Constitution: The Faith of Our Founding Fathers*. Grand Rapids: Baker Book House, 1987.

Federer, William J. *America's God and Country*. Texas: Fame Publishing, Inc., 1994.

Grant, George. *Buchanan: Caught in the Crossfire*. Nashville: Thomas Nelson Publishers,1996.

Third Time Around: The History of the Pro-Life Movement From the First Century to the Present. Brentwood, TN.: Wolgemuth & Hyatt, 1991.

Hamilton, Alexander, James Madison and John Jay. *The Federalist*. New York: The Heritage Press, 1945.

Hardenbrook, Weldon M. *Missing in Action*. Nashville: Thomas Nelson Publishers, 1987.

Hutchinson, David. *The Foundation of the Constitution*. Secaucus, New Jersey: University Books, Inc., [1928] 1975.

Kelly, Alfred H. & Winfred A. Harbison. *The American Constitution: Its Origins and Development*. New York: WW Norton & Company, Inc., 1948.

Kirk, Russell. *America's British Culture*. New Brunswick and London: Transaction Publishers, [1993] 1994.

The Conservative Mind: From Burke to Eliot. Washington, DC: Regnery Publishing, Inc., 1985.

The Portable Conservative Reader. New York: Penguin Books, 1982.

The Roots of American Order. Washington, DC: Regnery Gateway, 1991.

Langguth, A.J. *Patriots: The Men Who Started the American Revolution.* New York: Simon & Schuster, 1988.

McDonald, Forrest. *Novus Ordo Seclorum: The Intellectual Origins of the Constitution.* Lawrence, Kansas: University Press of Kansas, 1985.

McNeill, John T. *The History and Character of Calvinism.* New York: Oxford University Press, 1962.

Millard, Catherine. *The Rewriting of America's History.* Camp Hill, Pennsylvania: Horizon House Publishers, 1991.

Morgan, Edmund S. *The Birth of the Republic, 1763-89.* Chicago: University of Chicago Press, 1956 [1992].

Pilcher, George William. *Samuel Davies: Apostle of Dissent in Colonial Virginia.* Knoxville: The University of Tennessee Press, 1971.

Sanders, J. Oswald. *Spiritual Leadership.* Chicago: Moody Press, 1967.

Sandoz, Ellis, ed. *Political Sermons of the American Founding Era–1730-1805.* Indianapolis: Liberty Press, 1990.

Stokes, Anson Phelps and Leo Pfeffer. *Church and State in the United States.* New York: Harper and Row Publishers, [1950] 1964.

Storing, Herbert J. *What the Anti-Federalists Were For.* Chicago: The University of Chicago Press, 1981.

White, Morton. *The Philosophy of the American Revolution.* New York: Oxford University Press, 1978.

Wilson, Woodrow. *A History of the American People* (5 vols.). New York and London: Harper and Row Publishers, 1901-1902.

Endnotes

1. Bernard Mayo, *Myths and Men: Patrick Henry, George Washington and Thomas Jefferson* (Athens: University of Georgia Press, 1959), p. 18.
2. Ibid., p. 23.
3. Ibid., p. 2
4. M.E. Bradford, *The Trumpet Voice of Freedom: Patrick Henry of Virginia* (Marlborough, NH: The Plymouth Rock Foundation, 1991), p. 20.
5. William Wirt Henry, *Patrick Henry: Life, Correspondance and Speeches* (Harrisonburg, VA: Sprinkle Publications, 1993 [1891]), pp. 2:550-551.
6. In Moses Coit Tyler, *Patrick Henry* (Boston: Houghton Mifflin and Co., 1887), 145.
7. WW Henry, p. 1:4.
8. Tyler, p. 1.
9. Ibid., p. 5.
10. WW Henry, p. 2:251.
11. WW Henry, pp. 1:9-10.
12. Tyler, p. 5; George Morgan, *The True Patrick Henry* (Philadelphia: JB Lippincott Company, 1929 [1907]), pp. 25-26.
13. Morgan, p. 7.
14. David McCants, *Patrick Henry: The Orator* (New York: Greenwood Press, 1990), p. 12.
15. Morgan, p. 32.
16. Tyler, p. 44.
17. McCants, p. 12.
18. Tyler, p. 15.
19. WW Henry, p. 1:10.
20. Robert D. Meade, *Patrick Henry: Patriot in the Making* (Philadelphia: JB Lipponcott, 1957), p. 54. (Hereafter, Meade 1.); WW Henry, p. 1:9.
21. WW Henry, p. 1:9.
22. Morgan, p. 34.
23. Meade, p. 1:53.
24. Ibid., p. 52.
25. WW Henry, pp. 1:13-14.
26. Ibid., p. 15; Morgan, p. 57.
27. Meade, pp. 1:71-74.
28. Mc Cants, p. 23.
29. WW Henry, p. 1:16.
30. Tyler, p. 15.
31. Morgan, p. 37.
32. Ibid., pp. 37-38.
33. Ibid.
34. Henry Mayer, *A Son of Thunder: Patrick Henry and the American Republic* (New York: Franklin Watts, 1986), pp. 44-45.
35. Ibid.
36. Ibid.
37. Morgan, p. 41.
38. Mayer, pp. 46-47.
39. WW Henry, p. 1:19.
40. Mayer, p. 50.
41. WW Henry, p. 1:20.
42. Mayer, p. 53.
43. William Wirt, *Sketches of the Life and Character of Patrick Henry* (Philadelphia: J. Webster, 1818), p. 34.

44. Mayer, p. 58.
45. AJ Langguth, *Patriots: The Men Who Started the American Revolution* (New York: Simon & Schuster, 1988), p. 40.
46. Ibid., p. 41.
47. Ibid., p. 45.
48. WW Henry, pp. 1:38-39.
49. Ibid., p. 41.
50. Mayer, p. 65.
51. Morgan, p. 72.
52. Ibid., p. 74.
53. WW Henry, p. 1:51.
54. Ibid., p. 55.
55. Ibid., p. 59.
56. Clarence B. Carson, *The Colonial Experience, 1607-1774* (Wadly, Alabama: American Textbook Committee, 1992), p. 154.
57. WW Henry, p. 1:65.
58. Ibid., p. 68.
59. Mayer, p. 71.
60. WW Henry, p. 1:73.
61. Ibid., pp. 80-81.
62. Ibid., p. 83.
63. Tyler, p. 73.
64. WW Henry, p. 1:84.
65. Ibid., p. 87.
66. Jane Carson, *Patrick Henry: Prophet of the Revolution* (Brookneal, VA: Patrick Henry Memorial Foundation, 1979), pp. 13-14.
67. Tyler, p. 79.
68. Frothingham, *Rise of the Republic*, in Tyler, p. 81.
69. WW Henry, pp. 1:96-97.
70. Ibid., p. 100.
71. in Morgan, p. 111.
72. Woodrow Wilson, in Mayer, p. 109.
73. Mayer, p. 116.
74. Morgan, p. 113.
75. Ibid., p. 118.
76. J. Carson, pp. 19-20.
77. Washington in Mayer, p. 119.
78. Ibid., p. 125.
79. Mayer, pp. 126-127. Tyler says Henry moved to Scotchtown in 1771 not 1769.
80. Morgan, p. 116; Tyler, pp. 93-94.
81. Morgan, pp. 121-122.
82. WW Henry, p. 1:125.
83. Mayer, p. 160.
84. J. Carson, p. 26.
85. WW Henry, pp. 1:108-110.
86. C. Carson, pp. 159-161.
87. WW Henry, p. 1:132.
88. C. Carson, p. 161.
89. WW Henry, p. 1:143.
90. Ibid., pp. 154-155.
91. C. Carson, pp. 163-165.
92. Jefferson in WW Henry, p. 1:176.
93. Ibid., pp. 177-178.
94. Ibid., p. 183.
95. Tyler, p. 99.
96. WW Henry, pp. 1:209-213.
97. John Adams in WW Henry, p. 1:221.
98. Mayer, pp. 212-213.
99. WW Henry, p. 1:223.
100. Mayer, 216; David Barton, *The Spirit of the American Revolution* (Aledo, TX: WallBuilders Press, 1994), pp. 4-5.

101. Clarence B. Carson, *The Beginning of the Republic, 1775-1825* (Wadly, Alabama: American Textbook Committee, 1984), pp. 10-11; WW Henry, p. 1:255.
102. WW Herny, p. 1:227.
103. Tyler, p. 116.
104. Mayer, p. 223.
105. Tyler, p. 125.
106. Morgan p. 178.
107. Mayer, pp. 231-232.
108. Robert D. Meade, *Patrick Henry: Practical Revolutionary* (Philadelphia: JB Lipponcott, 1969), 19. (Hereafter, Meade 2) ; Mayer, p. 240.
109. Tyler, p. 135.
110. Mayer, p. 244.
111. in Tyler, pp. 140-145.
112. Mayer, p. 246.
113. Jefferson in Tyler, p. 155.
114. WW Henry, p. 1:279.
115. Ibid., pp. 280-281.
116. Mayer, pp. 259-254.
117. WW Henry, pp. 1:283-284.
118. Tyler, p. 163.
119. Ibid., pp. 164-166.
120. Ibid., pp. 165, 167.
121. WW Henry, p. 1:291.
122. in Mayer, pp. 261-263.
123. WW Henry, p. 1:296.
124. Tyler, pp. 170-171. George Ticknor Curtis, *History of the Origin, Formation, and Adoption of the Constitution of the United States; With Notices of Its Principal Framers* (New York: Harper and Brothers, 1854), pp. 31-40.
125. WW Henry, p. 1:302.
126. Ibid., pp. 298-300; Curtis, pp. 39-41.
127. WW Henry, p. 311.
128. Ibid., p. 313.
129. Tyler, p. 177.
130. Morgan, p. 221. See WW Henry, pp. 1:306-351 for a detailed account.
131. Meade, p. 2:95.
132. Tyler, pp. 181-182.
133. Washington, Writings, p. 3.309, in Tyler, p. 186.
134. WW Henry, p. 1:357.
135. Tyler, pp. 198-199.
136. J. Carson, p. 130.
137. WW Henry, p. 1:392.
138. Ibid., pp. 393-394.
139. Tyler, p. 198; J. Carson, p. 56.
140. WW Henry, p. 435.
141. Tyler, p. 207; See also David Hutchison, *The Foundation of the Constitution* (Secaucus, NJ: University Books, Inc, 1975 [1928]), pp. 9-10.
142. WW Henry, p. 1:424.
143. Russell Kirk, *The Roots of American Order* (Washington, DC: Regnery Gateway, 1991), p. 408.
144. For a full discussion see WW Henry, pp. 1:422-435.
145. Tyler, p. 208.
146. Ibid., pp. 208-209.
147. J. Carson, p. 58.
148. Meade, p. 2:123.
149. J. Carson, pp. 58-59.
150. WW Henry, p. 1:458.
151. Ibid., p. 548.
152. J. Carson, pp. 61-62.
153. WW Henry, pp. 1:558-559.
154. Ibid., p. 553.
155. Ibid., pp. 561-562.
156. Bradford, p. 11.

157. Henry in WW Henry, p. 2:43.

158. WW Henry, p. 2:52.

159. Ibid., pp. 2:193-196.

160. Ibid., pp. 2:198-201.

161. Bradford, p. 20.

162. WW Henry, pp. 2:273-275. See Huntingdon's letter to Henry in WW Herny, p. 3.257ff.

163. in WW Henry, p. 2:286.

164. Herbert J. Storing, *What the Federalists Were For* (Chicago: The University of Chicago Press, 1981), p. 9.

165. See Alexander Hamilton, James Madison and John Jay, *The Federalist* (New York: The Heritage Press, 1945), for the most explicit arguments in favor of the national position.

166. See Storing, in loc. I disagree with his conclusion that the Anti-Federalists lost the debate because they had the weaker arguments, p. 71.

167. WW Henry, p. 2:346.

168. This and all subsequent quotations from Henry's speech at the Ratification Convention can be found in WW Henry, p. 3.431ff.

169. WW Henry, pp. 2:350-351.

170. in Tyler, p. 336.

171. WW Henry, pp. 2:372-373.

172. in J. Carson, p. 65.

173. Mayer, p. 465.

174. Meade, p. 2:412.

175. Tyler, p. 365.

176. Meade, p. 2:417 ff.

177. Mayer, p. 466.

178. For the best discussion of Henry's land investments see Patrick Daily, *Patrick Henry –the Last Years– 1789-1799* (Bedford, VA: Patrick Henry Memorial Foundation, 1986).

179. Mayer, p. 468.

180. Tyler, pp. 383-384.

181. Ibid., p. 384.

182. Ibid., p. 384, pp. 389-391.

183. WW Henry, pp. 2:519-520.

184. Ibid., pp. 2:519, 575.

185. in Tyler, p. 395.

186. WW Henry, p. 2:575; Tyler, pp. 394-395.

187. WW Henry, p. 2:605.

188. Ibid., p. 2:606.

189. Ibid., p. 2607; Meade, p. 2:450.

190. WW Henry, p. 2:614.

191. Tyler, p. 421.

192. Ibid., p. 422.

193. in Michael Jesse Bennett, *Patrick Henry's Comments on Life, Liberty, and the Pursuit of Happiness* (Brookneal, VA: Patrick Henry Memorial Foundation, 1991), p. 39.

194. WW Henry, p. 2:594.

195. Bennett, p. 9.

196. See Weldon M. Hardenbrook, *Missing In Action* (Nashville: Thomas Nelson Publishers, 1987).

197. Tyler, p. 3.

198. WW Henry, p. 1:4; Meade, p. 1:39.

199. Morgan, p. 22; WW Henry, p. 1:4.

200. WW Henry, p. 1:286.

201. Ibid., p. 2:252.

202. in Bill Adler, *Motherhood: A Celebration* (New York: Caroll & Graf Publisher, Inc., 1987), p. 9.

203. Ibid., p. 75.

204. Tyler, pp. 4-5.

205. WW Henry, p. 2:251.

206. Froude in WW Henry, p. 1:15.

207. Loraine Boettner, *The Reformed Doctrine of Predestination* (Grand Rapids: Eerdmans Publishing Comopany, 1932), p. 382.

208. Ibid., pp. 389-390.

209. McCants, 23. For a more complete discussion of the political influence of Calvin in America see John Eidsmoe, *Christianity and the Constitution: The Faith of Our Founding Fathers* (Grand Rapids: Baker Book House), ch. 1-4; and John T. McNeill, History and Character of Calvinism (New York: Oxford University Press, 1962), ch. 20.

210. McCants.
211. George William Pilcher, *Samuel Davies: Apostle of Dissent in Colonial Virginia* (Knoxville: The University of Tennessee Press, 1971), p. 83.
212. Adler, p. 5.
213. Bennett, p. 10.
214. Tyler, pp. 12-14.
215. Ibid.
216. Tyler, p. 19; Wirt, pp. 9-13.
217. Tyler, p. 20.
218. Patrick Daily, *Patrick Henry—The Last Years—1789-1799* (Bedford, VA: Patrick Henry Memorial Foundation, 1986), pp. 29-30.
219. Meade, p. 1:55.
220. Daily, p. 29.
221. Morgan, pp. 211-212.
222. WW Henry, p. 2:489.
223. Mayer, p. 53.
224. Langguth, p. 45.
225. Daily, p. 75.
226. See J. Carson, p. 67; WW Henry, pp. 1:471-476; Daily, p. 82 ff.
227. in Tyler, p. 361.
228. Wirt, p. 312.
229. McCants, p. 90.
230. Ibid.
231. Daily, p. 114.
232. Tyler, p. 366.
233. WW Henry, p. 3.461.
234. Mayer, p. 72.
235. WW Henry, p. 1:77; Mayer, p. 74.
236. WW Henry, p. 2:167.
237. WW Henry, p. 1:281.
238. Norine Dickson Campbell, *Patrick Henry: Patriot and Statesman* (Old Greenwich: Devin-Adair, 1969), p. 288.
239. Tyler, p. 145.
240. Tyler, p. 145.
241. WW Henry, pp. 2:550-551.
242. Eidsmoe, ch. 1-2.
243. William J. Federer, *America's God and Country* (Texas: Fame Publishing, Inc., 1994), pp. 642-643.
244. American Dictionary of the English Language (1828; reprinted 1980, San Fransisco: Foundation for American Christian Education), s.v. "Providence."
245. Meade, p. 1:73. See also Ellis Sandoz, ed., *Political Sermons of the American Founding Era: 1730-1805* (Indianapolis: Liberty Press, 1990), p. 179 ff.
246. WW Henry, pp. 2:286-287.
247. Liberty Speech in Tyler, pp. 144-145.
248. Ibid.
249. WW Henry, pp. 1:61-68.
250. Ibid.
251. Patrick Henry in WW Henry, p. 1:81.
252. Ibid., p. 259.
253. in J. Carson, p. 46.
254. Liberty Speech in S. G. Arnold, *The Life of Patrick Henry of Virginia* (New York: Hurst & Company Publisher, 1845), pp. 107-111.
255. Liberty Speech in S. G. Arnold, *The Life of Patrick Henry of Virginia* (New York: Hurst & Company Publisher, 1845), pp. 107-111.
256. in Tyler, p. 148.
257. WW Henry, p. 1:259.
258. Rives in Morgan, p. 111.
259. WW Henry, p. 2:570.
260. WW Henry, p. 1:101.
261. Tyler, p. 88; Wirt, p. 66.
262. Tyler, pp. 11-12.
263. Morgan, p. 121.

264. WW Henry, p. 2:243.
265. J. Oswald Sanders, *Spiritual Leadership* (Chicago: Moody Press, 1967), p. 56.
266. Tyler, p. 172.
267. McCants, p. 104.
268. Tyler, p. 390.
269. Wirt, p. 408.
270. WW Henry, p. 2:419.
271. WW Henry, p. 1:547.
272. Sander, p. 110.
273. WW Henry, pp. 210, 81.
274. Ibid., pp. 285, 287.
275. J. Carson, p. 53.
276. in Meade, p. 2:124.
277. Morgan, p. 226.
278. WW Henry, pp. 2:435, 438.
279. WW Henry, p. 3.390.
280. WW Henry, p. 2:309.
281. Meade, p. 1:45.
282. WW Henry, pp. 2:286-287; Mayer, p. 466.
283. WW Henry, pp. 1:118-119.
284. WW Henry, pp. 2:272; 3.285.
285. Mayer, 15; WW Henry, pp. 2:353-354.
286. Tyler, p. 58.
287. WW Henry, p. 2:327.
288. Ibid., pp. 193, 196.
289. Virginia Bill of Rights, Article XVI, penned by Patrick Henry, in Bennett, p. 15.
290. Virginia Bill of Rights, Article XVI, penned by Patrick Henry, in Bennett, p. 15.
291. WW Henry, p. 2:570.
292. Eidsmoe, p. 308.
293. WW Henry, p. 1:43.
294. Eidsmoe, p. 313.
295. Mark Couvillion, "The Religious Faith of Patrick Henry," in James M. Elson, ed., *Patrick Henry Essays: In Celebration of the Fiftieth Anniversary of the Patrick Henry Memorial Foundation* (Brookneal, VA: Patrick Henry Memorial Foundation, 1994), p. 22.
296. Tyler, p. 393.
297. WW Henry, p. 2:570.
298. Couvillion, op. cit., WW Henry, pp. 2:198-201.
299. WW Henry. p. 2:409.
300. in Tyler, pp. 409-410.
301. in WW Henry, p. 1:113.
302. Daily, p. 151.
303. in WW Henry, p. 2:185.
304. Ibid., p. 203.
305. Anson Phelps Stokes and Leo Pfeffer, *Church and State in the United States* (New York: Harper and Row Publishers, 1950 [1964]), p. 69.
306. WW Henry, p. 2:207.
307. Stokes and Pfeffer, pp. 69-70; Daily, p. 151.
308. Sydney E. Ahlstrom, *A Religious History of the American People* (New Haven and London: Yale University Press, 1973), ch. 23.
309. in WW Henry, pp. 3.254-261.
310. Ibid.
311. Henry in Ibid., pp. 273-274.
312. PH Fontaine in Daily, p. 199; Tyler, p. 376.
313. Daily, p. 200.
314. in WW Henry, p. 2:631.
315. in WW Henry, p. 3.579.
316. Henry in WW Henry, p. 2:353.
317. John Henry in WW Henry, p. 1:9.
318. Roane in WW Henry, p. 2:521.
319. Grisby in Morgan, p. 261.
320. Daniel J. Boorstin, *The Americans: The Colonial Experience* (New York: Random House, 1958), pp. 110-116.

321. Greene in Kevin R. Hardwick, *Patrick Henry: Economic, Domestic and Political Life in Eighteenth Century Virginia* (Brookneal, VA: Patrick Henry Memorial Foundation, 1991), p. 26.
322. Morgan, p. 283.
323. WW Henry, pp. 2:558-559.
324. Morgan, p. 288.
325. in Bennett, p. 37.
326. Mayo, p. 23.
327. Patrick Henry to his daughter Anne in WW Henry, p. 2:306.
328. in Morgan, p. 381.
329. Edith Poindexter, "Patrick Henry's Children," in Patrick Henry Essays, p. 39.
330. Morgan, p. 242.
331. Meade, p. 2:381.
332. WW Henry, p. 2:518.
333. Mark Couvillon, "Give Me Poetry," in Patrick Henry Essays, p. 25.
334. Ibid.
335. Patrick Daily, "Patrick Henry's Last Years," in Patrick Henry Essays, p. 37.
336. Hardwick, p. 39.
337. in Morgan, pp. 243-244.
338. Hardwick, p. 40.
339. Ibid., p. 38.
340. Liberty Speech in Tyler, p. 141.
341. in WW Henry, pp. 1:207-208.
342. Adams in Ibid., p. 240.
343. Tyler, pp. 143-145.
344. WW Henry, pp. 2:397-398.
345. in Hardwick, p. 33.
346. in WW Henry, pp. 2:400-401.
347. Ibid., p. 608.
348. Ibid., p. 378.
349. Patrick Henry in WW Henry, p. 2:194.
350. in George Grant, *Buchanan: Caught in the Crossfire* (Nashville: Thomas Nelson Publisher, 1996), p. 13.
351. in WW Henry, p. 1:115.
352. Ibid., pp. 218-219; Wirt, p. 258.
353. in WW Henry, pp. 2:193-194.
354. Ibid., p. 1.ch.23; pp. 2:270-272.
355. Ibid., p. 1:113.
356. Liberty Speech in Arnold, p. 107.
357. Ibid., p. 107 ff.
358. WW Henry, p. 3.458.
359. Unless otherwise noted, the following quotations in this section are from the Virginia Ratification Speech in WW Henry 3.
360. Tyler, p. 141.
361. in George Grant, *Third Time Around: The History of the Pro-Life Movement From the First Century to the Present* (Brentwood, TN: Wolgemuth & Hyatt, 1991), p. 49.
362. Patrick Henry in WW Henry, p. 1:20.
363. Jefferson in Mayer, p. 50.
364. Mayer, pp. 231-232; WW Henry, p. 2:329.
365. Poindexter in Patrick Henry Essays, pp. 39-42.
366. Mayer, p. 15.
367. in WW Henry, p. 2:330.
368. Sanders, p. 124.
369. Patrick Henry in WW Henry, p. 3.436.
370. Patrick Henry in Morgan, p. 270.
371. Ibid., p. 284.
372. All quotations in this section are from the Virginia Ratification Speech, WW Henry 3.
373. in WW Henry, p. 1:431.
374. John 10.11 (KJV).
375. Virginia Declaration of Rights, Article Fifteen, penned by Patrick Henry.
376. Forrest McDonald, *Novus Ordo Seclorum: The Intellectual Origins of the Constitution* (Lawrence, Kansas: University Press of Kansas, 1985), pp. 70-71.
377. Daily, p. 40.

378. WW Henry, p. 2:520.
379. J. Carson, p. 3.
380. in WW Henry, p. 2:559.
381. Ibid, p. 592.
382. Ibid., p. 632.
383. Liberty Speech in Arnold, p. 107 ff.
384. McCants, p. 7.
385. J. Carson, p. 2.
386. in WW Henry, p. 2:493.
387. Ibid., p. 488.
388. in James M. Elson, "Patrick Henry, Orator," in Patrick Henry Essays, p. 15.
389. Meade, p. 1:71.
390. WW Henry, p. 2:248; Meade, p. 1:55.
391. in WW Henry, p. 1:267-268.
392. Alexander in WW Henry, p. 2:500.
393. Patrick Henry, Ratification Speech in WW Henry 3.
394. Daily, p. 41.
395. WW Henry, p. 2:184.
396. Washington in Ibid., p. 432.
397. Blair in WW Henry, p. 2:595.
398. Anonomous author in Morgan, p. 136.
399. Patrick Henry in WW Henry, p. 3.414.
400. Morgan, p. 31.
401. Morgan, p. 320.
402. Daily, pp. 46-56.
403. Edmund S. Morgan, *The Birth of the Republic, 1763-89* (Chicago: University of Chicago Press, 1956 [1992]), p. 8.
404. Meade, p. 1:52.
405. Patrick Henry in Daily, p. 66.
406. Mayer, p. 12.
407. McCants, p. 205.
408. Ibid.
409. Ibid., pp. 207-208.
410. Roane in WW Henry, p. 2:214.
411. Tyler in Ibid.
412. Patrick Henry to daughter Anne in Morgan, p. 244.
413. Meredith in WW Henry, p. 1:9.
414. Mayo, p. 9; WW Henry, p. 1:18.
415. Roane in Morgan,
416. Daily, pp. 25-26.
417. Tozer in Sanders, *Spiritual Leadership*, p. 66.
418. Patrick Henry in WW Henry, p. 2:274.
419. Patrick Henry in Bennett, p. 14.
420. Hardwick, p. 14.
421. Morgan, p. 42.
422. Mason in Tyler, p. 98.
423. Patrick Henry in WW Henry, p. 1:560.
424. in Bennett, p. 12.
425. Ratification Speech.
426. Hardwick, pp. 26-27.
427. Russell Kirk, *The Conservative Mind: From Burke to Eliot* (Washington, DC: Regnery Publishing, Inc., 1985), pp. 8-9; The Portable Conservative Reader, (New York: Penguin Books, 1982), xv-xxi.
428. Kirk, The Portable Conservative Reader, p. xvi.
429. Ibid., p. xvii.
430. Henry in Ratification Speech.
431. WW Henry, pp. 2:522-525.
432. Kirk, The Portable Conservative Reader, p. xx.
433. Patrick Henry in Bradford, p. i.
434. Eidsmoe, p. 52.
435. Russell Kirk, *America's British Culture* (New Brunswick and London: Transaction Publishers, 1994), p. 71.
436. De Tocqueville in Ibid., p. 72.

437. Boettner, p. 382.
438. Ratification Speech.
439. in WW Henry, p. 2:233.
440. McCants, p. 23.
441. See Article III of the Virginia Bill of Rights in WW Henry, p. 2:649.
442. Couvillion in Patrick Henry Essays, p. 22.
443. Ranke in Eidsmoe, p. 18. See also John Calvin, *On God and Political Duty* (Indianapolis: Bobbs-Merrill Company, Inc., 1956), for a fuller treatment of Calvin's political views.
444. Patrick Henry in British Debt Case, McCants, p. 150.
445. Kirk, America's British Culture, in loc. and Boorstin, op. Cit., p. 97.
446. William Blackstone, *Blackstone's Commentaries on the Laws of England* (Philadelphia: Robert Bell, 1771), pp. 1:41-42.
447. Ibid.
448. For instance Romans chapter p. 16.
449. Acts 5:29 (KJV)
450. Patrick Henry in Bennett, p. 34.
451. in Tyler, p. 392.
452. Ibid., p. 393.
453. Howe in Ibid., p. 384.
454. in Morgan, p. 405.
455. Patrick Henry in WW Henry, p. 2:625.
456. in WW Henry, p. 2:606.
457. Ibid., p. 320.
458. Ibid., pp. 286-287.
459. in Ibid., p. 477.
460. Fontaine in WW Henry, pp. 2:625-626.
461. WW Henry, p. 3.449.
462. Ibid., p. 459.
463. in WW Henry, p. 2:628.
464. Ibid., p. 629.
465. Wirt in Arnold, p. 257.
466. Mayer, p. 16.
467. See Storing, op. Cit, for an evaluation of the Anti-Federalists contribution to American political discourse.
468. Mayo, p. 10.
469. Ibid.
470. Charlotte Courthouse Speech.
471. Ratification Speech.
472. Mayer, p. 158.
473. Ibid., pp. 158-159.
474. Ibid., p. 160.
475. WW Henry, p. 1:112; Mayer, p. 165.
476. in WW Henry, 1:152.
477. Ibid., pp. 152-153.
478. Kirk, The Roots of American Order, p. 406.
479. See McDonald, op. Cit., pp. 50-53 for additional reasons that colonial Americans tolerated slavery.
480. in WW Henry, p. 2:166.
481. oane and Fox in Ibid., p. 117.
482. WW Henry, p. 2:168.
483. See Catherine Millard, *The Rewriting of America's History* (Camp Hill, PA: Horizon House Publishers, 1991), for numerous examples of secular revisionism.
484. in WW Henry, p. 2:627.